A Rough Piece of West Texas
And Other Interesting Places

Chronicles of Hardscrabble Hunting

May 2010

M. A. Piatt

D1795539

Acknowledgements

Every story and every place mentioned in this book are true. I would like to thank every person with which I have hunted and shared these experiences in these Interesting Places. We have all been uniquely privileged to have hunted in these places during our time on Earth. But most of all I would like to thank my wife, Kathy, for her patience all these many hunting seasons.

Table of Contents

Part 1

Interesting Places: Why They Matter

Chapter 1 - Opening Morning

Four O'clock AM. The hunter could only stare at the dimly lit clock lying beneath his cot. Of course he hadn't hardly slept at all so what difference did the time say now? How could he? This was the day. It was opening morning for the second season of the Colorado gun season. All those preparations led to this one moment, and there he lay in his sleeping bag almost frozen by the sheer magnitude of the day, of what MIGHT happen only a few short moments from now.

How strange it is to go through the normal routine of daily existence – getting out of bed, getting dressed, eating breakfast – when that day held such great promise of adventure. Who knew what lay out on the mountains in the early morning dark? A giant muley, maybe elk, a trophy animal which could define a hunter's career and validate his reputation may wait only a scant handful of heart beats away. That is why our hunter had to force his body out of the warmth of his down sleeping bag and into the sub-twenty something air whose dryness always cracked his tongue and split his lips on these trips. That is why he had to force his legs and arms into his hunting clothes despite them shivering in protest. "Take us back to the warmth" they cried out. That is why he had to force his feet into the cold frozen boots which would soon be carrying him over many miles of high Rocky Mountain terrain on this trip.

And that is why he had to force himself to eat breakfast. It wasn't due to the lack of companionship. After all, the cook tent bustled with all the hunters, his friends, as they busied themselves around the table. Each now brimmed with excitement at the arrival of yet another season in this very Interesting Place. No, it wasn't due to lack of community that made eating that morning difficult. Rather, his stomach churned at the excitement which pounded through every artery in his body. That adrenaline surge dulled his appetite, but he knew he had to eat for the day would be long one way or another.

Why the nervousness? Why the anticipation? At one level our hunter knew it was all a bit silly. After all it was only a hobby, an activity, and an expensive and an entirely optional one at that. In this age with its apparent safe provision of physical needs, why did he yet felt the need to hunt coursing in his blood? Food can be had at the store all safe and secure and always available. The land needed not to be tamed for that had already taken place generations ago. From a purely practical point of view there was no need at all for this effort, this expense, this expenditure of time and energy. Yet something drove him to do this "thing", this thing we call hunting. From what forgotten corner of his soul did this passion exist and why did he feel it so important to indulge it? There are no easy answers to these questions.

Our hunter, by all accounts, lived a perfectly normal middle class life in the richest nation in the history of mankind at the very heights of its economic prowess. From unspectacular beginnings he enjoyed an ordinary, largely carefree existence. It wasn't that he squandered his good fortune, far from it. He had done everything pretty much "by the book". He stayed out of trouble, made decent grades, and had gone to college to receive a degree which would allow him to continue his secure lifestyle.

Even that was a combination of good luck. You see our hunter lived at a special time in a special place where a person could go to a decent university and obtain such a degree at a rather reasonable cost. It hadn't always been so and there was no guarantee that it would continue (and every reason to think that it would not). From every angle he had been exceptionally blessed and fortunate. He hadn't done anything special to deserve it, but at the same time he hadn't done anything stupid to mess up the good hand he had been dealt. So why would a person like that be this place – the top of a mountain, in the dark – to do this thing called hunting? Where in a man's primal nature does this "thing" reside?

In some part perhaps the very security of his daily life provided the impetus for such non-practical expenditure of effort. Maybe deep within every man is the need to break out of confining roles we assume every day and live a different life, a life of challenge and adventure and risk and the unknown. The mask we wear every day, although it provides a measure of serenity, also weighs down a person's spirit to the point where it must burst out in spontaneous exuberance of risk taking. The hunger for an authentic experience is part of every human and that hunger builds and grows until it consumes all a man's thoughts. While we in the modern world often try to quell that hunger with the artificially contrived circuses of our entertainment age and stuff it into submission with the bread of our lazy gluttony, that hunger remains.

The mask we put on every day diminishes us in a very real way. Our hunter remembered that just before the trip a boss remarked upon hearing of his upcoming of where he was traveling "Really, you're going elk hunting. I never pictured you doing something like that." Our hunter felt a pang of slight humiliation inside "Well I'm not just a computer nerd. I do have a life outside this place." He thought quietly. But, he managed to hide his irritation and instead replied "Oh I go almost every year. It is my big hunting trip of the season." With that the supervisor, now fascinated and perhaps perplexed that he knew so little of whom this person really is, continued to ask questions. Our hunter gradually warmed up and opened up as he described the camping, the place, and some of the adventures he and his buddies had shared over the years. Maybe that is why he hunted. He had something to prove and that he mattered as a person, that he was more than a means to an end for someone else, that he was authentic.

And now that authentic experience lay just minutes away. That is why he now labored to complete the normal humdrum routines of morning. Several times he tried to calm his nerves and force down another bite of food. But with each bite he felt a slight nausea well up in his stomach. Valiantly he put on a carefree exterior for the others to see. In the darkness of the early morning, the kerosene lantern lit up the tent with brilliance and much needed warmth. It emitted a low hissing sound which normally one would find annoying, but in the vastness of this magnificent wilderness it provided needed reassurance.

Being one of the younger hunters, he sat at the far end of the table opposite from the tent opening and furthest from the sheepherder's stove. Each morning of the trip the scene would repeat: he would get into the cook tent first, light the lantern and stove, and wait for the others to appear through the tent door. After each hunter entered, he would warm his body in front of the sheepherder's stove. Our hunter would watch it all from his end of table; the lantern providing a little heat to keep warm.

What a strange sight it must be to an observer he thought. Outside in the dark the wilderness carried on much as it has done from time immortal - each creature fighting every minute to survive in the aspen thickets, in the evergreens, in the snow covered hillsides and along the sheer rocky cliffs. Did they ever stop to ponder the magnificent beauty of the landscape? Did they even have the ability to do that, or is that something that only resides with humans?

But inside the tent there existed a small piece of civilization, albeit a rather rough piece. Here in the artificial light of the hissing lantern the hunters gathered one last time before the day began. Here they felt no hunger as they woofed down their morning meal, and more importantly they had no real fear of hunger. The modern world provided security and that security, although smothering, is hard to deny.

Our hunter was struck by this paradox that morning as he first left the sleep tent and faced the bitter dry air. For one of the morning rituals that we can never escape is the call to nature. Now normally, in the comfort of home, we do not give this much thought. However in 14 degree weather one tends to give this mundane act a little more thought – and a lot less time.

But as he sat on the latrine tucked away in the aspens above camp, he couldn't help but notice a small mouse making its way through the snow and leaves that littered the ground. Quickly and with great business it sped back and forth through the little tunnels it had made in the snow occasionally popping out to the hunter's amusement. There as he sat somewhat put out at the lack of decent facilities, he could observe another creature fighting every second for its survival. Would it make it another day or would it fall victim to any number of predators? Our hunter wondered but didn't know the answer. The mouse would face the drama of survival that day with no choice to opt out. The hunter would enter into that same life or death struggle but do so voluntarily. The paradox could not have been starker.

Finally he had forced down the last bite of cereal he could stand. Often hunting camps are depicted as places where lavish meals of scrambled eggs, bacon, sausage and other goodies are cooked in great quantities and eaten heartily. Not so in this camp. These hunters did everything on their own and nobody wanted to cook. They wanted to hunt. That was why they spent the time, money and effort to be here on the mountain and not back in a hotel room in town. Breakfast was utilitarian and quick.

And so too were the lunches. He watched as the other hunters began making their sandwiches and packing their lunches. They might be back at camp for lunch but there was no guarantee. With luck, they expected to be far off the main roads and deep into the wilderness on the trail of elk and mule deer. Excitement increased among the hunters as they began to make their final preparations. Noticeably they spoke with greater enthusiasm and anticipation as they finished preparing lunch.

How they seemed so relaxed and eager, but our hunter knew that they too felt the same internal anxiety. He had often wondered why he would feel this way before a big hunt. As a new hunter everything appeared new and fresh. Often he didn't know that he was supposed to be excited. Eventually he would struggle to contain his nerves because he learned how each opportunity represented something special. Then he decided that perhaps all that was so much nonsense. He determined that the point of all this "thing" we call hunting was to enjoy oneself. If you got something fine, if not then it was no big deal. However when our hunter tried to apply that theory, it didn't work. Why bother at all if the goal is only entertainment? One could get that anywhere.

Now he welcomed the anticipation. He had learned that within this "thing" lay something special and unique. And that uniqueness required authenticity. The experience required this in order to be meaningful. That is what drew the hunter to this place, this very

Interesting Place, each year, the authentic experience is presented. Nothing that lay ahead was scripted or controlled or managed. This Interesting Place presented a stage for a drama which played out every moment of every day. Soon he and the others would be leaving the modern world behind and crossing over an invisible divide into another world where they would be enter into this drama and become participants on the stage. They would be absorbed back into a largely forgotten stage of existence which modernity seeks to level out but stubbornly refuses to die.

That is why he felt those butterflies in his stomach. It was a physical reaction to this crossing over from one world to the next, to the fact that the outcome remained unknown, and to the fact that he was going to loose a little bit of the control that we crave in our lives. All the hunters understood this emotion. This authentic experience was the reason they came here and this was the reason they hunted.

Companionship is nice, and enjoying nature is great, but they alone do not explain that primal drive which now was coursing through the hunter's veins. Crossing over into the realm of the Interesting Place where they would come face to face with an authentic experience explains it better. And in that crossing over they would be faced with challenges and opportunities for great triumph or bitter disappointment. That is why they had come.

Having completed their meal preparations, the hunters anxiously discussed their plans for the upcoming morning. One pair would go north of camp and scout for elk. Others would travel south down the main road to Long Point which in those days reigned as a supreme destination for mule deer. The Point road traveled down the spine of a long narrow mesa which stretched out several miles long; however, its width varied and at times it barely measured more than a hundred yards across. On both sides, deep draws and secondary canyons cut into the mesa at irregular intervals. The deer used these narrow parts as travel corridors to traverse the ridge between the valley (about 2000 feet below) and various bedding areas located on the slope faces.

Our hunter and his partner, the one who was known as Legend, decided to spend the first morning down the Point hunting muleys, so they left earlier than the others. Still dark with the first light in the east barely glowing over the mesa, he struggled to hike to the truck as his heavy boots crunching the frozen snow beneath. Now that the moment had arrived his muscles strangely rebelled. Perhaps it was one last subconscious call to hang back and not cross over that invisible divide, to not risk disappointment, to play it safe.

The hunter checked his geared one last time. The rifle felt oddly heavy as the cold metal stung his hands. He kept two bullets in his pocket for quick action. As he held them in his hand, the brass felt innocent and benign. How could such violence come from such a small object he wondered? What is it about humans where they can fashion such a simple, static device to such precision and to do such an improbable thing? In the great drama of nature, was this cheating? And if not at what point does such an advantage constitute an unfair advantage? These were questions he couldn't answer.

Slowly the truck ambled down the dirt road. As they turned onto the point road, the dark began to transform as the morning light brought the landscape to life. Carefully they glassed the side canyons and ridges for any sign. Far from the picturesque postcard mountains, this land consisted of high mesas strewn with sagebrush and open ground. Thick stands of evergreens grew down the steepest drop offs while aspens thrived in scattered patches in the shallower side cuts.

Although when viewed from afar the mesas appeared to be relatively flat, up close they contained numerous undulations and pockets any one of which could house a herd of elk or a giant muley buck. To most in the outside world, this territory appeared godforsaken, but to these hunters it was the very center of paradise. For in this overlooked land, adventure which could define a lifetime hid around every corner.

As they advanced down the Point road, the hunters took more time to glass every hillside and pocket of brush. Soon they began to spot deer, mostly does, but a few small bucks. Long Point was at its peak as a muley hotspot, and they were there to witness it at the height of its glory.

About halfway down to the Point they stopped to glass from one of their favorite high points. Slowly they hiked around the knob scanning the surrounding countryside in every direction. So many hours on so many trips they had glassed the hillsides. Suddenly as if it had appeared out of now where, our hunter spied a fine eight point mule deer buck on one of the secondary ridges that tied onto the main ridge. Quickly he un-shouldered his rifle and dropped down the slope opposite of the deer out of view in order to come around some brush and get a better look. Staying in a half-crouched position, he eased out from behind a sage brush thicket and glassed the opposite slope.

There he was! The hunter had successfully maneuvered into range without the buck detecting him. With the deer only about 250 yards away, he quietly set up his home made shooting stick (which he had fashioned from scrape wood after reading a hunting article) and placed his rifle in the small V at the top of the crossed sticks. The sun had just barely begun to peak above the mesa top filling the eastern sky with a brilliant display of red and orange colors, but our hunter was completely unaware of any of this. All of his concentration centered on the task at hand. Gone were the nervousness and the nausea from earlier. His entire world consisted of nothing more than a small brown patch of ground on the opposite slope.

Using extreme care, he worked the bolt quietly to round a cartridge into the chamber. This was one of the very bullets that he had held in his hand earlier that morning and marveled at how much violence could be had from such a small inanimate object. Now his mind could not and would not consider such ponderings. Instead his mind focused solely on the view in his rifle scope as he settled the crosshairs on the deer's shoulder.

As he instinctively felt the scope settle into the correct slot, the gun fired, startling him with its explosive percussion of sound and fire which ripped apart the quiet of the early morning. He held the view of the scope steady throughout and saw the muley buck crumple from the impact and disappear in the brush.

At first he felt no reaction except to round another bullet into the chamber, but he knew he wouldn't need it. This phase of his Colorado hunt was already complete. One deer tag filled with one elk tag left to go. Still he waited to make sure. Then he heard another shot from the other side of the Point road. It must have been his partner. He shouted over and indeed it was. The Point had produced magic again with two magnificent muleys taken on opening morning

Carefully the hunter hiked over to where he last saw the deer. His boots began to slip in the thawing snow which was beginning to melt in the morning sun. He didn't have to search very long for his prize. His trusty rifle in the hands of a now seasoned and experienced hunter had done its job efficiently.

At the sight of the buck, our hunter's reaction was a bit unusual. With all the emotional buildup and high adrenaline activity, his nausea returned – this time worse than before. Several times he had to kneel down and catch his breath. Each time he had to reassure his mind that this part of the hunt was over and he had plenty of time to deal with his kill. Still the excitement of the moment and the overwhelming sense of relief lingered on.

Deliberately but without wasting time, the two hunters dressed their kills and loaded them up. Working at altitude and in the now gloriously bright sun, they soon had to shed some of the layers of clothes to keep from overheating. That was always a problem in this place, freezing cold temperatures at night but warmer conditions as they exerted their bodies in the day.

Eventually they headed back down the Point road back north to camp. Discussing what had just transpired both hunters agreed that this was indeed a very Interesting Place. Would it always remain so? They weren't sure. Their minds told them no, but in that morning at the peak of their hunting careers in this very hottest of muley hotspots their hearts wanted to believe that these mornings would never end and that they would always return each year. Perhaps that was a naïve belief but a completely understandable one. These were the glory years of the Point, and it seemed that it would last forever with each season being as good as the last.

Slowly the truck ambled northward. They would not celebrate their success until late that night with the others at dinner and of course a few drinks. But for now the vast wilderness to the north beckoned them to elk hunt. There was an entire week with unknown adventures ahead in this most Interesting Place, and it was still Opening Morning.

Chapter 2 - The Primal Instinct

The Clamor and the Storm

In a forgotten time in the endless expanse of the North American continent there existed a golden age where Man could be considered relatively free to come and go as he pleased and purse whatever he sat his heart upon. In this age one such person, a hunter who would be known as Legend, set off on his own one day during quail season to a wild corner in the vast flyover country in the American heartland. This place, this very Interesting Place, could have been mistaken for the wilderness that existed before modern man arrived (if one overlooked the dirt roads and windmills). Trapped between a river and a series of bluffs this wild, unkempt stretch of land harbored wondrous habitat for all kinds of game great and small.

The Legend had decided on this day to hunt this place. Despite all the obligations of work and family he found a way to slip off with just his trusty hunting dog for company. The problems of home and career could wait. After all they had always been there and would always be there. To a hunter, there exists a primal instinct which at time rises up and must be heeded, or else the person dies a little. For it is in these few moments of a person's life in the field when a hunter can define his being for all time. How many days of job and family come and go without any memory of them. But one special day in the field can be remembered forever. It can even define a hunter as a Legend. That is the instinct which calls every hunter.

He planned on arriving early, making a quick hunt, and then to pass by some job sites on the way back (to provide a sort of cover for leaving so early in the morning and not being in the office). He could be in the office by mid-afternoon and resume his normal routine. Times were different in that regard in those days. A person didn't have the same feeling of being constantly monitored. One could come and go in a much freer way. Security at most places was barely noticeable if it existed at all. The level of trust was much higher and the threat of lawsuits much lower.

Still the Legend felt a little harried upon arriving. Quickly he got the dog out and off they went hunting the shaggy thickets which draped the bluffs. The weather, although cool and crisp, had a pleasant, autumn like feel to it. Soon the bird dog got wind of some quail, and within the first hour, the Legend had several bobwhites weighing down his game bag.

That would be considered a good performance by most - after all these were definitely not penned raised birds. Rather these quail were the survivors in a harsh and wild environment filled with all kinds of predators and environmental challenges. They often would not hold on the dog's point and ran in wild haphazard patterns through the thickets before bursting into flight at extreme shotgun range. Any successful hunter here needed to have stamina, experience, and a keen shooting eye.

But the Legend felt a little off his game in those opening covey rises. He missed several shots he normally would have made and several birds got up where he wasn't in a position to shoot at all. Perhaps he still felt a little out of sorts for coming here this day, but he was not at his best.

That is when it happened. The weather, quite stealthily, had changed while the Legend hunted. Now a thick dark line of clouds appeared in the northwestern sky bearing down on him and his dog. With that the wind suddenly kicked up and turned sharply colder biting into his face. And on the river, a great Clamor erupted - a Clamor so great that both hunter and dog stopped and turned to see. There on the river a great collection of waterfowl, like a scene that existed before modern man arrived in North America, exploded upward as one body. Their honking and flapping wings melded together into one great cacophony of noise as they rose above the land and filled the sky with their numbers.

It was as if this Interesting Place had been watching them and now laid before the hunters a challenge. The eruption of waterfowl signaled a change in the drama which was unfolding that day. The very stage of the drama cried out to the hunters (man and dog) and they accepted this Clamor as a challenge. So with the storm approaching they set off again with renewed determination. Now they hunted precisely and efficiently as a team. Now the dog found the birds and held them with ease and the man knocked down every shot he took. Like a crashing Storm they plowed over the bluffs and up the lowlands, though thick brush and cactus piles, they went until they had filled the limit. The weather storm arrived just as the hunting Storm finished with the last bird retrieved.

With the sky now spitting snow and ice, the hunters made a beeline for the truck. There they waited until the storm passed. Now exhausted both fell into a deep sleep. The day had started out like any ordinary hunt, but it ended with each hunter being pushed to his limits and each feeling the deep satisfaction of meeting those challenges successfully.

Why do we hunt?

One of the big problems with sport hunting involves attempting to explain to someone what, exactly, about the activity is so appealing. After all to the modern mind, the entire enterprise seems at best a foolish waste of time to at worst a needlessly violent act. In between these extremes, a modern may dismiss the pursuit (when he thinks about it at all) as nothing more than another way in which rubes of the less refined strata of society prove their manhood – thus filling some misguided psychological need. Or, maybe, they see the sport as a convenient excuse to get away from the pressures of daily life and party with the boys.

Thus, the typical image of a hunter is part unsophisticated redneck, part party animal, part murderer, and part idiot standing out in the freezing dark. In addition, the person has undoubtedly seen hunting shows on television. You know the ones where the hunter sits in a box as several dozen bucks with enormous racks but docile dispositions calmly munch about a feeder. The hunter stresses over which one to choose and finally – with the tension building as the background music increases – finally selects one. Then he takes what seems to be an eternity (at least it's an eternity for anyone who has hunted deer) to get the just-so-perfect shot and kills it. After a re-staged search, the hunter and his camera operator exchange obviously rehearsed celebratory excitement upon finding the carcass.

Afterwards they all retire to a lodge with accommodations and meals fit for Donald Trump. There they attempt – usually quite poorly – to justify the entire sequence with more scripted babbling about how great it is to experience the wild outdoors in all its majesty.

I don't know about you, but even as a hunter I find these episodes somehow strangely weird and artificial. I don't want to blame the producers; after all they have to create a drama that under the constraints of the television medium builds up the requisite tension and resolves the conflict all in a thirty minute time slot (minus commercial breaks). And I have seen a few shows that did a decent job. Nevertheless, these shows simply do not adequately capture the essence of hunting – the inner struggle of the hunter, the emotions, and the drive that makes us hunt. And I doubt that these shows really ever can adequately describe hunting to the non-hunter. However, they do create images that make that all the more difficult.

Against these images, a hunter has the devil of time explaining the why to another person. Often the ideals of conservation are invoked, and that is a good reason. Hunting has a great and positive track record in this regard and there is nothing wrong with emphasizing it. However to the non-hunter that may have been great in the past, but isn't necessarily a reason for the now. Also the question is inevitably asked "but why do YOU hunt". Also the hunter at times rambles about herd management. Normally this explanation is received with a slightly puzzled expression as if to say that "you've got to be kidding".

Other reasons often cited include enjoyment of the outdoors, time with family, relaxation, etc. But the question remains "why do you hunt?" Most hunters when they ask this question in their minds instinctively know the answer, but the words are difficult. Why? Why is it so maddeningly difficult to explain why we get up before dawn, hike in the cold, endure frustration and failure, stay in the woods alone, make outlays of money, and spend our few precious vacation days on hunting?

<u>Off on Friday</u>

The meeting was being held at a typical meeting room which is common at many businesses large and small. Each morning the staff of this operating unit of a large manufacturing facility located in the Midwest would meet to discuss the everyday problems and crises that exist in such a place. And although they didn't know it at the time, such places were special – and fragile despite their outward appearance of industrial might.

These facilities were fragile not due to the physical plant but due to economics. Globalization had just begun to rear its ugly head in the minds of the everyday person. Already they felt a deep sense of foreboding about what they had observed in the process. Discussions in the break rooms and union shops occasional broke out about something called NAFTA. Despite not really knowing what all it entailed – how could anyone at that point – impromptu debates flared up among the workers. Most were bitterly opposed to the idea. Some that in principle supported the concept behind the treaty still had reservations about how it would impact them personally.

One thing was for certain: the world in which they operated and lived their lives was changing. It would be a change that would affect them personally and profoundly alter the lives of their children. Against this backdrop, however, everyday life hummed along. The needs of the moment also seemed to push back these concerns from their consciousness. But no matter how busy they became, the changes sweeping the world economy and America never fully were displaced. Like tectonic plates beneath their feet hidden and powerful, the forces now unleashed inexorably were reshaping humanity, and they were being swept up in that change.

Yet the everyday challenges always screamed to be heard. And so everyday they met in the same room at the same time. The agenda droned on the same each day. How on this day it had a twist. Each Monday of the week Richard, the manager, would go around and determine who in his staff would be out of town or on vacation that coming weekend. On this Monday, nearly every member of the staff surprised him by announcing that this Friday they would be off. At first he was puzzled and confused over this. After all, it was not a holiday weekend. If fact it was the weekend before a holiday – Thanksgiving to be exact. Thoroughly puzzled, he had to know why almost his entire staff would be gone that Friday. Was it some kind of revolt? Was there some celebrity scheduled to be in town?

Richard grew up in California, the son of immigrants. He attended a prestigious college and received an engineering degree with honors. He had advanced rapidly up the hierarchy of this multi-national corporation. In fact this assignment, although temporary, was a bit of a set back. The corporate brass selected him to go to this struggling Midwest facility to "turn it around". The assignment would be a huge test for Richard, and an equally huge risk. He wanted to get the job done and get back into the political game at headquarters. He therefore had little connection to the culture of semi-rural America and almost zero contact up to this point.

"What's up with Friday?" he asked. Everyone in the room looked at each other a little nervously. After all each didn't want to be told that they couldn't have the day off. Finally one managed to mumble "Well sir, it is opening day of Illinois gun season". Leaning back in his chair, Richard let out a big grin "Ohh, I've heard about this from some people I worked with in headquarters. Let me get this straight. You take a day of vacation. You get up, how early?" "About 4:00 or 4:30" responded a foreman from the back of the room. "Wow, that early! Then you drive out to the middle of nowhere, park, and hike into the woods in the dark. And you're going to do this even if it rains or snows". "Umm, yea, that pretty well sums it up" responded one of the staff. "And you do this for fun?!?!" the boss added.

Nobody in the room knew exactly what to say at that point. Once someone put it that way, the whole effort did seem like madness. Why spend a day of hard earned vacation like that? Why not stay in the comfort of civilization? Why hike out in the middle of the woods in the dark in a cold rain (which was forecasted). Why indeed? Shaking his head Richard could only say "Well I wish you all good luck. I don't get it, but if that is what you want to do fine by me – just be safe". Everyone then chuckled slightly, relieved that he hadn't cancelled everyone's vacation. It had been a momentary meeting of two different worlds – two different ways of looking at life.

Chapter 3 – The Authentic Experience

The Great Leveling

A person can have all their physical needs met – food, shelter, clothing, protection from misfortune – and yet their life is incomplete. So that is why people ultimately seek authenticity in their life experiences. While artificially constructed experiences may provide for diversion and entertainment, in the end they leave one feeling unsatisfied, like something is missing but one can't quite put one's finger on it. While the technology employed may be spectacular and the planned experience executed with brilliant precision, if it is not authentic it will fall short.

In the modern world, we have attempted to replace the substance of authenticity with the style of celebrity and the glitz of technology. All of this is perfectly understandable. In the business of providing a service, one must control – as much as possible – everything connected to the experience being offered. That way a certain level of customer satisfaction can be more or less guaranteed; however, that comes at a price. The price is that what is guaranteed is that the process goes smoothly and in a safe, comfortable, and predictable manner. Therefore, the measure of the "success" of the service must be subtlety manipulated. No longer can the substance of an authentic experience be held as the standard – for that would be messy and unpredictable. Instead the style of the process is held out as the thing that qualifies as success.

One can see this most notably in venues such as packaged vacations, tours, movies, etc. There flash and glitz often replace a genuine search for authenticity. How many movies come out each year that present spectacular special effects but are based on vacuous plots? How many vacation destinations offer thrilling rides or wham bam entertainment spectaculars but hold out little in terms of lasting memories? This need from the business side to control the experience is driven is by a larger force which shapes modern life.

This phenomenon is a great "leveling" which grinds along continuously. It seeks to remove spontaneity and replace it with predictability. It seeks to remove uncertainty and replace it with order. It seeks to remove all the wildness from our soul and replace it with conformity.

This leveling cannot abide the messiness of uncertainty that comes from genuine spontaneity. Instead, it seeks to replace that with a sort of faux excitement generated by glitz and controlled by puppet masters operating behind the scene. All of this is done in order to guarantee a certain outcome. In order to accomplish this, this "leveling" attempts to remove all the effort and sacrifice involved with a pursuit and guarantee the result and the emotional state that goes with that result. The focus is on the emotional response not in the virtue of the efforts put forth.

Hunting has not been immune from this effect. This is the first great paradox of hunting. As hunting increased in popularity, it increasingly has come to be seen as a revenue source. Once that happened the need increased to provide a product which could be managed and controlled. An authentic experience cannot be managed so easily. Therefore the emphasis switched from the experience to the end result. With hunting that means antler size. That is something that can be quantifiably managed and controlled to some degree. Thus, as antler size increasingly became the standard to measure the hunting experience, operators could then manage their herds and control access. That is the paradox: hunting became popular for the intangible experience but that very popularity led to the intangible being replaced with a "leveled" product largely devoid of the very things that made that intangible experience so special.

Actually what has happened is that we have elevated the result over the cause. There is nothing wrong with pursuing a true trophy animal. At one time a trophy set of antlers represented the accomplishment of the outdoorsman. He was the one who had gone deeper in the wilderness, who had the best knowledge of the creature's ways, and who had the greatest perseverance. He was also the one willing to risk going home empty despite the expenditure of time and effort.

The trophy was a result of this experience, and a large trophy epitomized authentic accomplishment. To see a large trophy on display meant that real sacrifice had been made and that a wild, improbable story lay behind the mere physical result.

This is why Interesting Places, where they can be found, are so special. They are essential to that intangible, authentic experience which is at the heart of what make s hunting such a unique activity. Interesting Places are, for that reason, those few remaining strips and nooks of land, often overlooked and ignored which contain a remnant of unleveled magic. From the modern world's perspective they are often unassuming and quiet scraps that hardly warrant a second look. They are hard to find. They are often hard to get to. And often do not last long. That very humble and transient nature is what makes them so special and thus unable to be managed. However, they are necessary for hunting, because without them hunting becomes just another hobby. And this is the first principle of Interesting Places: in order to have an authentic hunting experience, one must first find an Interesting Place. That is a place that demands sacrifice, denial, and effort to hunt. Nothing is guaranteed, but everything is genuine.

Frozen in Time

Opening morning of the Illinois gun season always occurs on the Friday before Thanksgiving. The first season is only three days long, and tags can be scarce. For one hunter, he looked forward to that morning with tremendous anticipation. This would be his second year hunting in this prime deer country, and he had a great spot. Truly an Interesting Place, it was small by most standards – only about 60 acres. However, it was located on a rough patch of hilly terrain with a large creek bordering its east and south sides. At one time part of it had been farmed. You can tell that by the abandoned equipment left in the woods – an old Chevy with a tree growing through the spot where the hood had been, and an old plow which had fused with part of a tree trunk as it grew from a sapling to full adulthood. Obviously, most of the terrain was second growth forest with patches of a formerly plowed field now smothered in impenetrable undergrowth.

At one time before modern farming, people in these parts planted crops on every available square inch of land regardless of how difficult the terrain. This led to an almost complete denouement of the wildlife habitat. One could live their entire lives in that country and rarely see a deer, any deer. Over time farming became more mechanized and industrialized with the advent of petroleum driven equipment. You might think this would have destroyed what little remained of the natural habitat. However, it had the opposite effect. By increasing yields, less land needed to be put to the plow. The land that was left uncultivated tended to be the more marginal land in terms of productivity and accessibility. Thus the land became checker boarded with plowed fields separated by strips of land that had returned to a wilder state.

This created an almost perfect combination of food plots and cover for many species of animals including deer. Not only did they thrive after being re-introduced, this country became known for some of the largest animals around. This was achieved in the natural state without resorting to breeding or corralling. So far from being an enemy of Interesting Places, progress in and of its self can serve to actually promote and preserve them. It is the overzealous effort to capture the special essence of Interesting Places for short term gains that threatens them.

Our hunter had discovered a true gem of an Interesting Place in this environment. Once highly cultivated, the land now consisted of re-growth forest and cover. The vestiges of a by gone age now lay frozen in time and slowly returning to the dust from which they sprang. It was all re-growth except for the area right along the creek. Here one stepped back into an even more distance era. There the trees grew massive with trunks that made our hunter feel like a dwarf. These were old growth trees; perhaps one of the last remaining areas like that in this highly settled area. Beneath their sprawling canopies, sunlight didn't reach the ground. As a result, little vegetation grew around these giants. Stepping into this realm was like stepping into another world. When he first stepped into this area, our hunter couldn't help but feel a chill of primeval fear settle over his body. No wonder, he thought, that primitive people imagined all sorts of evil in such forests.

Another item which made this place unique is that he did not have to pay a ransom for the privilege to hunt here. That was another thing that made the place so special. Like a throw back to an early age, he had gained permission with a handshake and an understanding. Maybe that is why sports teams now have "throw back" days – it is to attempt to capture some of the humility and grace of an early age. The understanding was that he would make sure nobody trespassed on the property and that he would give the owner half of what he killed. For the rights to such an Interesting Place it was a remarkably straightforward offer.

That morning, he awoke early. A front was scheduled to hit that day, and the morning temperatures had already turned sharply colder. He went through the usual morning ritual, but as always he felt agitated and anxious. Opening morning always had that affect on him. Often he would joke that it was like being a little kid again waiting for Christmas morning except that in this case there really was no way of knowing if presents would be there in the morning.

He double checked his equipment one more time before cranking up the truck and heading off down the road. Slowly the heater began to thaw the frost on the windshield and warm his boots. It felt good, but he knew that soon he would forgo such civilized comforts for the hardships of a wintry morning in the field. Finally he turned off the blacktop leaving the last bit of the modern world behind. He was always surprised at how close the wild areas really are to the modern world even where civilization has made its presence for so long.

Soon he arrived at his parking spot. He sat for a moment in the truck after the headlights faded into black. Immediately he could sense nature closing in. He felt the bite of the cold air as it seeped into the vehicle. Now he faced that moment where he had to transition from one world to another. It was not just a physical change; it was a transition in the mind. He had to cross an invisible boundary between the modern world and its ways to the more subtle and slower rhythm of a forgotten world. It was at this moment that there is always a slight hesitation for crossing that boundary meant that he would become a part of an ancient drama which although played out countless times in the past had no guaranteed outcome in the future.

This was the moment where he had to deny the safety and comfort of home for an unknown end. This was the moment of doubt and of courage.

Quickly and as quietly as possible he gathered his gear and headed off. Due to the uncertain weather forecast, he had to take extra clothes which weighed him down. He had selected a relatively close stand for the morning. All the trees had dropped their leaves making a stealthy approach impossible. He decided that the best bet was to get to where he was going as quickly as possible, set up, and then disappear into the dark. He had pulled off this very tactic last year, and was rewarded with a nice buck.

On the path to the stand, he heard a loud sound from the brush to his right near the old Chevy with the tree growing through it. "Damn" he whispered. He knew he had bumped a deer; hopefully, it hadn't messed up the whole area.

Finally he found the stand and as quietly as possible crawled inside. Sitting alone in the cold and dark, even for a short time, has a certain effect on a person. In these moments one really wonders about why he is there and why on earth he pursues this quarry. The dark surrounds and closes in on the soul. With adrenaline surging, the senses are now heightened. One begins to hear sounds which normally would be ignored. "Was that a deer? Or maybe just a squirrel?" one will ask. This morning the sound of the tree branches, covered in ice, crashed in the angry wind. "How strange they sound. How odd they appear in the slowly increasing light" the hunter thought.

Finally the light increased enough to see. The landscape looked bleak and uninviting. The wind whipped leaves in small whirlpools. The naked branches swayed and creaked. He felt an uncontrollable chill overtake his body, but only for a moment. Furiously he glassed every spot in the brush around him for any sign of a deer. Although the ranges involved in this type of hunting are close, still it pays to use magnification especially in low light. He had the best optics which he acquired to scan long distances in the Rocky Mountains. Those same binoculars here seemed to be a bit of overkill. Still one learns to always use the best equipment that one possesses.

Suddenly he spotted movement. His heart raced at the sight. "Drat. It's only a doe." he thought. Renewed by that sighting, he re-focused his efforts. Someone not experienced in stand hunting may think it is relatively non-active. Often this is not the case. It requires a certain blend of skills to be successfully. One must be patient and constantly alert for the slightest flick of a tail may be the only clue of a deer's presence. Also one must be still, even in a box, too much movement can alarm that deer or other animals in the area. One must adopt a certain mental state: focused and calm but at the same time relaxed and nervous. It is not an easy state to achieve for a modern person. It is not a state that gives instant gratification. It requires sacrifice and demands subtle but intense effort with no guarantee of success. Modern man has to learn this skill and re-learn it every time he goes into the field for it is no longer natural to him.

Our hunter was well experienced in many styles of hunting including stand hunting. His skills had been honed with the effort of long hours hunting in numerous environments. His successes had been purchased by hard work, sacrifice, and his share of mistakes. Experienced, confident, and in his prime, he seemed destined for success that hunt – a trophy Illinois white tail. This would be his year to bag the big one.

He spotted a few other small deer in the brush. One young buck came out into easy range, milled around a small drainage in front of the blind for a good while. Our hunter was not interested. Unfortunately the deer disappeared as the sun passed higher in the morning sky. Now he made a decision. He would move to the far end of the property where the cover was dense and the location even more remote. He would set up at the edge where the old growth trees stood at a crossing over the creek. That was where he really wanted to hunt, but he didn't want to bust it up in the dark. Now that it was mid-morning, he could quickly back out and circle around to that spot with minimal disruption. During the off season he had built a ground stand there and planned on using it for an afternoon hunt.

To hike over to the other end also meant to cross a small creek which normally only had little or no water, but today after unseasonably heavy rains it ran full. Gingerly he navigated across. His waterproof boots and pants provided excellent protection from the frigid, near freezing waters. All of his equipment was top of the line. He had acquired it through years of trial and error (and I do mean a lot of error) in the unforgiving environs of the Colorado Rockies. Now, outfitted with the best equipment he worked even further into this little forgotten corner of wilderness. Now alone, he no longer was of the modern world, he had crossed over to a forgotten time and place.

Once settled into his ground stand, he noticed that the air had become more disturbed as the expected front approached. He settled in for an afternoon on the stand. Nothing much seemed to be happening. Earlier in the morning he continuously heard gunshots from all around. It is always like that on opening morning of gun season. The sounds had faded and now in the mid-afternoon hours, the surrounding woods had fallen silent of human activity. He was truly alone. The feeling seemed to at once bother him and energize him at the same time for these are the moments where magic can happen.

Towards late afternoon, he caught a glimpse from the dense thickets to his right. Instantly he knew it was a deer, and instinctively he knew it was a buck. Franticly he glassed the thicket, and he saw it again. It was a true Illinois trophy buck. Its body appeared to be built more like a cow's than a deer's. With experienced fluidity and careful stealth, he moved his slug gun into position. At that moment his heart stopped. The deer had turned with only its rear facing him, its body completely hidden in the brush. Only a few yards away stood a giant of a buck. He was so tantalizingly close but he couldn't pull the trigger. He waited for the deer to turn, but it never did. Eventually it slipped into the tangle and disappeared.

Still our hunter held out hope for another chance. He could hear the deer in the thicket and perhaps another. Finally he heard the deer move off, its giant body crashing through the brush. Maybe the deer had winded him despite his best efforts. Perhaps something else spooked it. We will never know. The only sound was the clacking of tree branches as they swayed in the gathering wind. The front was upon him.

He could see the clouds roll in low and heavy. The temperature dropped from its already freezing level to the sub-zero realm within a few minutes. Yet he held out hope until the clouds opened up and ice fell from the dark grey sky. Light failed quickly. Visibility dropped to below 20 yards. Despite his high tech, modern equipment, the cold began to settle deep within his body. Reluctantly he decided to pull back and try another time. It was the best percentage play, but that thought did little to soothe his disappointment. After all he had everything going for him: a great location, good scouting, the best equipment, tremendous experience, and practiced marksmanship.

Yet despite all that he couldn't get the shot. The prize had been oh so close, but it was not to be. He had been a part of a great and ancient drama. This time he left empty handed. This time his trophy was counted only in the experience.

As he left, the ground became covered with white as the ice turned to a heavy snow. It shone in the darkening light of evening. He turned back to look at the place where this drama had been played out. Now dark except for the white covering the trees and ground, the scene appeared to have been painted out of a memory - a memory frozen in time.

The Search for Self

One reason people seek out authentic experiences is the change these experiences make on the person. It is a part of our nature to require these experiences for proper development. These experiences must be authentic for them to have the desired effect. So profound is this need that when they are not available, people search for substitutes. Some of these substitutes are not all that bad in and of themselves; however, many, by their very artificial nature are unhealthy. By their very construct, substitutes must appeal to the emotions and satisfy the immediate craving. However they are like junk food compared to real nourishment. Ultimately they leave the person unsatisfied. How many addictions are a result of the unfulfilling nature of these experience substitutes? How much crime and other destructive thrill seeking stem from stunted personality growth?

Interesting Places are necessary to change a person, to develop a person properly. And this is the second principle of Interesting Places: they change the person who experiences them for the better. That is one of the positive aspects of hunting that is so hard to express. True hunting almost always changes a person for the better. Think about the hunters that you have known. Taken as a whole they are some of the best adjusted people you will meet. This often surprises people who haven't been around hunters much. "Gee you seem so normal" is a common reaction when the person standing in front of them fails to meet the stereotypes they had envisioned.

Interesting Places make that happen. For every passionate hunter, there is at least one place in the past that he remembers fondly. In that memory he can think back and realize how an Interesting Place changed him forever.

Weimar

For a young person, the act of hunting can be at once exhilarating and intimidating. There is something special about hunting with your father. It is as if each of us is hardwired to understand at a deep intrinsic level the importance of this act. This produces feelings that have no verbal description. So despite the modern world screaming at a person from every angle, this ancient instinct still remains. It cannot be drowned out. It is part of Everyman's need to be molded by those around him and by the experiences they share together.

This was true for one young hunter in his early teens. He had hunted with his dad on several occasions. Each outing had been a learning experience. Each time it seemed to the young boy that his father was larger than life. After all he appeared to know everything about the outdoors and about hunting. His shooting skills awed the young hunter on many occasions. Also the young hunter had heard his stories told many times. How could he live up to someone that sounded like a legend?

The one thing that had impressed the young hunter the most was his father's drive and determination in the field. The young hunter always had difficulty keeping up. Never, could he imagine his father slowing down. Now his father would take him to a truly Interesting Place – the Weimar lease. It was there that this Interesting Place changed him for the better.

The Weimar is located in northwestern Oklahoma. On its western border ran the Cimarron River – a flat sprawling river that dominated the landscape. From the river stretched a large floodplain which ended abruptly at a bluff of about 100 feet or so. Steep draws and crags broke the line of the bluff which provided excellent cover and hiding places for game. The uncultivated flood plain was filled with varying degrees of brush and tangles of thickets. An old fashioned windmill provided water on the southern end of the property. A far cry from the stereotypical images of Oklahoma with endless fields of wheat, this are was rough and wild with sharp changes in elevation. Much of the landscape had scarcely changed from primitive times. Truly this was a forgotten piece of land largely overlooked by the business of the modern world. This made the Weimar an Interesting Place by all accounts.

They arrived at the Weimar about mid-morning on that October Saturday. Quail season was going full steam, and the weather was crisp but perfect. The Weimar had everything that quail need to thrive and they often did in large numbers. Soon they had gathered their gear and let out the hunting dog with anticipation of a great day in the field.

The hunting started great. They first started out on the bluff top close to the edge where it dropped off the floodplain below. There they jumped several large coveys of quail. The wild birds scattered in all directions. The father knocked down a number, never did seem to miss. The young hunter struggled more. He missed a few and hit several. He didn't yet possess the years of shooting experience that his father had. The father, however, had perfected his marksmanship in early years in the great quail hunting grounds of eastern Kansas in days when quail numbers there were great. Few areas like that remained now. The Weimar was one of the few areas where wild quail could be found in numbers like that.

And these quail were the real deal. None had been pen raised and all were wild. They often didn't hold for a point and ran through the spiny thickets when pursued. Once they did rise, their flight was unpredictable and fast. Not exactly the type of shooting for an inexperienced hunter to do well. But this quarry in this place was an authentic experience. The outcome by no means guaranteed.

Soon the action tapered off with the warming of the mid-day sun. Still they pressed on stopping to take only short breaks and for lunch. Already the young hunter felt fatigue begin to take its toll. His feet began to hurt in the heavy boots. On this hunt, like the others, he stayed amazed by his father's drive. He had an almost maniacally zeal, that the young hunter could barely fathom – and barely ke`ep up with.

They worked the draws up and down very methodically. Then they worked the vast floodplain with its endless patches of cover. As the day passed into late afternoon, they began to encounter larger numbers of quail again. With the increase in action, the young hunter's spirits lifted. Soon they were knocking down birds in good numbers. Still, the old man always seemed to knock just a few more on each covey rise. The young hunter's aches and pains passed from memory as he felt his shooting rhythm improve. This was by far the most birds he had ever taken and that made this the best hunting trip he had ever been on.

At one point, the father stopped and announced "We better count our birds". With great joy, the young hunter produced the quail from his hunting vest which by now had been loaded down from the days' take. After counting, they knew that they were two birds short of a limit. With the action still good, they didn't think it would take that long to fill out. However, the quail would not cooperate so easily. The last two birds took an hour longer to acquire with several blown opportunities by the young hunter along the way.

Finally the last quail fell with a thud in a clump of long grass. The young hunter felt relief. He had done it! He had gone all day with his dad out in this wild place and had success. Now tired, sore, thirsty and hungry (teenagers are always hungry) he looked forward to the hike back to the truck. The hunt had been a great success.

However, his father had other plans. On the extreme far northern end he had seen some pheasants in earlier trips. Pheasants did not live in Oklahoma in great numbers, but there were a few in this are which was not too far from the Kansas border. The game regs allowed for three pheasants per season.

The plan (devised by the father for he was the one with the experience) called for each hunter to walk on either side of a small ridge which ran parallel to the bluff. The dog would work in front of them. After about a quarter mile or so, the ridge and the cover on the ridge petered out. They would use that natural feature as the "blocker" in their drive.

Once they started, the young hunter felt every muscle and bone in his lower body scream in protest. He had already put in a full day and this felt like overtime. The dog too started off gingerly obviously stiff from his day's work. By the time they started, the afternoon had given away to early evening. They had just enough light left to make this drive – as long as the hunters and the dog held up.

After they began, the dog soon perked up. He was onto something. Everyone, dog and hunters alike, forgot their bruises and aches and sprang forward with renewed energy. Soon a pheasant hen flushed from one side of the ridge. It startled the young hunter. He had begun to swing on it when his father barked at him to not shoot. Then another hen flushed. Then the dog bumped a rooster which flushed wildly in front of him. The father shouted orders to press on quickly.

A primal adrenaline surge flushed through the young hunter. He had never felt the rush of this type of excitement while hunting. A dog on point for quail was exciting and fun, but this was somehow different. It was a little like a big game hunt situation, and it was his first taste of that thrill. This experience was already changing him in this Interesting Place in ways that he didn't yet understand.

The dog now worked back and forth furiously appearing as fresh as the first hour of the day. Quickly they came to the end of the ridge as several more pheasants busted out in odd directions. The young hunter then became strangely aware of something to his right. At that moment a pheasant exploded from out of the grass with thunderous sound. The young hunter swung on it. Quickly he checked it over – definitely a rooster. Now he felt his mind focusing completely on the bird. The image of that moment would be forever frozen in his mind. In one day he had been transformed from a clumsy amateur to a seasoned marksman. That is what Interesting Places will do to a person. They require effort and sacrifice, but they will reward that with special moments in time that change a person.

He knew when he fired that he was solidly on the bird. Its wings folded up and then it crashed to the ground. He then heard another shot ring out from his father. He had also knocked down a pheasant. Forgetting completely his earlier exhaustion, he nearly sprinted to the spot where the rooster fell – he desperately didn't want to loose this one. There was nothing to worry about. The bird lay where it fell. The young hunter then felt a rush of emotion wash over his soul. For the first time in his young life, he felt the mix of pride, accomplishment, joy, sadness, and confusion that go with such a moment. It is a strange emotion, and it has no word to describe it. Perhaps it cannot really be described only experienced.

Now with light failing, the hunt was finally over. Slowly they hiked back to the truck and drove to the south end where the windmill continued to hum in the Oklahoma breeze. There they cleaned their kill in the near freezing water of the tank. The water there sparkled with a strange purity as the twilight danced on its surface. Hands now frozen from the water, the hunters gathered up and drove up to the top of the bluff. There they stopped to look back west at the last light of the setting sun. Sunsets in places like this are often incredible in their beauty. With no artificial light or pollution, the hues of reds, yellows, and oranges paint a brilliant canopy of fire across the western sky. As the last light faded into dark, the coyotes howled in the near distance. One could easily imagine this place as it was a hundred years ago for it would be little changed.

One thing that had changed that day was our young hunter. Although he didn't realize it yet nor did it show up right away, this authentic experience in this Interesting Place would remain with him forever. A seed had been planted and it would continue to grow for that is what Interesting Places do to people.

The Second Paradox of Interesting Places

One paradox about Interesting Places is that the very modern world that is constantly at work leveling everything in its path into a consistent mush of conformity also gives people of otherwise ordinary means the opportunity to experience these places. After all it wasn't that long ago in the United States that the average person could only dream of travel, let alone actually traveling to do something as optional as sport hunting. Life, for the average person, had to stay focused on necessities. Sport hunting was the purview of the rich. That is why the popular image of sport hunting is often dominated by images of rich European aristocrats hunting on exclusive land or the "Great White Hunter" in Africa. If the average person had the opportunity to hunt it was for whatever lived in the local area, and it was done primarily for food.

For a brief golden era in America, there existed a unique combination of two things: increased wealth which allowed the average person to be able to sport hunt, and remaining areas of wilderness or Interesting Places in which to hunt. This special combination is now fading before our eyes. Increasingly fewer people have the means to hunt and hunting opportunities become ever more expensive and exclusive. Thus the doors are closing on this golden era. For those of us that were lucky to live during that time and fortunate enough to take advantage of those opportunities, it was truly a magically combination.

No one should take this as a slam on other styles of hunting such as the high fence kind. Each person must decide what makes a hunt special to him. It is one thing that is truly relative to the individual. For what makes hunting such a unique activity is that it is the hunting experience that is the thing, not the end result. Of course, if there were no possibility of a successful hunt, then it wouldn't really have much of a purpose.

And that is the third principle of Interesting Places. There must be a reasonable chance of success – not too easy and not impossible. This balance is relative to the hunter involved for it is the experience to the individual that matters. Success should be possible, but should require dedication, effort, sacrifice, and the possibility of going home empty in order to make the experience important, because the experience is what builds a person's character. Interesting Places are there to set the stage for this drama to be played out. That is why we seek them.

Snow in Illinois

The hunter knew before he even set out that it would probably be a rather futile effort. There was good reason for him to feel this way. From the splendor of the Colorado Rockies to the wilderness of forgotten prairies in Oklahoma, he had seen and experienced much in his hunting career. Several times these places had tested him fully, and he had emerged as a seasoned hunter and skilled shooter. Although he perhaps couldn't boast of the trophies of someone who had been to Africa, his record would impress any knowledgeable hunter. Nobody could doubt the authenticity of his trophies or his experience, and that experience now told him that this was a low percentage quest.

You see, he was hunting on public land in a state long settled and tamed by the modern world. It had left a few scraps as almost a grudging nod to an earlier age. Of course these scraps of highly controlled and regulated "wilderness" were over hunted to the extreme. Still our hunter found himself in this place at this time. Due to a recent move, he really had no other place to hunt that year, so being the true sport he reluctantly decided that this was his only option on short notice.

Why would an experienced hunter go to such a place? Well the primal pull is strong in a person once he has tasted that indescribable array of emotions from an authentic hunting experience. So no matter what the odds, he will always give it a try. In this case, our hunter followed all the rules. He researched the available hunting lands carefully utilizing topographical maps and pre-season scouting trips. He knew that any public hunting land would be overrun once the season started, and to have any chance he had to have every advantage possible.

After checking out several possibilities, he settled on a public hunting area in a relatively remote part of the state. There during his scouting trip he found deer sign and trails deep in the woods in a nook that was bordered on three sides by private land. Using his binocs, he discovered two permanent blinds on the private land. That is always a good sign. It may sound obvious, but a good spot is often marked with evidence of previous or current hunting activity especially if the hunters go to the trouble of erecting structures.

On that scouting trip, a part of him actually began to believe that he could pull this off. If this had been private property he would have considered it a hot spot. Since it was public land, his mind had to overrule his hope. Even a doe would be a trophy in this situation. The rest of the scouting trip was spent in figuring out how to approach the target area. That would be tough. The regulations required that one park in a designated spot and check in (so much for the wilderness feel). There would be very few options for an approach. Still he plotted a course that hugged one fence line that seemed to give the best odds.

Opening day came on a nice but crisp October morning. At the designated time he checked in and began his hike to his targeted area. Just as he feared, a number of other hunters had also checked in that morning. The state game office did its best to try and distribute the hunting pressure. A lottery system decided who would hunt each area and on which day. Nevertheless, our hunter would be competing with other hunters, and they presented a wildcard factor not present in other hunts.

According to the regulations, the hunters had to wait until early light before leaving the station. From an organizing point of view this made sense. If you were in charge you would do the same thing. After all you don't know these people, and you don't want them stumbling around in the dark.

Yet for our hunter it was frustrating. He had hiked into wilderness country in the dark. He had trailed game in failing light in the Rockies. To be hamstrung by such seemingly cautious restrictions almost was an insult. Still he soldiered on as soon as possible.

By the time he reached his target area, the sun had already broken the eastern horizon. For an experienced hunter it all seemed such a waste – good hunting light for naught. Even then his hunting instinct kicked into gear. Diligently he scanned the brush for any signs of his quarry. In the distance, he heard shots, some not that far off. By all accounts this was prime Illinois deer country, but due to the fact that this property was public access, he knew his chances bordered on nil.

Still the primal urge stirred deep within his soul. For if he could pull this feat off – taking a deer, any deer, on public land – oh what a feather in his cap it would be. However, he needed some luck. Another hunter he knew would say that lightening would have to strike. He tried to conjure up that belief, but somehow he couldn't fool his mind. He would need a minor miracle to pull this off.

He had done everything possible to achieve success. He had scouted in the off season, scouring maps and topos. He had planned his approach, and now his final act of dedication: he planned on staying on the stand to the end. He had done this before. Here on this scrap of over hunted public land, he vowed to stay to the end. He had the equipment and the experience. His plan was quite basic: do everything to put the odds in your favor and wait it out with religious determination. He had learned this from his father as a young lad in hunts where they hiked for miles in search of quail. Then he witnessed the almost fanatical zeal his father displayed in the field. He came to appreciate that factor in hunting success. And here he would do the same.

Slowly the hours passed. He became absorbed into the small sliver of nature he had entered. Soon the small sparrows occupied his attention. The males of the species fought out with total abandon for dominance. Our hunter couldn't help but be amused. Of course from afar do not humans and their Machiavellian struggles appear similar? The squirrels came out and did the same. No matter how slow hunting can be, to a real hunter, once they become one with the woods, it all seems worthwhile. Gone were the concerns of career and family. Here once, again, he was in his primal element and a hunter.

Eventually the day passed. Despite playing his hand perfectly and despite not making nary a mistake, there would be no magic today. Lightening does not always strike, no matter how tightly we close our eyes and wish it so. According to the regulations of the game department, hunting ceased at an all too early hour. However, our hunter did not protest. In a different time and setting he would have been determined to stay on to the bitter end. He knew that many a deer were taken in the last moments of light - in the magic hour as it is known.

But in this case, no. The artificial regulations almost came as a blessing. The weather had turned to the colder right after lunch. Normally this meant more game movement. However in this patch of over hunted turf where numerous boot tracks already shown in the new fallen snow. Lightening was not going to strike, and our hunter knew it. Reluctantly he gathered his gear – accoutrements fit for high mountain adventures – and headed back to the parking area. He felt almost embarrassed. After all here he was, THE MIGHTY COLRODAO ELK HUNTER, reduced to a futile hunt on public land. It was a moment of hubris. And, of course, God hates hubris.

Upon approaching the parking area, he noticed that the winter storm had already covered his truck in a beautiful layer of fresh snow. Disgusted at the day's events, he hurriedly threw his gear into the back of the vehicle hardly taking note of the snow's effects on the landscape.

At that moment another hunter emerged from the woods with a wide grin on his face. He appeared to be a rather humble sort. Obviously his gear was not honed from years of adventures in far flung locals. Once he reached the parking area he stopped and greeted our hunter. "Isn't this great!" he exclaimed. "Isn't this the greatest thing in the world!" he continued. Our hunter now aroused could only ask "Huh". "Here we are hunting in a fantastic place. And now the snow is falling. Isn't this great!" he continued.

At that moment our hunter could only feel a mixture of humility and remorse. "Yea, yea this is the greatest" he responded. For at that moment he understood something more important than all the trophies he had ever taken. He understood that to that hunter this place was an Interesting Place because it had changed him. He learned a fundamental lesson about Interesting Places and at that moment that place became an Interesting Place because it changed him also.

Balance

What all Interesting Places require is balance. That is balance between offering a reasonable chance of success but only with effort and skill. It requires a balance to hunting's popularity in order to ensure that the sport is not distorted beyond recognition. It requires balanced economic growth that allows people the time and money to hunt without overheated growth that only leaves decayed wreckage in its wake. It requires a balance between skill and equipment.

Ultimately this balance would create a world of steady improvement in the human condition while creating a varied landscape of interesting and unique habitats (both natural and human). It is not anti-progress or anti-technology; instead this balance is the proper application of those things. This is a real trick to accomplish, and perhaps that is why Interesting Places are so rare. Instead the leveling process is an overheated, artificial growth that destroys uniqueness (both natural and human) and leaves in its wake a decaying mush of conformity. It is a result of human sin which hyper-stimulates certain economic aspects in the name of growth but only leaves popped bubbles as its legacy.

However, if we could pull off this balancing feat, we would have the best of both worlds by creating sustainable improvement in our lives which would also preserve Interesting Places in the balance. Interesting Places are fragile because they depend on this balance, and they suffer when we don't. That is the fourth principle of Interesting Places: they are fragile because they depend on a balance of many competing forces. I truly believe that this balance is natural and would occur without artificial meddling on human's part. It is our attempts to rig the system, usually as a result of lust for power and control that causes this balance to go out of kilter. The fix is on one hand easy, just stop meddling and let growth occur naturally. On the other hand it is difficult because to stop artificially stimulating growth just isn't something that our human society is set up to do.

Spring Season

Spring turkey season is a unique type of hunting experience for the avid deer hunter. First it occurs long after the deer season has closed. Just about the time that the hunter begins to long to be out in the woods, his thoughts begin to turn to the spring turkeys. It makes for a nice break during the middle part of the year. Second it is a chance to see old friends and reminisce about the previous fall's exploits and near misses.

The hunting is different also. Normally the weather is milder, and the hunter can be less concerned with dealing with his scent. This type of hunting often has a feel more like a camping trip with the added bonus of some adrenaline pumping excitement thrown in. Gone are the strenuous hikes up steep slopes in heavy winter clothing to protect from freezing early morning temperatures. In their place are hikes through green pastures along wooded draws in light camo gear. That is not to say that turkeys are less challenging than deer. In fact the opposite could justifiably be argued. It is that the feel and demands of the hunting is different.

But mainly what is special about spring turkey hunting is that the hunter has a chance to see and experience his lease in a way that is quite different than during the fall and winter months. Trees and fields have bloomed with green in the new season of growth. Wild flowers splash color in places that before were swaths of browns and grays.

Many times hunters seize this opportunity to do a little scouting for the upcoming fall season. Often such a hunter will find dropped antlers which are always interesting and always pose the question "Where were all these big deer hiding during deer season?" In many ways large and small, the hunter gains an appreciation of the property from different angles. Interesting Places have a habit of doing that. Every time you look at one from a slightly different point of view you find new surprises.

This one year had arrived at camp for the spring turkey season full of energy and confidence. He had a very good fall deer season, and he had looked forward to this hunt. Upon arriving at camp, he felt relaxed and ready to go. The early scouting reports from the rancher were good, and all the hunters were in a jovial mood. One thing about hunting turkeys for deer hunters is that the atmosphere is usually a little less tense. Of course once in the field each hunter wants to score and it doesn't hurt if that score is a big gobbler. But overall each hunter felt less pressure since each had already ready gotten a good deer in the fall. Now would be a time to enjoy the experience of turkey hunting.

In other ways turkey hunting is different from deer hunting. Although one can rattle and call during deer hunting, mostly the idea there is to find several good spots and hunt them hard. Usually this involves long hours on the stand between moments of action. With turkeys, the hunter is actively involved in the mating rituals of the birds. As long as there are at least some turkeys in the area, the hunter will at least get some action calling, and hopefully if he is skilled and lucky perhaps a shot as well.

Our hunter picked one of his favorite turkey spots for the morning hunt. Located down in a draw among a number of large live oak trees, it had produced consistently over the years. The morning began well. He exchanged gobbles with a number of birds right off the bat. Several times he worked a gobbler in using his hen call, but it always hung up. That is what gobblers often do. They don't come in to a call all the way. Instead they "hang up" just out of range or out of sight. Then the hunter must either try to make his call as seductive as possible to bring him in or the hunter can make like a hen and work towards the gobbler. Once our hunter tried that but with no luck. The other time he stayed back but the gobbler never came in. Instead he moved off slowly.

Now you might think that this story is going to be about this particular hunter taking a nice gobbler after hunting hard for several days. However the story focuses on something else. See, from the first light of day up until noon, our hunter had been part of the drama. He had many factors in his favor and came close a couple of times. Totally absorbed in his hunt, he had scarcely noticed anything about his surroundings.

However after lunch the action died down. There on the stand, he began to see other things. Slowly he became less of a participant and more of a spectator. Imperceptibly he had slipped all bonds to the hectic world from wince he came. Now completely transformed into part of the nature that surrounded him, his eyes were opened to new realities.

Soon he observed the cardinals. It was their mating season also. Each male had his perch, the favorites being an old bare stick that gave a good view. From these perches the males displayed their bright red plumage for all to see. They also would viciously swoop down to repel any potential invader. To the hunter they appeared to be almost evenly spaced throughout that area – almost as if they had been programmed in that fashion. It occurred to him that in some ways humans were very different than these creatures. After all they had the capacity to transcend the mere daily struggle and look on such a scene from afar. In other ways, maybe we are not so different. Most of our lives and energies are devoted to struggles just like the cardinals. Our Machiavellian power struggles may be just as amusing to the birds (if they could understand them) as their mating rituals are to us.

Our hunter now pondered such questions in his mind all through the long afternoon hours. Eventually other animals - rabbits, armadillos, raccoons, a doe with here new fawns, even a snake – appeared as if to be presented on a stage for our hunter's observation. Each creature went about its business as if it was the only business in the universe. He carefully studied each animal's habits. At once he could sense a gain in understanding, but also sense that his understanding was and always would be incomplete.

Everything in this Interesting Place appeared to be in balance. Each being appeared to be independent but at the same time connected. The overall purpose of all the activity seemed directed toward a purpose, but that purpose was obscure. Our hunter understood that he was no different in a way. He couldn't fully understand that purpose because he was, by his very physical nature, a part of the process and couldn't fully obtain the correct perspective. Yet he could sense it and admire it. He could peer into the looking glass but see only a poor reflection. He could see in part and know in part. Someday he may know in full.

Interesting Places were put here for a reason. They are a necessary part of creation, not for sustenance but for understanding. Without them we may not ever step out of our own narrow daily worries. They are not here just for entertainment but for growth of our being. We cannot fully explain why and we will never be able to explain. Perhaps that is their ultimate lesson.

Chapter 5 - Hunting as Philosophy

Philosophy in Action

Hunting is an expression of philosophy put into action. At least it is one of the most accessible action expression to which the average person in modern day America has access. The reason for this is that the biggest problem with any philosophy which has been described is death. Every philosophical system runs into death like a bug hitting a windshield – the end result is not pretty. Many attempts have been made over the centuries by very intelligent writers to somehow work around this problem. However, all human rationalizations come up short. The normal treatment is to quietly ignore or gloss over the issue and move on. This is somewhat understandable because death is a disagreeable subject, and writer and reader alike probably tacitly agree on that maneuver. Hunting, by its very nature, deals intimately with death; because, let's be honest, that is the ultimate goal of the pursuit.

Although every human based system of philosophy falls apart when confronted with the question of death, one system does not. That system is the Christian belief system. And in that theology, death is not dealt with or explained by human efforts but instead it is defeated by God who created all. So instead of dancing around the question of death, Christianity confronts it head on. Death is a necessary part of our existence because it forces us to accept our limitations (that we are not gods). Once we accept that we have no logical choice but to humble ourselves before God.

Hunting is an expression of philosophy because it forces us to deal with death as a natural part of creation, and should cause us to ponder our own mortality and our relationship to creation. In hunting we see the creation not as a static completed thing but rather as an ongoing process in which we are privileged to participate.

The second problem with any philosophy is that in order to mean anything, it must be put into practice. That is, without action in the real world in which we live, it doesn't really mean anything regardless of how internally well constructed it may be. To a very real extent the purpose of life, as a whole and in the individual, can be viewed as a testing ground of concepts that are put into concrete action. Viewed in this light, what we call existence is not the end in and of itself but a means to an end. Although it is quite real, the physical world is temporary and only exists to serve a higher purpose. That does not mean that what happens in our lives is unimportant. Quite to the contrary, it matters a great deal because these events change us and prepare us for a larger reality.

That is why we are implored to judge people by their works. That is because our actions matter. The ultimate test for any philosophy or theology is to see how it plays out in individuals and in the world. How does a particular philosophy change the individual, Society, the world? Many systems appear at first to be good or beneficial; however, once put into practice they prove disastrous. Socialism is a classic example. It all sounds so good to our mortal ears – each according to his needs and each according to his means. But every attempt to implement that philosophy in the real world has produced only destruction and death on a large scale. Death can be seen as necessary in order to weed out our wrongheaded notions about morality and God.

To achieve the desired result, events and experiences in our lives must meet several criteria: the experiences must matter – that is they must be permanent, the events and experiences must be authentic – that is they cannot be artificial, and the events and experiences must have an unknown outcome – that is they cannot be scripted. Another item that becomes apparent is although we have some insight into what is occurring, we cannot know fully all the reasons of why. The reason is that we ourselves are part of this process. As participants in the unfolding drama, we are also being sculpted towards an end result. Therefore, we cannot have privileged knowledge of all the whys or it would make the process artificial.

We can look in the mirror – that is step out of the daily grind and take a peak at the larger purpose of life. But we can only see a poor reflection. Everything cannot be known at this point. At some point in our existence we will know but not in this world.

Why do I make these claims? There are two reasons. The first is that we instinctively crave and seek out situations where we can have these necessary experiences. We understand at a level that cannot be put into words that these experiences are necessary, not just for mere physical survival, but in order to grow in a non-physical way in which we do not fully understand. Man does not live by bread alone. We need to constantly test our concepts and see what is real.

One result of this effect is that many people attempt to feel this fundamental need through a variety of odd, dangerous, and sometimes illegal activities. Often one hears about someone doing some crazy thing and claiming that they did it "to feel alive". So far from being a sign of mental derangement, the fact that people participate in destructive and dangerous pursuits is actually a sign that this instinctive need is not being met by any other experience in their lives.

Our society is infused with post-modern ideology. In this way of thinking a person is implored to look inside themselves to discover who they are and to use that knowledge to create their own reality. This system does not accept absolute truth for our life purpose but instead assumes that we can mold our own version of what is true. In reality post-modernism is nothing more than a dressed up version of the old lie that we can be gods ourselves. Most hobbies and entertainment activities today revolve around this post-modern way of thinking. More than mere escapism their temptation is to convince us that we can create our own truth. Often this is supposedly done by reaching deep within and "discovering" that we have this capacity to become godlike.

Hunting confronts us with the opposite of post-modernism. Here we witness and participate in a drama which forces us to accept that there is some higher purpose to life. This purpose drives forward independent of our wishes to the contrary. Death acts as a constraint on thinking and behaviors. Although it may appear from our current perspective to be cruel, without it we would have to admit that our hubris would be even greater than it is. How we think about death will go a long way in shaping the type of person we ultimately become. By confronting the uncomfortable reality of death head on, we discover that we cannot shape our reality, but instead must adapt to the absolute truth we see in nature. We do not discover our inner "god", but instead it is a discovery of our own humility and mortality.

The second reason for my claims is that while we have a fundamental need for these experiences, we at the same time shirk from them out of a sign of fear. This may sound contradictory but it is not. Remember that when we place ourselves in this great drama, we are testing our concepts our ideas, and ourselves. Through this process we learn what is real about ourselves. That idea can be frightening. Many times we try to hide from these challenges. However, we really can't hide because as actors in the play we cannot leave it. Eventually reality seeks us out and creates these situations regardless of our wishes. Sometimes we face these unexpected events and come out better and sometimes not for the outcomes are never known to the actors beforehand. But the mere fact of the uncertainty of troubles is proof of my claims.

One unfortunate result of the second reason is that when people shy away from these necessary experiences, they often try to remove the possibility of them all together. This is a false attempt to create a "safe" world in which to live. Thus they attempt to replace the uncertainty and messiness of these challenges with a predictable security. Of course, as actors in the drama there is no real escape. Our efforts are themselves are part of the possible outcomes of the play. By choosing these paths we may achieve an extra level of comfort but at the expense of stunted growth of our being.

This should not be confused with the same thing as trying to create a better world for all. Those efforts are legitimate challenges that focus our talents and energies to productive ends. Here we face tests whose outcome is not known and whose effects are permanent. Often people gain a level of satisfaction from their jobs that is something more than just the monetary aspect. Instinctively we know why this satisfaction exists and that it is necessary beyond meeting our physical needs.

However, when people fear uncertainty, they run to those that offer a false comfort. The process of these efforts to trade our birthright for temporal comfort is, however, not only an individual choice. The collective decisions of our society accumulate to create a force which relentless seeks to level all uncertainty and remove doubt from our lives. This "leveling" process grinds on and reduces the options for individuals to find necessary experiences.

The act of hunting is one activity in which we can have the experiences and events that matter in the development of our being. For when we hunt, if the situation is right, we become an integral part of the drama which is unfolding all the time in nature. Our actions have consequences which are real and permanent. Obviously this is true for the animals that are hunted but it is also true for us. We cannot predict the outcome of any experience, and we are at the mercy of actions by other actors which are out of our control.

For that reason, the actual taking or the attempted taking of an animal is crucial to the authenticity of the experience. Without the element of death, the entire pursuit becomes nothing more special than sitting at home and watching a game on television. Without the potential taking, the person no longer is an actor in the drama, but merely a bystander, which is not a bad thing; it just isn't a unique experience anymore. However, once the hunter becomes a participant on the stage, his actions have a permanence which affects nature and his being forever.

And crucial to hunting's positive effects are Interesting Places. They are not the thing to be worshiped, but instead, like all of creation, are here for a purpose. With these Interesting Places, we can have an authentic experience that is essential to understanding our place in the world. That is why we instinctively and sometimes desperately seek them out. Out of a lifetime of mostly monotonous existence, Interesting Places can produce moments in time that shape our beings forever.

First Deer

The young hunter had never been on a deer hunt before, so when his father invited him to his lease it was a moment of jubilation mixed with apprehension. He had never really contemplated seriously the idea of shooting a deer. Such an act seemed so much larger than he could imagine. Of course, he had heard his father tell numerous stories of his exploits.

This only added to the mystery and awe of such an event. Now the thought that he would go into the woods in pursuit of deer filled him with a sweeping rainbow of emotions. How would he react? He didn't know, nor could he know. One might say that well it doesn't matter because nobody will know but you. Well for some reason it did matter and he knew that. There is that part of every soul that seeks to discover itself. The act of this discovery both fascinates us and terrifies us. It is in these moments that we learn who we are and what the world is, for it is by actions taken that have permanent consequences that we discover the answers.

And to set the stage for these questions we need Interesting Places. They would be going to one very Interesting Place. It was in some respects only a typical Texas deer lease. However, it was run by a rancher who believed in doing things the old fashion way. Agreements were by handshake. Lease costs were modest. The hunters did not use feeders instead they hunted out of both blinds and by still hunting. A variety of game was available, and although the deer were not huge by antler size, the hunting was wild chase and challenging. All these things combined to make this lease a truly Interesting Place for it was a throw back to an earlier era before the big money operations and their emphasis on antler size alone. In other words it was a perfect place for a new hunter. Here one could learn what hunting was at one time and experience the sport in its natural state.

There had been times in the past where he wondered about big game hunting. He secretly would sneak a look at his father's rifles. They seemed larger than life. So much so that he had trouble imagining ever using one in the field. He even had half talked himself out of the idea all together. "It's too boring sitting in a blind all day. I'd rather be hiking like in small game hunting" he thought in such moments. But in reality he knew that this was a bit of a cop out. There was a part of him that wanted to be put to the test, but there was also a part that feared it.

Nevertheless, here he was in the vehicle riding to the lease – a lease that he had heard so much about with so many stories that it almost had become some mythical place in his mind. Now he would actually be there. When one must travel long distances to hunt as many modern Americans must do, there is plenty of time for discussion. And as they drove, he became more and more fascinated by his father's description of the place, of the various spots, of the style of hunting. More and more he felt his soul being drawn in by the sense of adventure, and more and more that adventure loomed large due to the nature of the quarry at stake.

Eventually they arrived. As soon as they crossed the gate, he felt an almost electric energy in the air. It was a truly Interesting Place – wild, mostly unkempt, hidden and remote, and for a weekend it would be theirs. The place had a variety of habitats. There was a large cultivated hay field bordered by hills covered in native grasses. There was the normal Texas brush broken by draws covered with large oak trees. There were even a couple of sizable ponds on the place. All in all, the place provided the type of variety and edge habitat that a number of species of game loved.

Of course one issue with all hunting leases is where do the hunters stay, and here the answer was equally unique. The quarters had been fashioned out of an old oil field mud logging trailer somehow acquired and transported with effort. Now fully settling into the Texas soil, it was obvious that it would spend eternity right in that very spot. Still for a young person, such accommodations only added to the allure of the place. Everything about this property fit in with what an Interesting Place was all about. The land was not overgrazed or over cultivated. Obviously a working ranch, it had the variety that can be had with sustainability.

During the course of the drive, our young hunter carefully soaked in the verbal instructions that his father gave him. Since this would be his first time hunting for large game, he felt some pressure. And it was this pressure that focused his mind on the task at hand. Yet the question of how he would react in this setting remained to be determined. He would find out soon.

On the first morning hunting he, for obvious reasons, hunted with his dad. Driving over the dirt roads, he quickly became disoriented in the dark. Several times they spotted deer as they sprinted away from the vehicle. In the headlights they loamed up like ghostly spirits. They hardly seemed real. Each time they spotted one, the young hunter could feel his heart drop into the pit of his stomach. Emotionally he was becoming pulled into the hunt for reasons he didn't understand. He was in the process of crossing over from the modern world into a more primal past that he didn't even know existed in his being. Now his hesitation about hunting deer had long since faded into his past. How could I have ever thought that way? He asked. It was almost as if he had been transformed. The old person had ceased and a new one born in its place.

Once in the blind that first morning, they had to wait and be quiet. It felt strange to the hunter to sit in the dark and basically, well, do nothing. Imperceptibly the dark gave way to light. Slowly the hunters adjusted to the quieter pace of nature. This requires that the hunter recalibrate his sense of time. Once this is accomplished, nature presenting a stage for the day's events, and the hunters are now actors on that stage.

Soon the elder hunter spotted something. Whispering to the young hunter "There's a buck over to the left in the brush". Frantically the young hunter scanned the area but saw nothing. "Quick get ready" but the young hunter, being inexperienced, reacted too slowly. He did catch a glimpse of the buck through an opening in the brush, but couldn't get a shot off. In a few years with his sense sharpened by numerous trials this would have been a relatively straight forward shot, but today his inexperience showed.

The elder hunter was quick to not criticize. He simply pointed out what went wrong. Disappointed the young hunter was shaken a bit. He hadn't expected that it would be so demanding on the nerves; however, he was also hooked and he knew it. Maybe that is how it was supposed to unfold. If the hunter had scored easily, would he have felt the same passion for the chase take hold within? We will never know.

After the morning hunt, our hunters spent the afternoon hunting quail before taking a late afternoon stand. Along the edges of the hay field, excellent cover hid good numbers of quail, and our hunters did well. Quail hunting was something of a break for the young hunter. He had done that before and taking a few birds buoyed his spirits.

However, they didn't see much during the evening stand. Maybe the young hunter had been just a little too clumsy in his approach or perhaps the warmer temperatures caused the deer to not move. Even so it was a bit disappointing. By now he had become fixated with the idea of taking a deer. The trip would somehow seem somewhat empty if he didn't.

When next morning arrived, our young hunter awoke with confidence. Everything appeared to set for his first deer. The weather was cool and crisp, and the time felt right. He had already been baptized a couple of times in the stand and he understood more what he had to do. Once again they arrived at the stand in the dark. This time, the process of becoming absorbed by the unfolding drama felt a little less strange. He knew what to expect. Already with a little experience he alertly scanned the brush in the early morning light.

Then his father, once again, spotted a buck. Barely containing his excitement, he motioned to the young hunter. However, once again, our young hunter was a bit clumsy and late to see the deer. These deer were not tame and they required sharp sense and keen reflexes to hunt.

Fighting the ever increasing disappointment they hunted the rest of the day switching to still hunting at the other end of the property. Here there were several bluffs overlooking a stream which was on the next ranch. They approached the bluffs from several points and carefully crept over the edge allowing their scent to waft over down the slope. Once they jumped a group of about five deer – all does and yearlings. The young hunter almost took a shot, but he knew that he was never on any of the does. It appeared more and more likely that he would not get his first deer on this trip.

The elder hunter made a decision about the evening hunt. It would be their last time to hunt on this trip, after that they be forced by the work and school schedules of the outside world to head back. Up to that point, the father had selected stands that provided for close shots. He figured that if they did see a deer he wanted the shot to be doable by a novice rifleman. However, the downside of those selections was that they hadn't seen many deer, and when they did the shots – although not long – required quick reactions.

This time he picked a stand used by one of his friends. This friend had the reputation of an expert long range marksman. In fact this friend had taught the father many things about hunting and long range shooting in Colorado. This hunter preferred a place where he could scan and shoot at long ranges, and this stand fit that bill exactly. The stand stood at the top of a relatively high mound where one could see out in three directions several hundred yards. Opposite of that mound was the north facing slope of another larger mound. Deer often traveled on several trails along that slope.

The thing about those mounds is that they were round to an almost unnatural degree. People over the years had found Indian artifacts and arrowheads throughout the property. In fact there were the remains of a settlement on the bluff slopes where they had jumped the does earlier. Nobody knew exactly what these mounds were. Some had suggested that they were not entirely a product of geological forces alone. They stood out in an obvious way that made them suspicious.

Nevertheless the one made for an excellent stand location to take a long shot. From that perch a hunter had a commanding view of the landscape. This is where they hunted on that last evening. The elder hunter thought that at least here they would see deer, and he would allow the young hunter to take a shot. After two days of close calls, he felt that the young hunter deserved at least that.

As the afternoon hours rolled by, the father discussed the ins and outs of long range shooting. He also instructed the young hunter on the ranges to various points on the other slope. To the young hunter these ranges struck him as impossible. Still he eagerly absorbed everything that his father told him.

Soon after the sun touched the horizon they began to see several deer off the east moving towards their location. They appeared and disappeared in the cover as they worked along the slope face. Both hunters knew there was a good chance of them coming into range, but they were also running out of daylight. It would be a close race. Just as the evening dark began to take over the landscape, the deer popped into range on the other slope. The young hunter picked out the closest doe, but it was still a good 250 yards out. He had never dreamed of attempting such a shot and now he was faced with one.

"Go ahead and get your gun ready" whispered the father. Now practiced from several failed attempts, the young hunter quietly brought he rifle up and settled the fore piece on the window sill of the blind. He almost had to command his movements as his mind felt only distantly in control of his body. Remembering the elder hunter's instructions he aimed at the shoulder of the deer now facing to the west. He decided that if he missed, he would miss trying to do as instructed.

The last thing he remembered is the sensation of trying to squeeze the trigger. When the gun went off, it startled him unexpectedly. In the last evening light he could distinctly see the flames erupt from the barrel for a brief moment. It was a sight picture he would never forget. But that was all he saw. Almost sheepishly he turned to looked at his father would strained through binoculars to see what happened. "You hit it!" he exclaimed in a surprised tone of voice. For a moment the words failed to register. "Quick, reload" he added.

With that the young hunter snapped out of his daze, and smartly worked the bolt to bring another round into the chamber. Intently he scanned the hillside through the scope for any sign of movement. After a few minutes, the elder hunter stated "I think it's down. We better do a search before dark." With just enough light left they stepped out of the stand and quickly marched to the spot. There the grass had grown knee high and was thick. The elder hunter now had a worried look on his face. He had expected the young hunter to miss. Now in last light they had a hit deer, and they needed to leave that evening. Privately he questioned his call at this moment.

"Let's split up, and search using a corkscrew pattern." The young hunter knew this drill well. They had used it many times quail hunting. The idea was to mark a spot where you thought you last saw the animal. Then starting at that point circle out in a corkscrew to pick up any sign. The elder hunter started where he had last seen the deer. The young hunter started about 10 yards further west. Suddenly the sight of an animal emerged in the grass in front of the young hunter. It was belly up with all four legs held in an upright position by the grass. "Hey, dad here's a deer. Maybe it's the one I shot". His father relieved looked at him as if to say "Of course it's the deer you shot, dummy. What do think? That there are freshly killed deer lying around everywhere?"

At that moment the enormity of what he had just done hit the young hunter like a sledgehammer. HE had done this. Suddenly he felt his body washed over with an incredible flood of emotions. Pride, relief, joy, sadness, understanding, confusion, and every emotion named by man. It was an unexpected and intense sensation. Momentarily it stunned him like a taser.

There was no time to waste however. The elder hunter wanted to get the deer field dressed quickly so they could be on their way. By the time they finished dressing the animal they had broken out the flashlights. After they loaded the animal into the back of the vehicle, the young hunter's emotions began to recalibrate to normal. Now he began to understand what had happened. He was part of a drama with meaning that was permanent, and was authentic. To have that experience required an Interesting Place and this place was definitely that. The experience had changed him in ways he didn't understand.

But one thing he did understand was that he was now a deer hunter. He understood in a way that cannot be put into words what that meant.

On the long drive home, the hunters at first remained mostly quiet. Exhaustion from the long weekend had taken their toll. Already both men had begun to cross back from the world of hunting to the modern world. Thoughts of assignments and work schedules had already intruded into their minds. Finally, the elder hunter asked the young hunter how he felt. The young hunter tried to explain but stumbled for lack of the proper words. The father understood perfectly.

Paleo Man

An aspect of our modern world is the incredible variety of outlets that people have in which to "express" themselves. In fact much of what makes the modern world is exactly that: people franticly trying different things in order to see what is "good" or in other words what gives meaning. The outlets for these endeavors are vast with new ones coming on the scene all the time. Our consumer society has become expert at spotting new fads and capitalizing on them. All of which creates a confusing blizzard of choices which are loudly pushed upon us from every conceivable media outlet.

We can attempt to try them all to see which "style" fits us. Thus the style or at least the outer expression of that style becomes "us" in some sort of way. So the question becomes: does a person really create his own reality in the Post-Modern sense or instead does all a person do is select from some preconfigured options (provided by our consumer society) and then wear that as an outer covering? Is that all that our free will entails – simply selecting an outer persona to project an image of who we think we would like to be? As the popular song implores us to "Strike a Pose", this Post-Modern quest becomes a frenzied search for meaning while at the same time a cop out to avoid who we really are.

As it is written:

> *"I denied myself nothing my eyes*
> *desired;*
> *I refused my heart no pleasure.*
> *My heart took delight in all my work,*
> *and this was the reward for all my labor.*
> *Yet when I surveyed all that my*
> *Hands had done*
> *and what I had toiled to achieve,*
> *everything was meaningless, a*
> *chasing after the wind;*
> *nothing was gained under the*
> *sun."*

In the end these endeavors which we set about every day seam at once necessary in order to live one's life; however, we instinctively know down in hidden part of our soul that they are indeed *"Meaningless, Meaningless"* for in the end what comes from them?

So we busy ourselves relentlessly so that we don't have to face this fact. The modern world happily obliges us in these pursuits and we try not to think about the ultimate meaning of all our labors and pleasures.

As mentioned before, death is a big obstacle and so we often try to ignore it or wish it away. But it remains there as a testament to our futility. We are really creatures of a paradox. We can in one sense remove ourselves from the daily struggle found in nature, but not entirely and not permanently. This fact enrages some and they rebel against their nature as if to say that God doesn't know what He is doing (and of course THEY could have done it so much better. Isn't that one of the meanings of the original sin)? This produces outlandish and sometimes criminal behavior. These are the ones that deny the physical reality and attempt to become gods in their own minds by denying the Natural Law. Their rallying cry is "if it feels good do it." The irony is that by trying to deny the Natural Law and attempting to create their own morality, they become consumed in their carnal nature and often destroyed by it.

Others rail against this seeming contradiction in our nature by going the other way. They deny anything not immediately connected to the physical world, and instead immerse themselves in the daily struggle for existence completely. Their motto is "he who dies with the most toys wins." Yet in their attempt to deny the moral law they loose what humanity they have and despite their outward sophistication and education become little more than drones whose life's work vanishes with their physical existence.

The balance between these two extremes is difficult, especially in our modern civilized world where from every direction there exist diversions which tempt us with the promise of fulfilling our lives. It is impossible to cover them all because there are more numerous than the stars; however, one stands out in part for its oddity and also for what it attempts to do.

This fad is the caveman movement of which there are several variations. In its most basic form it revolves around a particular diet. The idea being that our bodies are designed to eat a particular diet which consists of a mix of food far different from what we consume in the modern industrialized world. Consumption of the modern diet has contributed, or even been responsible, a great many of the physical aliments which people now days suffer. For example heart disease, type 2 diabetes, and certain cancers are a result of our diet and lifestyle for which are bodies are not adapted.

And it is the lifestyle area that advocates of the caveman principle really get contrarian. They believe that in addition to changing a person's diet to something more akin to what our primitive ancestors ate one should also change their entire lifestyle. To do this they try to simulate the lifestyle of a Paleolithic person. For example, their exercise routines consist of "natural" yet strenuous activities which a primitive might do during the course of his (or her) daily struggle to survive. Thus they do somewhat bizarre things such as carrying large rocks around in the hot sun one day, while the next time they might climb ropes. The whole idea is to use modern tools and knowledge to re-create the Paleolithic lifestyle (minus all the really nasty things like hungry predators, actual starvation, lack of sanitation, etc.).

What does this do with hunting? Well it occurs to me and from my experience that hunting, and by that I mean wild chase hunting, is a pretty good approximation of the lifestyle our "cavemen" ancestors led. And our physical bodies are superbly adapted for that lifestyle. I am always amused when I read something by a paleontologist who blathers on about how early humans had no special physical adaptation to survive in a primitive state except for their large brains and perhaps their opposable thumbs.

Nonsense! Our bodies are exquisitely molded to perfectly fit the demands of such an existence. Everything from the breadth of our shoulders to the operation of our ankle joints has an exact purpose in the art of survival which gave our ancestors all the advantage in the wild state. Basically we are designed to be hunter gathers with the ability to use tools and forage over a rather large area. Although we may lack the more obvious physical abilities of other animals, such as speed or raw strength, that doesn't mean that we had no physical adaptations. Instead what our bodies are adapted to do is to use tools.

And anyone who has gone elk hunting in a place like the Rocky Mountains can appreciate that fact. For when a hunter steps back into that primitive mode of existence, even just for a short while, he can see exactly why his body is built the way it is. A human is designed to carry a certain amount of gear and be able to amble over a certain amount of territory at a certain speed. This gives the human all the advantage he needs to survive and as we all know eventually conquer nature.

So, in their own rather bizarre way, the proponents of the caveman lifestyle have it right in concept. But a really easy way to live like a caveman is just go on a wild chase hunt!

Gingerbread Man

Both hunters had stopped at one of their favorite perches in order to glass or use binoculars to scan the surrounding countryside. Here on top of a mesa in Colorado, they had already hunted several days for elk with no success. Several times they had spotted elk and gone after them but each time things just didn't quite click.

Then as they glassed from that spot early in the afternoon, they spotted him: a giant bull elk. He stepped out from an aspen stand located far off on another slope several miles away. That stand of aspens trees formed what looked like a gingerbread man when viewed at a distance, hence its name. Now these hunters faced a problem. The big bull had holed up in a perfect spot – for him. That is because these aspens lay across a steep valley with a creek at the bottom. There was really no easy way to get up on him undetected. So for a number of minutes, the hunters weighed their options and continued to watch the bull move in and out of the thicket.

Finally they decided that this bull was too good to pass up. It would take a while but they could hike down to the bottom of the valley and then set up on a small ridge still on their side of the creek. From there they could reevaluate the situation.

Gearing up for an all afternoon elk stalk always takes some planning. Everything must be evaluated for its potential usefulness versus the extra weight it would add. Obviously one has to take a rifle and sufficient ammo plus the all important shooting stick which serves two purposes: walking stick and rifle rest. Binoculars, range finder, knife, and other accoutrements are necessary as well. But other items need consideration. Should one actually get a big bull down, then what? So into the backpack goes more gear: game bags, a saw, a hatchet, rope, food for the evening and of course water. In addition, with overcast skies, the hunters had to carry foul weather gear just in case. By the time these hunters had finished packing, each carried around 50 pounds which was carefully and thoughtfully distributed over their bodies.

For each hunter, the first day had been quite a shock to their systems. To come from the soft, sedentary life to the mountains always hits a person's system hard. But by now, the third day they had both transitioned over to that primal past that lives within every human. Several hard stalks later and they had returned to a forgotten way of life. Yes they missed the comforts of home, but in a very strange but real way they instinctively knew that this is what they were made for.

One last time they glassed the great slope with its huge aspen thicket in the shape of a gingerbread man. Why do people do that? Why do they see shapes in the stars and in nature? It seems that humans have not just the ability but the programmed drive to discern patterns in their environment. Is this only a survival skill or is there more to it than the mere physical realm?

With one last discussion they set off towards that slope. They planned to use the natural contours along the way to shield their approach. This would involve more effort, but they knew a straight on track would be detected easily.

That is why that big bull was hanging out there. He didn't become a big bull by being careless, and it would take all their skill to get a chance at him. But such an animal taken in a wild chase manner would be a trophy that can define a hunter's career.

They crossed over a ridge that ran parallel to their intended destination and kept low. That path two days earlier would have elicited protests from their still citified feet and muscles, but they had quickly adapted to a more caveman state so they now covered the ground swiftly and with the fluid grace of a seasoned Indian guide.

Within two hours they have covered the distance and stood below the nose of the ridge they had targeted. Now with great deliberation they eased up the back side of that ridge until they barely crested the nose. Staying low, almost flat to the ground, they glassed the aspens which now lay across the valley and slightly above them. It became immediately clear that with any further advancement they risked totally busting up the area. Once they attempted to cross the creek, they would be completely exposed. At that, they began a long discussion about what to do next.

They had several options, none of them great. They could remain on that nose and hope to get a lengthy (about 500 yard) shot. That's if the elk came out again low and retreated to the creek from the bottom of the aspens. Or they could try a two man drive. However, with the lay of land, they simply couldn't figure out a good way to do that. There were too many potential escape routes the bull could take without the hunters seeing him.

Finally they decided on the first option. One hunter remained on the far side of the nose while the other dropped back to come around the other side. From there they set up and waited.

Was it the right choice? It is hard to say. The cold fact remains that they never saw the big bull again. They may have been detected before their arrival, despite their best efforts. Maybe elk ambled off without being seen. We will never know. A sane person might look at this stalk as a perfect waste of time and energy better spent back in camp or better yet in town. However, as these hunters stayed on the stand they couldn't help but feel that this very thing is what they were made for. Gone were the tensions of the modern world along with its distractions and temptations. They had fully transfigured into the rhythms of a forgotten way of life. Sitting on that hillside in a remote wilderness with every piece of their bodies perfectly fitted for the effort, they felt a type of peace that is largely unknown in the world. Perfectly adapted for that way of life, they were the ultimate carnivores. For a short moment in time they were cavemen again.

<u>Conclusion</u>

In actuality, whatever lifestyle we choose is an action expression of our personal philosophy. How that expression pans out is a demonstration of how closely that philosophy agrees with the Natural and Moral law which are constant. In this manner the physical reality exists to prove out truth and error. Thus what happens in the physical world – although it is temporary - reflects what is true in the metaphysical reality which is permanent. The modern world presents a blizzard of options and begs, even demands, that we waste our energies in trying them all. Perhaps that is how the world attempts to prevent us from true understanding – by burying us with choices.

Hunting represents one such option; however, it is the option where our physical bodies most closely fit what they were designed to do. That is why Interesting Places are so important. Their existence allows us to know this lifestyle if only for a little while. They stand contrary to the other options for our time as quiet and mostly overlooked reminders of an early epoch etched in our being.

Part 2

Pasture No. 6

Pasture No. 6 truly fit the definition of a very Interesting Place. Located in western part of Texas, at first it would not strike anyone as anything special or unique in terms of hunting properties. However, in an era where hunting became more and more commercialized, this place maintained features (some not intentional) that made it stand out in numerous ways. In order to understand how this lease stood apart, we must first look at what had become of deer hunting and hunting leases during that time.

Texas Hunting

Originally going back many years, hunting occupied at best only a side show for most Texas properties. Ranching was the main thing, and hunting existed just to bring in a little extra income for the landowner. The hunting on many places consisted of whatever happened to be on the property, and the hunting style was pretty much left to the hunter. This was long before the days of high fenced properties and fixed blinds with feeders. This type of situation is what I like to call wild chase. In other words, the property is not set up specifically for deer hunting, and the hunter has pretty much free rein to hunt it as is. Traditionally there were two classic methods of hunting in those circumstances. Often that consisted of some combination of scrape hunting and using whatever terrain was available to set up for a shot.

Scrape hunting is, by many opinions, the purest essence of the sport. In this method, the hunter uses his knowledge of the animal's habits, and skill as an outdoorsman to hunt for scrapes first. Scrapes are markers left by bucks which designate his territory. Often they form a "buck run" and there will be a number of scrapes along a circular route which the buck travels during the rut.

Scrapes are made by the buck pawing the ground with his hooves forming a dinner plate sized area that appears to be "scraped" out. Then the buck leaves scent in that scrape, thus forming a marker which lets other deer, both does and other bucks, know about him.

Many times the scrape is accompanied by a "licking branch" which is a branch from a nearby tree or shrub that hangs over the scrape at about eye level for the deer. The buck also leaves scent on that licking branch.

The object in this style of hunting is two fold. First the hunter must locate the scrapes and the trails where the scrapes occur. Second he must figure out how to hunt them. Often this involves picking out several sections of the trail where the hunter will have good cover but at the same time be able to see enough in order to have a good shot. Normally this type of hunting entails getting down in the brush and up close and personal. Also the use of rattling antlers and calls are often used in this type of hunting with good results.

To achieve success, the hunter needs to able to enter and set up stealthily without busting up the area with his scent, sight, or sound. That is why normally the hunter picks out several sections of a trail to hunt – to have different options depending on the wind and sun conditions. He must also be able to remain on the stand without messing up the spot and execute the shot which may be close and quick. Because of the up close nature, this method of hunting is suitable for either rifle or archery. Since the exact set up location can vary, this type of hunting normally doesn't involve fixed blinds. Although in some situations portal blinds can be used, typically the hunter must use the available cover or pre-construct ground blinds during the off season (ground blinds are normally used in most of Texas due to the lack of large trees). This leaves the hunter open to the vagrancies of the weather, so not only must he be equipped for stealth, he must be prepared to face the elements.

The other type of hunting method in a wild chase scenario involves locating a position that allows the hunter to glass a variety of trails and areas at a distance. There are two ways to achieve this in places where the lack of trees prevents hanging a tree stand. One is to construct a tower in a location that allows the hunter to see at a distance. Of course, this is a major investment and cannot easily be moved.

The other method is to use whatever available elevation changes exist as a "tower". Many times it doesn't take much height in order to be able to see quite a bit. With a little strategic pre-season brush clearing, a knowledgeable hunter cannot locate several natural stands that provide flexibility depending on the wind, time of day, and observed deer movements.

While this method may not sound as "pure" as scrape hunting, it requires skill, knowledge, and planning. Long range shooters prefer this style as it places much greater emphasis on long range shooting skills. Stealth is still required as the hunter may be more open than when he is deep in the brush. This is particularly true if the hunter is using this method in combination with a glass and stalk where he is hiking a ridge and glassing into different areas.

Often these two methods can be combined. That is the hunter can locate scrapes and active trails and then use the terrain to gain elevation. If this is possible it allows the hunter more options to hunt a particular hot spot. This combination technique can be quite effective in a place like West Texas where there is sufficient elevation changes.

Both styles of hunting have several key points in common that qualify them for wild chase. First, in both the hunter must first locate the place or places to hunt and then figure out how to hunt them - no artificially made hot spot created with feeders. Second both methods require pre-season effort in terms of scouting and planning. Finally the emphasis is on the hunter's knowledge of the game, his skills as an outdoorsman, and on his shooting prowess.

With both there is no guarantee of success for nature can be finicky. However, any deer taken by either method is a real trophy regardless of its size. For at one time a large deer represented a trophy that demonstrated the skills required to succeed in the field instead of representing the results of a controlled breeding program.

At one time taking a trophy deer required determination, patience, quick reflexes, and calm nerves and good fortunate. The trophy, although it physically was the end result, was not the thing that was treasured.

Instead it was a physical token of the hunter's achievement. Behind every trophy taken by wild chase methods there lays a story or stories and many lessons of perseverance and skill.

Up Close and Personal

On Pasture No. 6, one area in particular vexed the hunters on the lease. The area know as No. 3 consisted of a large flat area of West Texas scrub brush sandwiched between a road which formed the western boundary and a complex of ridges that ran along the east side. In some years the combination of overgrazing by sheep and the West Texas drought reduce the area to something that resembled a moonscape. One would hardly give it a second look. However after several wetter years in which no sheep had grazed, that area became overgrown with thick seemingly impenetrable brush. Once that happened the area transformed from its previous desolation into an almost jungle like setting with a maze of numerous game trails crisscrossing the flat.

The hunters on that property had tried over the years a variety of methods to hunt the area. They had hunted out of tripod stands; however they proved difficult and somewhat unsafe. First is that they tended to stick out above the brush just enough to expose the hunter so that he could be easily seen. Although the brush grew thick, little vegetation grew high enough to brush in a tripod. One might think "well put in a tower stand." The problem with a tower is that it would have needed to be massively high in order to see much of anything and such a structure would not be portable thus severely limiting its effectiveness.

Also the hunters had hunted the area from perches on the ridge to the east. During drought years this approach provided good views and long range shot opportunities. However as the years got wetter and the brush got thicker this became less and less effective.

The peculiar nature of the West Texas brush – being both thick and not that tall – presented a unique challenge to these hunters. Normally the problem would be solved with a combination of a tower and a feeder. The tower provides the cover and height to see and the feeder provides an artificial hot spot to bring the deer in. For our hunters they gradually drifted away from hunting that area and instead hunted on the ridges and on the draws hoping to see deer on the move in those laces. Over the years Area No. 3 became less and less hunted.

One year that changed. Our hunters always attempted to locate scrapes and buck runs on the property. Normally these were located in the steep draws that ran throughout the property; however, the density of activity moved around from year to year. That year they noticed a distinct increase of scrapes in the thick brush on the flats and area number three was located right in the middle of that. In addition our hunters had observed deer crossing the road on several major trails leading right through the heart of Area No. 3. Obviously this deer had been patterned to some extent by the feeder schedule on neighboring leases. Once the deer had made their morning rounds, they crossed into Pasture No. 6 and holed up there for the day.

Now the question became how to hunt the area. Over the course of dinner and several drinks two hunters discussed their options for the morning hunt. One might think "Why was that morning so important." Well for one thing, it would be the last morning of that hunt before they both had to return home. Also they had two other factors that made that morning potentially critical. First the rut was on. Second they expected the weather to be cool and crisp. All these factors pointed to a potentially good morning. And both hunters knew that with the uncertainties of work and family schedules, they needed to make the most out of every opportunity. That is one difference for most average hunters. They never really know if they will get another chance.

The more experienced hunter, the one who was known as Legend, argued that the best option was to keep hunting from the ridges. They had found several good scrapes right at the base of the ridge between Areas No. 2 and 3. He felt that the odds favored continuing with that tactic. However, both hunters had hunted the area several times in that manner and had not seen much.

The younger hunter wanted to try a different tactic. Instead of approaching from along the ridges, he wanted to cross the fence on foot downwind of the two trails and set up where he could see a portion of one of those trails between the road and an area where several scrapes had been found. It would involve getting up close and personal right in the thickest portion of the brush.

The two men respectively discussed both options and decided that each would try their own approach in the morning. The elder hunter would drop off the younger hunter along the road on the north side of the trails since they expected the wind to be out of the south in the morning. Once dropped off, the younger hunter would cross the fence and stealthily sneak into position. He planned on using one of the numerous cedar bushes as a shield. In addition he planned on putting out some scent and rattling.

However, when morning came, the weather had thrown his plan into disarray. Instead of being out of the south, the wind shifted during the night and was coming out of the north. In addition, the temperature had dropped sharply. Our hunter had to quickly revise his plan. Instead of hopping the fence to the north of the trails and hiking a short ways in, he decided to approach from the south after going through the main lease gate. This entailed a much longer approach, but there was an old and unused jeep trail which he could use to make a quieter approach.

Once dropped off, our hunter took his gear and began to move towards his target. He didn't take much - basically a rifle, shooting stick, and rattling horns. After all, he figured his plan would either work brilliantly or not. Either way he wouldn't be out on the stand for very long. The fresh north wind bit on his face as he swiftly and silently worked to the trail.

One effect of the longer approach from the south became obvious soon. By the time he reached the area, it would already be shooting light. That wouldn't be all bad. If he bumped a deer he could see it for a possible shot. Also he could see clearly where to set up. Actually the timing proved perfect. Once at the trail he quickly set out the scent attractant and found the perfect cedar bush about 30 yards away. Big enough to completely conceal him, it provided a gap beaten two branches for him to shoot through. Also a southern approach meant that the rising sun would be at his back – another fortunate development. So he set up and waited.

He didn't have to wait long. Well before the deer normally crossed the road, a shooter buck deer magically appeared on the trail in front of him. Where it came from, he had no idea, but it was obvious that he had hit the jackpot. Quickly he centered the crosshairs of his rifle on the target. It was almost too easy of a shot. With a single blast, the deer, hit hard, took off. But he didn't go far. By any absolute standard of antler size, this was not a trophy; however, for our hunter it easily qualified as one. For it was the manner of hunting used, the skill of the hunter, the planning, the ability to adjust those plans, and a little luck that combined to make this deer a true trophy.

The Current Situation

One of the big problems with hunting is that it has been a victim of its own success. This is the first paradox of hunting which has resulted in a peculiar situation currently. With the increase in popularity two distinct branches of hunting have emerged: one is high dollar game management hunting, the second is for everyone else. The end result is that truly Interesting Places have been continuously squeezed out and with them real wild chase hunting.

The first type of hunting is at once easy to understand and at the same time vaguely repulsive to many people. Those hunters at the high end of the economic ladder have, over time, demanded better deer and higher success rate. The market has responded with the high dollar, high fenced lease with managed deer herds. And to further accommodate their high paying guests, these hunting properties popularized the use of feeders so that the deer would arrive at a more or less predictable time and place thus eliminating all the uncertainty associated with a wild chase hunt.

The high fence eliminates competition and allows the property owner to "manage" the herd. That is to improve the antler size through breeding and selective harvesting programs. For many people (including many hunters) the idea of managing the deer population in this manner is a contradiction in terms. After all if an animal is bred, tracked, and priced then it is no longer wildlife at all but livestock. The goal of these places is really putting the reward before the victory – sort of like handing out a trophy to a team that didn't really win. Remember that a trophy sized deer should represent physical proof of a hunter's knowledge as an outdoorsman, his skill as a marksman, and his dedication to his craft.

That is why these types of properties ultimately do not satisfy. The experience is not authentic therefore it is not really that meaningful. It may be fun in the same sense that an evening out is fun, but there is no life changing moments possible, no lessons to be learned, no mountain top experience possibility. Everything is predictable and guaranteed. After all as the price paid goes up, the clients demand more predictability for their money. The market responds and substitutes the end result (big antlers) for the thing itself (a wild chase experience).

An unfortunate effect of these high dollar places is that the same attitudes have permeated down the price chain to properties at the other end of the spectrum. Land owners, seeing the money making potential of the high end leases, naturally wish to capitalize also. They begin to see hunting as less of a sideshow and more of an important money making operation of their land.

This leads to several things happening. The first is that the land owners wish to maximize their income by increasing the number of paid hunters on the property. However that immediately poses a dilemma for on a typical property – even a large one – namely that there are a limited number of really good areas in which to conduct a wild chase type of hunt. The solution, borrowed from the high end leases, is to utilize the timed feeder. With the feeder, a number of artificially created "hotspots" can be manufactured which can increase the hunter density. Unfortunately for the hunters, they become reduced to hunting out of a box and staring at a feeder a short distance away with the ability to actually hunt only a very small clearing and a few trails leading up to that clearing – hardly the stuff of grand adventures and life changing moments.

For the property owner this method of hunting does several things. First it allows more paid hunters on the property. Second it controls the hunting. Hunting is by its nature a somewhat messy affair and not the safest activity available. One cannot blame a property owner for wanting to control the placement of the hunters and where they shoot. Finally, by spacing the hunters it allows the rancher to utilize the rest of his land for more intensive grazing on the bulk of the property.

However there are negatives. The most obvious is that the hunt is reduced to a rather predictable experience of sitting in one's designated blind and watching a feeder. Although normally deer will come around, on the typical lease the chance of seeing a big buck is somewhat less likely. The idea is that by patterning the does to the feeders the bucks will be hanging around during the rut. Sometimes this can happen, but even when it does it is not exactly a grand adventure. Feeding can inflate the deer population, but it can also increase the number of varmints, especially feral hogs. These have grown in number and destructiveness as artificial feeding has increase. That combined with overgrazing by livestock has rendered large parts of west Texas overgrown with cedar which often reduces the natural feed and cover.

So what we are left in the typical setup is a property overgrazed by livestock, overgrown with cedar, and overrun by destructive varmints. The hunting is reduced to sitting in a box and watching a small area around a feeder. Due to the density of hunters and the thickness of the overgrown cedar that is about all a hunter can do. A few deer routinely make their rounds from one hunter's site to another. This allows the hunter to see a few deer and hold out hope of getting a big one. While there is a chance at a buck, most hunters on a given property do not see a true shooter during the course of a season. So after a couple of bucks are taken by a lucky few hunters, the remaining hunters take their does or cull bucks and call it a year.

Battle in the Blind

This story is not about an Interesting Place rather it is a story of a typical place. The only reason it is here is for that reason only – to illustrate typical places. Of course that presents a bit of a dilemma. After all typical places don't make for good stories. With the standard setup of a timed feeder and a box blind about 100 yards away, there isn't a whole lot of room for much drama or unexpected occurrences. What can one say about such a place? "Well I got up. It was really dark and cold. I drove out to the stand. I got in the stand. There I waited until sunlight. The feeder went off and several does came in. Then I saw a buck hanging back in the cover. He stepped out and I shot him." While that may have been an intense adrenaline filled moment, it doesn't really make for great story telling.

Now by most standards this typical place was not a bad place. In fact it contained many elements of a good hunting lease. The hill country terrain varied in elevation enough to create a variety of habitats. Several natural springs, well maintained by the rancher, provided good water sources. An old ranch house provided decent accommodations as long as one didn't expect the Ritz Carlton. The price was definitely not on the high end. And most importantly the lease contained a fairly decent amount of game. A hunter could count on several family groups visiting his feeder almost every time which at least gave him something to look at. One could probably count on a deer as long as one didn't get too picky and there always existed a chance at a decent buck.

However in most ways it didn't qualify as an Interesting Place. Each hunter had an area which consisted of one or more feeders and a blind all contained within a few acres of visible clearing surrounded by brush. The areas were spaced strategically in order to maximize the density of paying guests. By rule, each hunter was not allowed to wander from his designated area. In fact our hunter had only seen the lease in its entirety once when the rancher showed him the place before he signed up. Other than that he only knew his area (quite well) and that of his partner. So the hunting consisted of getting up into the blind and hunting the feeder - no other options existed. The name of the game was waiting and waiting and waiting.

Now for our hunter, on the one and only year he hunted this lease, he couldn't complain too loudly about the hunting. After all he killed a buck and a gobbler that season. In addition his partner did the same that year. And at any time they could have each taken their allotment of does but chose not to do so. By any objective this lease could not really be faulted.

However with only one way to hunt, the hunting quickly became mundane – even bordering on boring. After all how many times can a person sit in the same box all morning and all afternoon and stare at the same patch of ground without getting restless? So what's this story about? Well it is about the endless boredom of sitting in a box all day. Well that and the most interesting encounter our hunter had during his time on the lease.

That morning started off much like every other morning that season. Get up early before dark, have breakfast and drive out to the stand. Normally both partners hunted at the same time. Our hunter would get dropped off at his area first and his partner would then drive a little ways to his area (regardless of whose vehicle was used). That morning a cold front had moved in so when our hunter got out of the vehicle he felt the sting of the fresh air on his face. Actually the cold weather would be a blessing. Normally he had to sit in a sweltering box warmed by the sun. A little coolness in the morning would be a nice change from the normally monotonous Texas heat. The walk to the stand, although easy, ambled along for a good quarter to half mile. This provided a chance to stretch the legs before getting cooped up in the stand for the morning.

It had been about a week since our hunter's last trip to the lease. During that trip he had spent several long days on the stand. He had seen several deer – does and small bucks, and he decided that on the next trip he wouldn't mess around much. The first decent enough deer he saw, he would take it. After all he had already tired of the monotonous style of hunting, and besides there was little chance that waiting any longer would produce a monster on this place.

Such was our hunter's thought process when he arrived at the blind. Normally he didn't hunt out of tower stands, but since that was the style on this place he had little choice. This tower however stood quite a bit higher than normal and required some athleticism in order to climb. In order to enter, one had to go through a door located on the bottom of the box after climbing the stairs to that point. Deftly and with deliberate care he navigated this obstacle and soon found himself inside his now all too familiar stand waiting alone in the dark.

The tower offered a commandeering view. He had the good fortune of inheriting this structure from whoever hunted there last. Probably it had been there for several generations of hunters for it could not be easily moved. Carefully he began to scan his feeder area with the binoculars. They amplified the light allowing him to see items long before shooting light. He did not particularly like the idea of a long morning hunt inside that box; however, once it became light enough to see, he quickly became absorbed in the hunt. After all early morning is always a great time and he being a hunter would hunt hard. Perhaps he could end his day early with a kill.

Soon he could make out the familiar shapes of deer as they milled around waiting for the feeder to activate. Early on they appeared as shadows moving back and forth. At times he couldn't tell if they were real or not, but slowly, oh so slowly as the light increased he could see that they were indeed deer. However the morning breakfast call consisted of all does and yearlings. Even though he decided to shoot something that morning he just didn't feel like taking a doe. So he watched them as they bolted away at the sound of the feeder spinning corn out. They soon returned and grazed on the feed for a good thirty minutes before heading off to the next site.

Now our hunter faced a long wait in the blind before he could leave and return to camp for lunch. So he settled in and did what any overworked sleep deprived person would do. He took a nap. Of course there is a skilled art form to napping on the stand. One never goes completely asleep. Rather one always opens an eye from time to time to monitor for movement. It is actually a good technique for it helps to keep a person from squirming around too much in case ole big boy come nosing along.

Soon in the warming temperatures of the sun he did sense movement. At first he couldn't quite pin down what had alerted him. His interest rekindled, he glassed the now all too familiar brush for any sign. Then he realized what had alerted him for right next to his face crawling up the wood were several hornets! Our hunter now understood to his horror that since the last time he hunted, hornets had built a nest underneath the box and there he was trapped on top of them as they slowly came to life in the warming air.

His mind raced with what to do. He had no spray or repellant of any kind. Then he thought of a quick escape before the beasties got too warmed up. However once he opened the door in the floor, he quickly shut it. Hornets had already gathered on the underside of the box. Then he thought of one way to fight back – with his hunting knife. Quickly he used it to cut the hornets in half one by one. At first he could keep up, but soon they buzzed about in larger numbers. Still he kept cutting and avoiding the pests.

Our hunter had a real dilemma. How would he escape? Fortunately his answer came later that morning for the hornets had their own agenda. Soon the majority of them flew off. As lunchtime approached, our hunter bravely bundled up as best he could and quickly made his way down the ladder and out to safety.

That was about the most interesting story from this most typical place. It wasn't a bad place just not an Interesting Place. Oh, and like I mentioned, our hunter later took a deer but what he will remember the most is his fight with the hornets!

Pasture No. 6 – An Interesting Place

So just why was Pasture No. 6 different? What made it an Interesting Place? Well there were a number of things beginning with an unexpected fact. Nobody really wanted it. See it didn't fit in with the traditional idea of a Texas deer lease at all. Technically Pasture No. 6 was part of a larger ranch which consisted of a number of "pastures" or leases. To the rancher each pasture existed as a separate lease property; however in actual fact a number of hunters on the various pastures (consisting of most the land of that particular ranch) had pooled their land together into one mega-lease. This mega-lease consisted of thousands of acres and several dozen hunters. Each had a stand and a feeder which he maintained. But since they pooled the leases the group had developed a rather complex system of determining who could hunt where. In addition this group built and maintained a common bunkhouse which involved its own rules.

One can easily appreciate that in order to make such a system with that many hunters and that many stands work required the strong arm of a single leader. Otherwise the arrangement would quickly break apart. And that is where Pasture No. 6 comes in. See for some reason it never got included in this original pooling. The hunters on the lease never really knew exactly why. Several times they made overtures but these never went very far. It seems that the strong man had made up his mind and Pasture No. 6 simply would not be considered. It could be that Pasture No. 6 was physically separated somewhat by a county road from the other leases. Or it could be that Pasture No. 6 didn't appear to have enough good spots for traditional stand hunting and didn't fit in with the large group approach. Whatever the reason, once the head man said "No", that was final. Pasture No. 6 would continue to be an odd, little satellite lease separate from but adjacent to the large acreage of the pooled leases.

And ironically enough that was to be to our hunter's advantage (although they didn't know it at the time). For one important requirement of an Interesting Place is that is a forgotten little corner that is easily overlooked – a hidden gem. Without the rules of the larger group, the hunters could hunt it as they pleased. This allowed them to explore other options than traditional stand hunting.

Another reason why Pasture No. 6 qualified as an Interesting Place was its inaccessibility. This is probably another reason that excluded it from being pooled with the other leases. Getting to Pasture No. 6 required only a truck. However getting around on that pasture could be difficult. There were a couple of old oil field roads long since fallen into disrepair from lack of maintenance. That and the extremely rough terrain meant that there existed only two spots that could be hunted in the traditional manner. So not only could our hunters hunt the place in non-standard ways, they were actually forced to try new techniques. Sometimes these efforts didn't produce immediate results but sometimes they did. And when they did lightening struck for our hunters.

In every way, the place wouldn't strike a person as particularly attractive, and in fact its first impression would probably be the opposite: that of a Rough Piece of West Texas hard to get to and hard to hunt. But in that rough patch of sticker bushes and thickets it held surprises and unexpected adventure. For although the place didn't house a lot of deer, hidden in the steep canyon crevices and in the deep, brush choked washouts that crisscrossed the land lay the perfect hideouts for big solitary bucks. And that is why Pasture No. 6 was an Interesting Place.

Canyon Deer

Our hunter looked forward to the opening of gun season every since he hunted on the lease during archery season. During that time he had seen a number of good bucks at Area No. 4 located on the far north end of the lease. In addition to seeing a number of deer in the area, he and the other hunters had located a number of scrapes along the trails that ran at the bottom of a large canyon which ran from the ridge at the east to the large flat area to the lease's western boundary. And he had his eye on one deer in particular. It was a true monster by any standard and especially so on a low fence wild chase property such as Pasture No. 6. Large and heavy horned he encountered this beast first during the archery season.

It occurred after a final work day in October in preparation of that for the upcoming gun season. Our hunter and two others did some final touch up work on the far southern end of the lease. Afterwards he planned on an evening archery hunt in Area No. 4 on the northern end. Basically it was a scouting mission, but always once in the field with a weapon one never knows what will happen.

Already tired and sweaty from the morning's work, our hunter donned his camo gear and began the hike into the area. Now October in West Texas can be very hot and that day was exactly that with afternoon temperatures in the 90's. Soon after he began his hike, our hunter began to shed clothes fast. By the time he navigated the almost half mile trek uphill he was sweating uncontrollably. There, before he got into his ground blind at the base of a steep ravine at the bottom of the canyon, he paused to cool down and take a drink of water. Fortunately the ground stand utilized a large cedar bush as cover which provided some protection from the glaring midday sun. Still it looked to be a long hot day on the stand.

He located this ground blind in an area which had a good view of several trails which intersected about 20 to 30 yards in front. In addition, they had found several good scrapes which indicated activity. After he put out some attractant he settled in for a long wait. Although he wanted to maintain cover, the incessant heat forced him to cool off. Soon his water bottled ran empty, and he seriously considered abandoning his quest but still he pressed on.

Eventually the sun dipped below the horizon and the temperatures fell quickly. It always amazed him how fast the conditions changed in this semi-desert environment. As the sun fell, the scene in front of him sprung to life with small animals scurrying about. Then he spotted several deer including a small buck which seemed to appear out of nowhere like ghosts as they always do. Encouraged by the activity he forgot about his earlier discomfort. He was hunting now.

As he studied the small buck, suddenly all the deer became startled and fled. "Damn" he thought. At first he couldn't tell why. They didn't seem to be alerted to him. But then he saw what spooked them. A huge, monster buck charged into view from the rear brush. Head down he quickly staked claim to the scene. Our hunter froze at the sight. Then he forced his hands and arms to move the bow into position when the big boy disappeared behind a thicket to his right. Everything was going according to plan. He had placed the attractant at that spot in hopes of using that ticket as a chance to pull his bow before a deer stepped out broadside.

But not all plans work out exactly right and monster bucks do not get that way by being careless. Somehow as our hunter just began to draw the big buck sensed movement and charged out of the thicket straight at him. Frozen in a half draw position that he couldn't hold for very long our hunter tried not to make eye contact. The big buck stomped in closer. Finally it looked away and our hunter tried to come to full draw. However the old cagey buck was just playing a game as he quickly snapped his head back to try and determine what was up. That time the big boy busted our hunter and he quickly left the scene.

Now that gun season arrived, our hunter set out for redemption. Between seasons he often dreamt of that monster with its heavy symmetrical antlers and buff almost white colored body. This time he would hunt the area from up on the canyon using the rim rock and the brush as a natural blind. He had hunted from this spot before and it provided a shooter's view of all of Area No. 4 including the ravine bottom.

On the first day he hiked up to his spot. Instead of going straight at the spot, he always tried to hike in from the back side of the ridge and then quickly move down into position trying all the while to minimize his visibility. How different that day in November was? Before the temperatures smothered him in dehydrating heat, now the cold drizzling conditions forced him to wear multiple layers in order to be able to stay in the stand all afternoon. Soon he settled into position and waited.

Evening came much earlier now especially in the overcast conditions. Patiently he waited until finally just as the sun started to set he spotted some does moving in from the east. Switched to full hunting mode he thoroughly scanned the area as the darkness began to fall.

Then from the other side of the ravine in the same thick brush he spotted a deer. It was a buck and a really big buck. With light failing he swung his rifle into position. It would be a bit lengthy at 200 yards. But that didn't bother him for he had taken much longer shots in the Rockies and felt comfortable at that distance. No, what made this shot (and shots like it) testy was the quickness required. Unlike what is often depicted on television, wild chase bucks in this country do not often stand around and let a hunter inspect them thoroughly before deciding on a shot. Instead a hunter has to decide whether to shoot and then execute the shot in as little as a second – and that takes real skill.

Our hunter, now with his rifle fully ready waited patiently until the buck moved out just enough so he could see his antlers and front shoulder. He had to make a fast decision and he made it to shoot. The buck was definitely a buster. He settled the crosshairs on the shoulder and with the sound of the gun firing, the buck kicked hard and staggered off.

As soon as our hunter shot and saw the deer move away he instinctively knew that it wasn't the same deer he had seen during archery season, but it was going to be a good deer nonetheless. After he hiked down to the opening, he found copious blood and other signs of a lethal hit. Now dark, our hunter followed it with a flashlight which wasn't hard. It looked like someone had carried a bucket with a large hole in the bottom.

Confident that he would find the deer piled up anytime, our hunter puzzled at the sudden end of the blood trail in front of him. Here he would discover something truly amazing about this Interesting Place. For where the trial ended, brush hid an incredibly steep washout which went down a good 5-10 feet. Hidden from view until one gets right on top of it, these washouts were formed by flash floods and choked with vegetation. They crisscrossed all of Pasture No. 6 in the flat areas below the canyons and ridges.

His buck lay at the bottom of this particular washout piled up and twisted in the thorny mesquite brush. Normally our hunter would have been thrilled at taking such a nice buck. But in this case he knew he shot the second best deer on the lease. The best one still roamed out there somewhere. Nobody ever saw that monster again. Maybe that is why such a deer is a real trophy. In a wild chase setting on an Interesting Place, they are a symbol of skill, determination, planning, and a little luck.

Our hunter got a measure of satisfaction. As he drove back to camp he encountered several members from the pooled acreage. You know the ones that didn't want Pasture No. 6 included in their club. Once they saw the deer they could hardly believe their eyes. They all agreed it had to be one of the largest ever taken on that ranch on any pasture.

Pasture No. 6 didn't look like much from the outside – rough, hard to hunt, and unimpressive. But it was a true Interesting Place with many secrets.

Camping

One might inquire as to why the hunters on Pasture No. 6 wanted to throw in with the other leases in the first place. After all, if that lease was such a hidden gem why share it? Well of course there are several reasons. First is that these hunters didn't at first understand that this Rough Piece of West Texas was indeed so special. In the first few years they didn't do much good primarily because they didn't understand it and attempted to hunt it in the typical manner. Also during those early years, the rancher ran a number of sheep on the place which didn't do much for the hunting. In fact they almost got off the lease after the first year due to their discouragement with the place. But that is another story.

Actually the real reason had to do with camping accommodations. This is a problem with many hunting arrangements. Where are we going to stay? That is always a concern with any lease especially one located out in the middle of West Texas. The hunters on the other pastures had solved that problem by pooling their land and therefore their resources. With that they could and did construct a rather impressive facility for camping and sleeping. Obviously several members of their group had experience and connections in construction for their structure showed it. The building came complete with excellent sleeping quarters, kitchen facilities, heating, cooling, and even a system of water for bathing.

Far from being only a matter of comfort, such accommodations definitely aide one's hunting success. After all if a person can't stay comfortable, then how can one spend much time in the field? These hunters had traded exclusive use of their property for a larger overall area and a good camp. In addition they had more rules to follow, but overall nobody can fault them. They had a great deal.

For the hunters on pasture No. 6, however, things were definitely more rustic. They slept in a single popup trailer. It had grown long in years as evidenced by the deteriorating canvas which each year thinned and tore just a little bit more than the last. They did have a working propane stove, but no bath facilities and no heating and cooling. Most of the time, they made it okay. However, numerous times they cast an eye towards the bunkhouse down the road. How nice it would be to throw in with that group! Their camping problems would be solved.

Frozen Night

Once again two of the hunters on Pasture No. 6 approached the group to inquire about pooling No. 6 in with the other pastures. It was in the heart of the Texas gun season and a number of hunters from the large group were hunting that week. Our hunters had already experienced some success and that proved to be an ice breaker to get a conversation started. One thing led to another and the large group ended up inviting the two Pasture No. 6 hunters over for dinner. They graciously accepted for the offer of stew sure sounded a lot better than the simple meal they planned on having.

So they came over along with the young daughter of one of the hunters. And a good thing they did. The meal was delicious! Some unknown law of nature states that stew cooked and eaten out camping and hunting tastes ten times better than the same stew eaten at home. And eat they did for all three were quite hungry from the hard hunting and rather meager rations of cereal for breakfast and sandwiches for lunch they had eaten for the last couple of days.

A good meal always greases the social skids and this night proved no different. Soon all the hunters, now in good spirits, exchanged stories from previous hunts and leases and generally had a good time - although it should be noted that each side maintained some secrecy about recent hunting on their respective properties. The members of the large group agreed that these guys and their little lease would make for a good addition to the group and promised to inquire with their head hunter about doing just that. Eventually our hunters returned to their little popup full but, truth be told, a little envious but also hopeful. Maybe they wouldn't need their ragged popup trailer for much longer. Maybe they would soon be included in the group with its excellent accommodations.

The weather that evening and for the whole trip up to that point was pleasant. A light jacket provided all the protection one needed. Soon our hunters settled in to their respective sleeping bags for the night without a care in the world.

That changed suddenly when one of the hunters woke with a start shortly after midnight. "Damn its cold" he thought. A front had obviously moved in and the temperature had dropped considerably. Still when he looked at the thermometer in the trailer he could scarcely believe his eyes. "Fourteen degrees" he blurted out "That's Colorado weather." By now everyone had awoken to the sudden drop in the mercury. Of course they hadn't planned on any tough weather that trip and only had light sleeping bags totally unsuited for the conditions they now encountered.

"Are you cold?" he asked his daughter. "I'm FREEEZZING" responded the daughter unsurprisingly. He now knew he had a real problem. She, having grown up in South Texas, had never experienced such conditions and this was shock treatment for sure. The hunters started up an electric space heater they used on occasion in the mornings, but they dared not leave it on during the night. For the rest of the night our hunters slept fitfully and woke often to warm up with the space heater. However nobody got much sleep that night as you can imagine.

It sure would have been nice to have slept in that big warm structure with the other hunters, but then again that was part of hunting at Pasture No. 6.

Like I mentioned before, Pasture no. 6 certainly did not impress as a great spot. Consisting of a smallish scrap of rough, overgrown terrain, the lease was difficult to hunt using the typical Texas hunting style of a blind and feeder. Hard to access without busting up the place and requiring hard work and patience to hunt, most hunters would quickly scratch it off as a possibility. Overlooked and unloved, this place certainly qualified in every way as a Rough Piece of West Texas.

Overview of Pasture No. 6

Consisting of a little less than 800 acres (which is very modest by Texas hunting lease standards), Pasture No. 6 formed a roughly semi-circled, oblong shape running from north to south, more or less. On the eastern edge, a large ridge ran snakelike along the entire length of the lease. This ridge rose up about a hundred or so feet from the bottom and was steep enough that it could only be climbed in a few spots. Along the face of the ridge, facing east and north, a number of canyons cut into the ridge in an irregular fashion, which of course provided a number of possible hiding places for bucks. The ridge flattened out to a mesa top which provided easy walking once one got up there. Just below this mesa top, rim rock jutted out forming a shear drop off of about 10-20 feet depending on the locale.

Two very large canyons, one near the south end and at the north end, cut deep in the ridge and formed very large secondary canyons. Overall the varying and irregular nature of the ridges and canyons provided numerous places to perch and watch over large areas from a commanding height.

Down below the ridge, a large flat area paralleled the ridge along the west end of the property. This flat area was crisscrossed with numerous trails that ran through the brush in various directions. In dry years this area often became barren and desolate; however, it wetter years it became a veritable jungle of overgrown mesquite bushes.

In the basins of the two secondary canyons, deep ravines or washouts had been cut from the runoff from the ridges. The extent of these ravines were hidden from view and not very wide, but they grew as deep as 10 feet and were choked with thick brush. They formed natural travel corridors for the deer. Several ran away from the ridge into the flat area for a good distance. These plus the almost impenetrable thickets provided the deer a method to cross over into the Pasture No. 6 from other areas virtually undetected.

A county road formed the western boundary and provided vehicular access to two gates - one located on each end. However, the "roads" on the lease were hardly that. Normally after entering one of the gates, the hunters would pull off behind some brush quickly and continue on foot from that point.

Overall there were four identified hunting areas on the lease, each with a feeder of some sort. Although Pasture No. 6 didn't lend itself to feeder hunting much, one needed feeders if for no other reason than the other pastures around had feeders. So a type of arms race forced the hunters on Pasture No. 6 to at least provide some feeders although most of the memorable action didn't involve them much. Starting from the south the areas were named as follows: No 1, No.2, No. 3, and finally No. 4. These may not seem like very imaginative names, but they worked. Areas No. 1 and No. 3 were located amongst the brush in the flat area while Areas No. 2 and No. 4 were located in the steep secondary canyons that cut into the main ridge. Generally speaking when one of the hunters said that he was going to hunt Area No. 4 that didn't mean a specific spot. Instead that could be anywhere in that part of the lease more or less around Area No. 4. So basically the areas represented different quarters, roughly, of the lease with each covering 100-200 acres of area.

Hunting Considerations on Pasture No. 6

One might be tempted to use an ATV in order to allow better access. There were two trails to two of the four hunting areas (Nos. 2 and 4) that could be accessed this way. The only problem in using an ATV, or any other vehicle, once on the lease would pretty well bust it up. The deer had a commanding view of everything that happened on the lease from their holdups along the face of the ridges. They bedded down on the north facing (or generally north facing) slopes and could see from these perches anything that moved down below.

That is one of the things that made hunting on Pasture No. 6 so challenging. One had to access the place from the county road, but in doing so one could easily be detected by any number of sharp eyes and ears. Areas No. 2 and No. 4 could be hunted by the typical method of driving up to a stand and hunting a feeder, but the odds of success would be lower than other typical methods. Perhaps that is one reason why that pasture never got invited to join in the larger area of pooled pastures. There were really only two "spots" to hunt in the typical manner, and they were difficult to hunt without stirring up the place.

Typically our hunters found that the best way to hunt the lease involved parking the truck quickly, getting one's gear without making a lot of noise, and hiking quickly but as quietly as possible to the target spot. Once there the goal was to disappear into the background. For afternoon hunts, our hunters had to allow for sufficient time for everything to settle down again. Deer may be wary, but they don't exactly have the mathematical skills needed to keep track of how many people went in versus back out. So if a hunter had the necessary skill, he could slip in a relatively quiet manner and then blend into the background and remain hidden until evening.

Morning hunts proved to be somewhat problematic. One had to pick out a location and try their best to get in as silently as possible. This was made all the more difficult by the fact that loose, broken slates of shale rock covered Pasture No. 6 everywhere one went. The large ridge was composed of several different layers of rock which could easily be discerned. The layer that formed the rim rock obviously came from a harder material than the other layers which over the years had weathered away leaving the ground below smothered in broken shale. In order to hike in, either in the morning or the afternoon, one had to walk with the up most care. Otherwise, the normal silence would be shattered with the sound of shale clanking and grinding together underfoot. And in those canyons the noise generated by the slightest misstep would echo off the walls like a fire alarm to the deer. To walk stealthy in these conditions was a skill that had to be learned and practiced by the average office dweller that occasioned there.

Silence is not something that modern people do well at all. In fact we learn from our everyday environment to do exactly the opposite. We are told and even encouraged to be heard, to fight to be the next to speak, to scream like lunatics at sporting events and gatherings. Our culture rewards the loudest and acknowledges the most outlandish attempts to generate attention. We absorb these lessons so well that we hardly become aware of them. In every way – clothes, loud music, tattoos, or any other obnoxious behavior - we scream "look at me." Why just this afternoon, my attention was diverted by a motorist who insisted on playing his bass load enough to be heard by everyone at the stoplight. Why did he do that? I don't know, I guess he just couldn't stand the idea of not making a bunch of noise for five minutes. It is the ego which seeks to dominate its surroundings, which demands to be the center of attention on all things great and small.

This is our nature which is at odds with the nature required for success at an Interesting Place like Pasture No. 6. There we must learn to move quietly like a ghost because our prey moves about in that manner. To be successful we must mimic their ways, and to do that requires that we unlearn everything the modern world has taught us despite how second nature it feels to us. That is one of the great benefits of hunting, especially at an Interesting Place. In those situations, we learn just how self centered and out of touch with the natural world we really are. In those places, we must humble ourselves and learn everything anew, even mundane things like how to walk, how to move, even how to blink. We think we know these things until we get in a wild chase hunting situation, then we realize that we don't. Interesting Places are like that. They teach things about our nature that we otherwise would never even be aware.

Of course being a wild chase hunt and all, certain things fell outside of a hunter's ability to control. ATV traffic on a nearby property, an oil company pumper checking something out next door, or even an occasional truck driving down the county road affected the hunting. With hunting pressure everywhere in that country, these deer were very wary, they had to be. That aspect definitely is a drawback to low fence hunting, but that also adds an element of uncertainty that a skilled hunter needs to consider in order to be successful.

Double at No. 2

Area No. 2 had always been a promising looking place. Situated in one of the two large secondary canyons that split the main ridge, the area consisted of steep slopes covered with dense brush which led down to a narrow and rough basin. There at the foot of the canyon began a sharp washout that then winded through the flat area until it petered out near the county road. The entire area overwhelmed one with the feel that this was a big buck hideout.

Naturally such a hot looking spot could not be approached easily. And despite the rough, wild terrain, our hunter, the one who was known as Legend, had spent more than a few afternoons and mornings on the stand here without seeing a darn thing. On those days the hours often would stretch on forever. Once up on the ridge slope, he could look out across the landscape for miles around, the view fading out in the misty, atmospheric haze. To pass the hours he would glass across to other leases and try to see what was going on there. From his perch he could make out numerous blinds on other properties. They seemed to have been set by some kind of giant hand with each one was perfectly spaced apart on a square pattern.

On those long days, he often wondered what had he done wrong. Why wasn't he seeing any deer? He had done everything as correctly as he could. He opened the gate quietly, parked without making any noise, hiked in as stealthily as possible. Yet he sat – no deer, no sign of any deer. Of course he knew Pasture No. 6, and it could be like that – one could do everything with great skill and still the slightest misstep may alert every deer in the area. That was hunting, and that was hunting in a low fence, wild chase lease like Pasture No. 6.

This day he would hunt Area No. 2 again. By all accounts it looked to be an ideal time. All evidence indicated that the rut was on, although often in that part of the country the rut is a rather smeared out affair. In addition the weather that day looked to be ideal for hunting with an overcast sky, cool temperatures, and misty rain. These hunters had learned from experience that bright blue skies often meant no deer. With the only possible approach from the north and west, the sun would light up any movement like a neon sign making the hunting just that much more difficult.

Another factor played to our hunter's favor – the day of the week. On weekends during the season, the hunters on other pastures would inevitably ramble about, often in ATV's. The level of activity had to be noticed by the game for the simple reason that it was so much out of the ordinary, and deer notice what has changed. In fact the hunters on the lease often joked that could the number of deer they would see was inversely proportional to the number of ATV's buzzing about in the morning before dawn.

However this day was in the middle of the week and all around Pasture No. 6, quiet ruled the land. Our hunter went through the familiar ritual of carefully and quietly approaching his intended stand. Once through the south gate he pulled off behind a large pile of mesquite brush. Then he silently assembled his gear and began the trek east towards the ridge. Although most of the hike covered the flat area, it wasn't all that flat once on foot. The flat area rose constantly as the ridge approached. Once at the ridge, our hunter used a nose that sloped down to the bottom for access. This nose provided one of the few places where the grade was gentle enough to allow a person to hike up to the top.

He had a selected a stand location slightly below where he normally sat. In the past he often chose to sit at the base of the rim rock using it as a backdrop. Several places along this contour provided cover behind cedar bushes and the rim rock ledge helped to shield against the sun and wind.

However, in Area No. 2, selecting a stand was a bit of a balancing act. Because the two slopes that formed the secondary canyon ran away from each other, the distance between the shooter and the opposite slope increased dramatically as one ascended. But, on the other hand, the higher one got, the easier it became to peer into the brush and see openings and trails on the opposite slope. So there was a tradeoff. This time our hunter would set up lower, which would not only shortened the shot, but perhaps also would provide for more concealment.

Once in place he settled down for a potentially long afternoon on the stand. After all, he had experienced just that many times before. Because of the day of the week, everything around him fell silent. In this country, it is often eerie just how quiet the world can be away from civilization. At least at first it is eerie. Then one adapts and crosses over into a pace of life somewhat forgotten – a pace where nature reveals itself on its own terms. Once a person crosses over to this ancient reality, he becomes not just a mere guest but is absorbed onto the reality and becomes an actor on the stage of the drama which constantly unfolds everyday.

Our hunter did exactly that. Soon the civilized world with its demands and its incessant drumbeat of light and sound faded away. How strange such a place seems once a person leaves it. By that I mean really leaves it totally - in mind and spirit as well as physically. Despite its triumphant blaring of invincibility, the modern world appears somewhat odd and even fragile when viewed from afar.

His mind now had totally adapted and he now actively participated in the drama before him. With deliberate efficiency honed by years of experience, he skillfully glassed the opposite slope for any sign. This time he didn't have to wait long. Almost inconspicuously a slight movement caught his attention. He didn't know exactly what had caught his eye but he now focused even more intently on that area. Slowly he scanned every opening for anything. Perhaps it was just a bird flitting through the shrubs or a smaller animal.

Then he caught what had grabbed his attention. Almost invisible in the brush a doe's head slowly turned to look behind her. Instinctively he got his rifle ready for he knew that she might be looking behind to see a buck. With complete concentration he waited, watching the scene unfold in the rifle scope.

His gun was his old trusty 25-06 which he had used on many deer hunts and made many great shots on deer from Oklahoma to Colorado. He relied on it for long range shooting and this time would be no different. Although the shot would be shorter than if he was higher up on the slope, it was still lengthy. And because he sat lower on the slope, the brush would provide fewer openings for shooting. That is one thing that a person unfamiliar to hunting in that country has to experience to appreciate. The shots are not like they are depicted on television where the shooter has considerable time to scan over the buck and settle down for a shot. Here in this wild chase country with wary and educated deer, the shots are lightning fast. Normally a hunter has only a fraction of a second in which to make up his mind to shoot and then pull the trigger. Forget about slowly squeezing the tripper. Here it is more like point and click. That added to the fact that our hunter would be shooting from a sitting position using a shooting stick, made for a very challenging shot of the highest skill level.

Very soon after the doe moved off, he glimpsed a good mature buck, head down, on the trial behind her. He swung the rifle scope to get on the deer; however, it kept moving in an erratic, unpredictable manner as they often do when on the trial of a hot doe. Finally the buck stuck the front part of his body out from behind a cedar bush just enough for a shot.

At the sound of the rifle, our hunter knew he got a solid hit, but the deer disappeared in the smoke. Once again the landscape fell silent. Our hunter knew enough to wait and so he did. Eventually he hiked over and quickly picked up the trail. Soon he found his prize piled up behind some brush. While not a monster deer by high fence standards, it still was in every way a respectable, mature buck taken with skill, experience, and determination.

So why is this story titled "Double at No. 2"? Well about a month later, our hunter decided to give Area No. 2 another try. It was almost repeat performance with the weather conditions, stand selection, and time of day. The main difference being that this buck wasn't just moving through the brush, he was running! This made for an even more challenging shot as he darted from side to side on the trails.

That is what makes hunting in a wild chase environment always unpredictable. After a number of days stretched over several years of hunting in Area No. 2 without much success, our hunter doubled up from the same spot in less than a month. That small adjustment in where he set up must have made all the difference. That is why hunting in such Interesting Places is always intriguing.

Methods of Hunting

Previously I mentioned before that at Pasture No. 6 there were really only two places that could be hunted in the typical Texas manner (with a blind and a feeder). And they posed certain difficulties using that technique. ATV's were basically a non-starter due to the noise they generated and the problem that these areas (2 and 4) couldn't be driven up to without every wild animal on the ridge seeing all the commotion. Of course for many people, ATV's are as integral a part of hunting as camo, and not being able to use an ATV takes out a lot (or maybe most) of the fun.

For these people I don't really have much of a complaint except that I admit that I don't get the ATV thing. For me they are useful in the off season for servicing feeders and to get to areas to scout for scrapes and sign – in other words off season use only. Even then I was always a bit leery of them. My theory is that one's hunting lease should always be treated like a wilderness even in the off-season. The reasons are two fold. First even during the hot summer months, a lot of banging around can't be good for the deer. I might be a bit overly cautious, but especially at a big buck hangout like Pasture No. 6, one wants to maintain it as a buck sanctuary. It is hard enough in a low fence area to get and keep good bucks on our pasture. Why chase them off several times a year with a bunch of racket?

The second reason is psychological. I am of the opinion that once a person steps onto their hunting property, they need to switch on their hunting instincts. That means leaving the modern world and its ways behind and entering that ethereal realm of our ancient ancestors. That means to tread lightly and disturb as little as possible. If one does this then the little things – walking over broken shale silently, not banging the truck door, using the brush continuously as cover – become more instinctive when the season arrives. That may be little things, but an Interesting Place like Pasture No. 6 is often sensitive to the little things.

For these reasons, success at Pasture No. 6 required different approaches. Our hunters adopted two basic techniques that were actually variations of the same thing. One involved using the ridges as natural lookout posts for makeshift stands. This allowed flexibility in where the hunter could set up. Depending on the wind and sun conditions, a hunter could adjust his stand location to optimize (hopefully his chances).

To do this well, he needed to have two things: good knowledge of the deer habits and good shooting skills. The need for good shooting skills is more apparent. By locating up on the ridge faces, the hunter immediately put himself in a position for a longish shot. This is quite different than the typical blind method of setting up 80 to 100 yards from a feeder. The shots from up on the ridge not only could range out to 400 yards, the hunter had to be ready to take a variety of different shots depending on where a deer came out. The hunter didn't have the advantage of a solid blind with its window rest. Instead he either had to improvise a rest or use a shooting stick. Either way he had to be able to adapt his shooting stance quickly as the action unfolded.

Using the ridges as stands required more skill and knowledge of the deer habits than it may seem at first glance – as our hunters found out. Simply plopping down anywhere up in the ridge face where one had a good view wasn't enough. Very careful attention had to be paid to the approach so as to get in with as little disturbance as possible.

Also the hunter had to pay attention to his cover and wind direction even up high. The irregular nature of the ridges and canyons caused the local wind direction to swirl and suddenly change direction which often left a careless hunter with the wind against him. With the sharp changes in elevation and the dry semi-desert conditions, the wind direction within a local canyon varied during the course of the day as the top of the ridge heating and cooling at a different rate from the bottom. This led to micro wind currents that could and often did vary in direction from the overall wind pattern in the area and changed from morning to evening.

Another huge problem about using the ridges as stands involved the sun. Deer like to bed down on north facing slopes for a reason – they can us the sunlight to illuminate everything in front of them. Many hunters think of deer as primarily creatures of scent, and of course they are. Their sense of smell is legendary for good reason. However do not think that they cannot see. They can see quite well, and when sportsmen hunt in more open terrain such as West Texas, they find this out. For our hunters on Pasture No. 6 they more often than not had to simply bite the bullet and take their chances with the sun. Occasionally they could set up where they had both sun and wind to their advantage, but usually not. That was one of the big reasons why Pasture No. 6 was so maddeningly difficult to hunt, and why much of our hunter's successes occurred on overcast and bad weather days.

Locating scrapes and hunting over scrapes was the other technique our hunters utilized on Pasture No. 6. Here the idea is to locate a buck's scrapes and make out his "buck run" and then figure out how to hunt that. Which sounds all good in theory but in practice is much more difficult. For one thing finding scrapes in the rock hard, stony ground could challenge even the most seasoned of white tail hunters. Many times the hunters would carry out the following conversation:

"I think I found a scrape take a look at it."
"Is that a scrape, I can't tell."
"Well I thought it was, now I'm not so sure. Maybe its from a raccoon or something."
"Okay let's make a note of it just in case."

Making scrape identification all the more difficult, the area didn't have a lot of trees for rubs and licking branches. However that could work to one's advantage because where one could find a licking branch along a trail above a scrape, that helped to confirm buck activity in that area if some of the other located scrapes were doubtful.

One of the things that always puzzled our hunters is that the buck activity always seemed to vary from year to year. Some times Area No. 4 had deer sign everywhere. The next year nothing, but the base of the ridge in Area No. 3 had good scrape activity. Possibly this had to do with the changing rainfall and sheep grazing from year to year. After all West Texas is arid and changes in climate on a yearly basis can affect the deer population greatly. The advantage for the hunters is that every year Pasture No. 6 always hunted like a different lease and kept them on their toes.

To hunt the scrapes was another problem entirely. One could attempt to get down in the brush and hunt a section of trail. Our hunters did this on occasion. However normally they used a combination technique where they first located an area of scrapes and buck activity and then figured out how to use the ridges to set up natural stands over those areas. This combination technique allowed them to maximize their use of hunting, stalking, and shooting skills making Pasture No. 6 an every changing Interesting Place.

Lucky Charm

A daughter's first hunt with her dad is an unforgettable experience for both, and certainly this was the case for one of the hunters on Pasture No. 6 and his child. Only a fourth grader, she had always overheard her father talk about these trips. Of course he added a certain amount of embellishment which was understood except perhaps for such a young child. To her these stories carried the weight of unimaginable adventure, for this was the real deal not some television show or movie. There is something about that very fact in hunting – the authenticity of the experience which no technological wizardry can quite match. Even a young person can appreciate this even when she probably didn't yet consciously realize that fact.

For that reason, the trip understandably produced a certain amount of anticipation in the child. Adults sometimes forget this. To them any given trip is just another hunting trip, some are successful many are not. However, to a small child – one who hasn't yet grown to that point where they don't want to be seen with their parents – a trip like this one can loom up large in their mind. After all while they may want to be a part of the action, they also can secretly dread it. They do not want to be seen as being the cause of a trip's failure. Now an adult has the background to understand that many things go into whether a particular trip produces game or not, but a little child may not have that understanding.

And so it was on this trip. It began innocently enough. The dad picked up his daughter early in order to get a head start down the road. She already was filled with excitement. For one thing she had gotten new boots and clothes and that, of course, is always a big deal for a little girl. Now she could look forward to some quality one on one time with her father.

The hunter planned on arriving at Pasture No. 6 in early afternoon, getting unloaded at camp, and hunting Area No. 4 in the evening. He figured that an evening hunt would be a better first time experience than a crack of the dawn hunt where they had to hike out in the dark. By all indications, the timing appeared to be good. The rut was on, and the weather looked to be a little on the cool side and overcast. Everything pointed to a good time and a great adventure.

On the trip, our hunter naturally had to explain and stress the safety rules. For while the daughter would not be carrying a gun or shooting, hunting is still a very serious endeavor and our hunter needed to make sure she understood what she could and couldn't do out there. It was then that the daughter began to get really nervous.

For perhaps the first time in her young life, she felt that feeling known to all who hunt. That feeling is an indescribable sense of dread which can well up, and which causes the person doubt about what they are getting themselves into. It was in that moment that this child first felt the emotions of leaving the modern world behind and crossing over to a largely forgotten past – that hidden corner of our primal soul which is hardwired to be a part of the great drama of nature. For a seasoned adult, this emotion can be difficult to overcome, for a child who never knew such a state existed, it was downright debilitating.

And that produced the first great crisis of the trip. Unfortunately for the child, the sudden welling up of these powerful emotions caused her to get sick. With the drive half completed, our hunter didn't know exactly what to do. With great care he tried to calm her and reassure her. Still he thought "Maybe this wasn't a good idea, perhaps I should go back." It is possible that he could have been using this as a convenient excuse himself. However a call back home convinced him otherwise. If they turned around now, the child might blame herself. Finally she and her father settled their nerves and pressed forward.

Then came the second crisis of that trip. Just as they started to get within shouting distance of the lease, the cool overcast skies opened up and a cold rain fell. This caused our hunter a great deal of concern. The hunters on Pasture No. 6 didn't use blinds much and anyway he had learned from previous experience with an older child that little ones don't particularly like being cooped up in a box. He had planned on hiking up to one of his favorite perches on the slope above Area No. 4. He figured that even if they didn't see anything, she would enjoy the scenery with an extra set of binoculars he brought. He could stand a little precipitation; however, he didn't want to have his daughter in any bad weather. If the rain continued, it could threaten the entire trip.

With the rain hitting the windshield, he kept silent. He didn't want to say anything until he knew if they were going to hunt that afternoon or not. Once they turned off the blacktop, it let up miraculously. Now at the little popup to unload their gear, the youngster once again expressed some doubts, not with her words but with her expressions. The campsite now appeared a whole lot less than what she had envisioned. Gone were any remaining notions of romantic adventure, now she faced the harsh truth of being out in the wilderness away from the comforts of home. Still little kids are resilient and she kept any doubts to herself.

Sensing this, the dad decided that they should get out to the pasture before she decided that a hotel back in town sounded like a better idea. Now the weather had cleared up and it was perfect for hunting which caused our hunter to start to kick into full hunting mode. He could feel the excitement of crossing over to his primal past stir up inside. Whether or not the daughter felt this at that time, well it's hard to say. For her everything was new and different. At this stage out so far from home in this strange and wildly untamed place, all she could do was trust her father.

They entered the lease through the north gate and pulled off as usual. Then they began the hike up to the stand area. Adults often forget that what seems to be a rugged but modest hike to them can feel like the Baton Death March to a fourth grader. The loose, rocky shale combined with the steep ascent proved quite a challenge to her. After all she had never done this before. Heck, before this trip, she could never have imagined that she would do this in her wildest imagination. That is one of the great things about taking young people into the outdoors: they quickly learn the difference between the reality of nature and their assumptions based on television and the movies.

The hike took much longer than normal and much longer than our hunter liked. He knew that one of the keys to Pasture No. 6 was to slip in quickly and quietly, then set up and disappear into the background. Now he knew with a young child this would greatly diminish his odds (after all young children are by nature NOT quiet and can NOT simply vanish into the brush in a motionless manner). Still he wouldn't have traded this opportunity to be with his youngest for any deer in Texas. If they got something, then that would be great. And if not, well that would be just as special to him.

Finally they arrived at the stand. It was one of our hunter's favorite places. Located at the base of the rim rock, there lay several large stones which created a natural ground blind which had been built up with smaller stones placed over the years by human hands. Several cedar bushes just down the slope broke up their outline and provided more cover. The rim rock acted as a backstop.

Soon after they set up, our hunter described the area and the deer habits and movements to his daughter. The hunters had located several scrapes and good deer sign along the trails in the bottom. Eagerly he described how the bucks use the scrapes as markers, how they leave rubs, how the rut works, and how and why the deer bed in certain areas using his hands to gesture the large expanse of open scrub brush laid out before them. What did the daughter think of all this? Well we'll never know but certainly couldn't have been like anything else she experienced.

By now the hour had barely passed 3:30 PM. They had been on the stand, oh maybe thirty minutes. Then came the third big crisis of the trip. "What time does the feeder go off?" she asked. "Uh, about 5:30" answered the father. With that her little shoulders visibly slumped down and forward. Adults forget that children just don't have the patience that we do. Staying on a stand takes practice and a certain skill. It doesn't have the non-stop excitement of television or video games. That is, of course, part of what makes hunting unique and special, but that is a difficult lesson to learn on the first trip.

Our hunter realized that they may not make it till dark. He tried to get her to read a book he had brought, but she wasn't interested. He tried to get her to eat a snack and drink a soda. That helped but it didn't last long. He was beginning to run out of options to keep her entertained.

At that moment, our hunter happened to glance up the canyon to the east. There he spied several does milling about. They were way to far out – more than 500 yards in thick brush – but he thought that his daughter might be occupied by watching them. Perhaps they would later come in closer for a shot. As he did this she announced "I see a deer." "Wow" he thought "She must have really good eyes to see those does without any magnification." "You see those does way over there?" he asked. "No I see a deer down there" she confidently declared.

Confused our hunter pulled down his binoculars to see what she was talking about. Then he saw her pointing down to the canyon bottom to the WEST. Hurriedly he scanned the bottom. Although she didn't have the experience, she sounded sure so he had to check it out.

Then he saw it. It was a buck, mature but not a huge one by any stretch. At first he hesitated. But then he thought "If I shoot this deer, she'll have had a great time and we can be in town for dinner at the steakhouse." This might not sound like the best thinking when deciding if a buck is a shooter, but once he confirmed that it was mature and a bit of a rag horn, he decided to take it. He gently grabbed his daughter's arm. This was the predetermined signal that he was about to take a shot and he whispered "Don't move a muscle."

Of course Murphy's Law came into play at that point. As soon as he decided to take it, the buck immediately became elusive. It was obviously on the trail of a doe and was moving, head down, in an erratic back and forth manner. Several times our hunter tried to get on the deer but couldn't get a clean shot. This type of shooting is very different from what is depicted on TV. The deer are constantly moving and the sticker bushes allow only brief openings.

After several attempts to get a shot, the buck had worked well off to the east side of them and was angling away, up the opposite slope. Our hunter knew that he was running out of time and chances. He gently touched his daughter's arm again and again warned her not to move. The buck had vanished in the brush; however, he knew which trail the buck was traveling. He made a decision to set up his shot at an opening up ahead on that trail. If he guessed right he would have a split second shot at more than 250 yards.

What began as a simple introductory hunt for his child now had turned into a life and death drama. What was once a borderline shooter buck now had become that hunter's quest. Totally fixated on the task at hand, the hunter's breathing slowed down and became methodical. His heart rate steady, his entire consciousness now consisted only of that one opening in the brush. All of his years of experience hunting deer in a variety of locations, all those hours of practice at the range now were being brought to bear on this one moment. He had completely crossed over to that primitive state of being where he no longer was a mere observer but actually part of the eternal drama of nature. In that state he had no consciousness of any other reality. This is the authentic experience which cannot be faked or controlled. It can only happen and then just for a fleeting moment.

After what seemed forever, the buck stepped out into the opening. As it came into view, our hunter bore down on him through the scope visually focusing on the one spot on its front left shoulder. If his eyes had been lasers, he would have burned a hole completely through the deer to the ground below, such was his concentration. Without warning the rifle fired. Our hunter's sight never left the buck as the gun recoiled. He knew instantly that the deer was hit hard when it rolled its shoulders down and staggered off out of view.

Still focusing through the scope sight he searched for the deer again trying to determine if it had gone down. He heard it crash through some brush a short distance from the place of the shot and then nothing. At that instance, he realized that his youngest child had been next to him during that time. Concerned at how she would respond to what she had just seen, he quickly made sure she was okay. Not only was she fine, she was thrilled. She wanted to go recover the deer right away; however, our hunter had to teach her a lesson about allowing enough time to make sure the animal was down. During that waiting time, he took the opportunity to discuss what had happened and why the buck was behaving like he did. Finally he said to her "It's a good thing you were here. If you hadn't seen that deer, then I probably would not have seen him. You must be my lucky charm." With that she beamed with pride. Not only had she been part of the hunt she had also contributed.

Eventually they climbed down the slope to where the deer was last seen. Here they encountered the fourth great crisis of the trip. For once they got there, very little could be seen. Our hunter then started to wonder if he had really hit that buck as hard as he first thought, and he realized that he now had the problem of tracking this animal over rough country and through sticker thickets with a small child.

At first he tried to convince his daughter to wait for him in the spot where the deer was shot, but she would have none of that. He then used the opportunity to teach her about tracking. He showed her how to spot blood and followed the ground which had been disturbed by the deer's hooves as it bolted off. They started at the last known spot and began to go in an expanding circle pattern to pick up more sign. Our hunter silently let out a big sigh of relief when they began to pick up good blood on one of the trails. Filled with confidence they followed a little ways until it turned sharply to the left and then disappeared. Slightly confused, our hunter stopped, marked the last blood sign, and scanned ahead. Then he spotted what appeared to be a signal foot sticking up out of the ground. He motioned to his daughter to look ahead. Finally she saw it too.

The buck had run into one of the steep washouts that ran through Area No. 4. These ravines can literally swallow up an animal and that is what happened here. Once our hunter(s) retrieved the deer, now they needed to field dress it. The father didn't particularly want his child to see that part, but she insisted. It is strange that when children are exposed to the outdoor sports at an early age, they adapt to its demands easily. It is only when they are conditioned by the modern world and its messengers that they learn to view such things negatively.

The plan had worked perfectly. Our hunters had a great adventure with an animal in the truck to show for the effort. And best of all, there was still enough time to go the steakhouse!

Buck haven

Many things made Pasture No. 6 a difficult and somewhat unattractive place to hunt. However, these very elements made it a buck haven. The large ridge which ran the length of the property created untold numbers of crevices which provided bucks with hiding spots. Naturally the bucks hung out in those places which provided them the maximum advantage of both wind and view – that was the tradeoff.

The lease didn't support a large number of resident deer. Due to the semi-desert conditions, does normally had to travel in order to browse and the better areas for that were located elsewhere on other pastures. Does did travel through Pasture No. 6 – especially during the rut. That was the best time to hunt, like it is all in deer hunting. However at Pasture No. 6 these hunters learned that simply couldn't just hunt during the rut in the typical manner and have success. Once they figured out what kind of place it was, they had to adapt their hunting styles to fit the property. On one hand the place was a perfect big buck hideout, but on the other hand with the low density of animals and the lease's difficulty to approach meant the chance of success often hinged on the small things that can easily be overlooked.

So if a hunter was careless in his approach – or just unlucky – chances were good that he wouldn't see any deer and that happened a lot. Many times our hunters would hike up to one of their perches on the ridge or hunt a scrape area in the brush and not see a thing. Those are the times that truly test a hunter. It is easy when the deer are all penned in. It is quite another to stick to it when they are not, and the hardscrabble land doesn't look like it could support any life at all. So Pasture No. 6 wasn't a place to see a lot of deer. It was a Rough Piece of West Texas which made it a buck haven.

But when one did see a deer, he better be ready for odds were good that it was a buck, and those opportunities didn't happen every time so when they did a hunter needed to be ready to capitalize. That is what made Pasture No. 6 unique and that is what made it an Interesting Place.

Jumped Deer

I certainly do not want to give the impression that all hunts on this Interesting Place ended with hunters posing with their deer while a partner snaps pictures. In fact the overwhelming majority of the time our hunters didn't even dirty their barrels (They often joked that one advantage of not shooting anything was that they wouldn't have to clean their rifle when they returned home).

Numerous times they didn't even see anything at all anything to look at. But just about the time they were ready to give up on the place lightening would strike. The problem often being that the opportunity was fleeting and required a fortuitous set of conditions in order to score. Some of these conditions fell within the hunter's ability to control but many did not and that is one thing that always made Pasture No. 6 an unpredictable adventure.

On this particular trip, our hunter set out to hunt the area below the main ridge between Areas No. 3 and No. 4. At the base of the ridge ran a well used game trail and the hunters had previously located several scrapes along that trail. The problem was that these scrapes tended to concentrate at the location where the ridge nosed down gently to the flat area. This presented a problem of how to hunt that spot because that nose was one of the only places for a human to climb from the bottom up to the ridge top. If a hunter tried to get up on the ridge face above the place where the scrapes clustered, he would have to walk right through the area busting it up. Once again Pasture No. 6 would pose a challenge of access. To slip in undetected would require skill and a little luck.

Our hunter had set about in his mind to hunt whatever buck had made these scrapes. They were just too numerous and well used to ignore, and to hunt a buck over his scrapes and trails is the epitome of classic white tail hunting techniques. Once before, he attempted to hunt the area from the ridge. On that morning he decided to hike to the ridge top from a different access point further down the ridge. It would be rougher and steeper but he felt, since he was in good physical shape, he could get in without making too much noise. However half way up when he was climbing almost hand over fist due to the steep ascent, a covey of quail busted out in front of him. In the early morning quiet they sounded like a machine gun going off. Needless to say that he didn't see a thing that day.

Another time he gave the old "up and personal" technique a try. Setting up in the brush on the opposite side of the area from the ridge, he hunted the trail through an opening. The problem with the "up close and personal" method is that by definition you aren't going to see many deer, mainly because you can only see a relatively small opening. He did his best Indian tracker imitation on the way in and set up in a good spot. However, either the buck(s) detected him or it just wasn't his day. Once again he saw a grand total of zero deer.

A couple of weeks later he decided to give it another go. This time he would hunt in the afternoon. That would allow time for the area to settle down after he hiked in. Also he determined that if he moved down the slope a ways to the north, then he might be able to see a different part of the flat area between Areas No. 3 and No. 4. Using his long range shooting skills to his advantage, a setup there would allow him to possibly take a long shot towards the location of all the scrapes while at the same time allowing him a good view of the flat area and its trails to the north.

As usual he tried to be as careful as possible as he made, once again, the arduous climb up the slope away from all the scrapes. Slowly and deliberately he picked his way towards his intended setup place. Due to the many cuts and ravines in the ridge, this wasn't as easy as it might seem. These undulations added considerable distance to the hike, and because of their remoteness, they were choked with brush. So numerous times a hunter had to carefully backtrack in order to avoid busting up the area.

One of the rules these hunters followed as they hiked into an area, especially as they hike up ridges, was to keep their firearms unloaded – for safety reasons. No one wanted an accidental discharge as a result of a fall. While this is certainly prudent, at times it can cost a hunter an opportunity, and that is what happened here. The good news was that our hunter must have done a good job being quiet and stealthy in his approach. For just as he rounded the end of one of those mini-cuts in the ridge face, out jumped a huge buck directly in front of him. The distance could not have been more than ten yards.

The bad news is, of course, his rife sat slung over his shoulder – unloaded. Old big boy didn't wait around long enough to see if he could un-shoulder his firearm for a shot as he bolted straight up the ridge face within rock throwing distance past our hunter – at least he got a really good look at the antlers.

Quickly our hunter got his rifle un-slung and loaded (he always kept a couple of rounds handy just in case). Now, it is always quite amazing how fast a practiced hunter can get his rifle loaded in such a situation and this time was no exception. Numerous hours he had spent going over just such a situation – getting a round out quickly and working the bolt. Maybe in this situation all that work would pay off for him.

Fortunately for our hunter the buck stopped just at the top of ridge. Quickly our hunter kneeled down to steady the gun; however the brush didn't cooperate. He didn't have a clear shot at anything but the deer's rear end. In a split instant he decided to pass on that shot and shift his position slightly to his left for a clearer view. That turned out to be a fateful decision for both the hunter and the prey. That is the nature of the hunt in a wild chase environment. Little things matter in a life and death drama which has been played out countless times in countless situations across time. The outcome is unknown. So far many little things had gone right for our hunter. Would this decision be the last little thing that made the difference?

After shifting, it took just a tiny fraction of a second longer than it should have for our hunter to re-acquire the buck who had also moved slightly. Maybe the animal's ability to blend into the background was just enough to delay the hunter. Perhaps the hunter's vision or focus wasn't quite fast enough. In any case, our hunter did find the deer once more and immediately put the scope on his prey.

As he tried to settle the cross hairs for a shot, old big boy decided he had had enough and trotted over the top and disappeared. Our hunter, naturally, tried to climb up after it, but once he topped the ridge, the deer was nowhere to be seen. So close, so many things he had done right, but even the tiniest details in this high stakes drama can make all the difference for both parties. That is one of the things which make wild chase hunting on an Interesting Place so authentic and special.

Our hunter never did get that deer although he tried several more times. He would have made for a fine trophy, but even though he "failed" in a sense, he did come away with a trophy – the memory of those moments.

Chapter 8 - Calling in a Deer

Perhaps this title should read Screaming in a Deer. For that is what happened. Admittedly, it wasn't exactly a textbook example of highly skilled rattling timed and pitched to the nuances of a particular phase of the rut. Nothing here should the reader take as a lesson in technique or hunting skill. Instead it is a tale of what can happen when hunters are in the field and improvise to meet unexpected challenges.

This story began with one of the hunters on Pasture No.6, which as you know by now was a forgotten, overlooked rough patch of West Texas thus qualifying it as an Interesting Place. This hunter had reached that stage where many hunters end up, that of father to a young, enthusiastic hunter raring to get his, or in this case her, first deer.

The desire to pass on the tradition of hunting to a younger generation is certainly one of the great joys of hunting, but it is also one of the most delicate things a father can do. After all hunting is not a game. By its very nature, it is dangerous. Also, the rhythms of the hunting experience are foreign to a young generation brought up on fast pace video games and action packed movies with high tech special effects.

With hunting there are no special effects, just nature operating at its own pace with its own rules. But the difference, of course is that the hunting experience taps into a reality at the most primal, intense level. It is the intensity of life itself. And in this intensity, the outcome is never known for certain. With so much at stake, everything for the participants, the drama played out between hunter and hunted must unfold carefully.

To a disinterested observer, it is a painfully slow process. But to the participants, their every move in the play is carefully made through ageless instinct honed by experience. With each step, the intensity within each soul focuses every corner of their being into the purest flame of awareness only achieved by loosing the consciousness of self.

Such an intensity burns so hot that it is at once craved beyond else and at the same time feared for its power. The modern world seeks to contain it, to mollify it, to allow a person to get a taste while at the same time protecting from danger. Many substitutes are thus tried. People turn to thrill seeking, vice, intoxicants, power, even evil just to try and experience once this purity of being. For it is in this total concentration of the mind that a person can connect to their soul, connect to humanity past and future.

However, the modern world levels and this leveling is incompatible with this passion. So a deal, of sorts, is struck. Weak substitutes are temporarily offered. Style substitutes for substance. Variety replaces patience. Excitement displaces drama. But the style proves empty of value. The variety produces a numbing safety of false choices. And the excitement soon gives way to the dull boredom of over stimulation.

The subtle ways of the hunt at first seems to be lost in a hopeless contest against these false substitutes. But the hunt has the advantage of a hunger which gnaws relentlessly if quietly. And this hunger cannot be forever denied. It is the person that must learn to accept that hunger and embrace it, not for the hunger to be made acceptable to the person.

So the hunter, who had experienced these things but could only express them in obtuse metaphors, was faced with a dilemma. He must introduce his child to the mysterious ways of the hunt. Yet the full brunt of these ways experienced all at once by a person so young carried the risk of alienation. This is particularly true when the young person is going to be carrying a weapon for the first time in order to feel the awe of being a central participant in this eternal drama.

The first thought of our hunters was to take up a position where they would have the greatest chance of seeing deer and getting a shot. In that year, the top place to fit that bill was Area No. 4 located on the northern most end of Pasture No. 6. Each year the density of deer activity shifted around to different parts of the property. The reasons for this baffled the hunters but everyone generally agreed it had to do with a combination of conditions: the amount of foliage as result of that year's moisture, the mast harvest in the deep slot canyons that ran throughout the lease, and changing hunting pressure on neighboring properties.

Anyway, Area No. 4 was always a good hunting location and this year it was particularly so. The area was dominated by a steep canyon running to the northeast which nearly severed the dominate north south bluff in two. In a way, Area No. 4 was almost a lease apart with its own gate entrance and road. That year, numerous scrapes could be found in the steep canyon bottom along the wild maze of trails that appeared and disappeared near the numerous narrow slot canyons along the bottom. These slot canyons had been cut by water and were choked with brush. They faded in and out of existence in a random manner; however, in places they were very deep. The deer used these slot canyons along with the indecipherable system of trails to move about undetected.

The area was normally very productive, but demanded sharp hunting skill. Deer would appear like ghosts and vanish like a dream in these tangled travel lanes, which gave the hunter only the briefest moment to act. It required extreme patience, stealth, attentiveness, and most of all calm nerves to shoot between the heavy brush at long distances in the poor light of early morning or dusk. Often a quality deer would only present itself for the fleetest of seconds. The shot making was extremely tough. Every hunter on the lease agreed that that it was some of the most demanding they had experienced.

If you are thinking that this isn't exactly the type of deer hunting often depicted on television you'd be right. Time normally did not exist to mull over a deer or size it. The hunter had to be alert enough and skilled enough to make a decision to shoot almost instinctively. Often a hunter had to pick out a spot in the brush, in dim light, and make a "point and click" shit.

If you are thinking that this is a tough environment for a young person to try for her first deer, you'd be right again. So our hunter did what he thought would give them the best chance. That would be to go to Area No. 4 and go up the bluff on the north side. The idea was to get up above the bottom area in order to peer into the brush. Also by getting up high, it would hopefully provide them with scent and sight protection. Finally, they would be not only be hunting the bottom trails but also have a view of the north facing slope across from them.

And so they went for their afternoon hunt. The hike along the road and then up the bluff wasn't exactly like going up a mountain, but it was tougher than expected for our young hunter. We often forget that young people simply don't have the stamina that more seasoned hunters have developed. That is probably as good a lesson as one can get from this story.

However, eventually they made it to one of our hunter's favorite perches in the area. It was located at the base of the rimrock that lined the top of the bluff. From there several good places to hunt could be easily found. They provided shade, cover, and a good rest to shoot. Looking down, the canyon bottom was about 200-250 yards away. Longer shots could be taken in the flat area behind the bottom most trails out to as long as a shooter dared.

Of course the idea of hunting from this perch was to maximize the possibility of seeing a deer. Once they arrived and set up, our hunter realized that the plan simply was not going to work at all. It was quite a lot for a young person to sit still until sunset. After all, a young person wasn't used to the gentle but demanding skills of such technique. It was quite another thing to ask that a person to make such a challenging shot under conditions that would test the best marksman.

Our hunter could tell from his child's body language that this arrangement was simply not agreeable to her. Even more importantly, it wasn't going to be a positive experience for the youngster. This created a dilemma that had no easy solution. From the hunter's perspective, he had three options: stay to the original plan and possibly taking any opportunity himself, basically punting on the idea of serious hunting in order to use the situation as a teaching moment, or move to ground stand located at the canyon bottom for a closer shot. The ground stand was an old archery spot located right in the middle of several trails in thick brush.

Each option had its positives and negatives. By staying put, they had a much better chance of seeing deer and a much better chance of not messing up the hunt with scent or movement. However if they moved to the ground stand the young hunter would have much better chance of making any potential shot. The drawbacks here were that they would be in the middle of heavy cover with little chance of seeing any deer, let alone a shooter. The prospect of sitting still in the brush for several hours while not seeing hardly as much as a sparrow didn't seem to the hunter to be a very positive option either.

The other option of giving up hunting in a serious way and instead using the situation to teach the youngster about deer hunting didn't appeal to the hunter either. He understood that a young hunter could tell when a particular hunting trip was not a serious outing. And besides, this young hunter was beyond that stage. If they attempted anything less than a serious effort could possibly be a serious letdown to a young hunter.

However, the hunter knew he had to do something. It was at that moment that he realized he could combine options two and three while at the same time provide a way to stave off any boredom. He had in his backpack an old grunt tube (he could have kicked himself at this point for not bringing rattling antlers, but since he originally planned on hunting off the bluff didn't think of them). They could move down to the ground stand directly below without stirring the place up too much. Then after things settled down, he would let the young hunter use the grunt tube. This would cut the dullness of the hours that lay ahead and at the same time allow the hunter to pass on some lessons to the next generation.

The hunter knew that moving again after getting set up was not the highest percentage play possible. The deer on this Rough Piece were spooky and extremely sensitive to any unnatural movement. By moving to the ground stand, they would seriously decrease their chances. After all there would be not one, but two hunters smack in the middle of any potential action. It is difficult enough for one experienced hunter to pull this off successfully with these hard hunted deer. It would be doubly difficult for two to set up in these deer living room with a decent chance of scoring.

So with this dilemma, this hunter fell back to his old instincts about setup: choose a stand location first for the shot and second for the chance of seeing a deer. Some hunters hold to the opposite school of thought. And I'm sure any group of seasoned deer hunters could hold a lively, if futile, debate on these two approaches. However, in this case with this young hunter, he decided to trust his instincts and move. The young hunter was in full agreement, and so off they went.

The hunter led the way, showing the inexperienced youngster how to use the available cover to descend as quickly and quietly as possible. Soon they disappeared into the thick West Texas brush at the bottom of the draw.

The old archery stand was pretty rough by any standards. Basically it was a cleared area under the boughs of a cedar tree. An old log provided for the only seats. The cedar not only provided cover form the sun, but also its strong scent provided protection from the sharp noses of the hunters' quarry. You might wonder why no tree stands? Well in that Rough Piece of West Texas there simply weren't any trees. People did try to use tripods, but let's face it, if you have ever tried to hunt out of tripod, you probably figured out real fast a different approach.

So the hunters slipped in and set up. Our hunter had long decided that for safety's sake, there would only be one loaded gun and one shooter at a time. His trusty deer rifle had several rounds in the magazine but none in the chamber. It was placed behind him - only to be used for a follow up shot. The young hunter's rifle was perched on a bipod shooting stick ready for action, and held but one bullet (Barney Fife style), loaded by the elder hunter. If a shooter deer was seen, the elder hunter would reach around and take the gun off safety. That would be the cue for the young hunter to shoot. In this manner, the elder hunter would be certain that the target was valid, and perhaps more importantly, he would be certain to be behind the young hunter when the rifle went off.

After letting things settle down a bit, our hunter produced the grunt tube out of his backpack. After a brief instructional session, the young hunter gave it a try. To the hunter's delight, the tube worked. By that I mean it worked in the sense that it gave the youngster something to do, not in the sense that it produced a buck.

However, the plan was working. Certainly they were hunting in a serious manner – they were in a great spot at a good time of the year. The youngster was the lead shooter and, by all accounts having a positive experience. And let's face it, a fun outing is by far the most important thing for a first time shooter. And besides, despite busting up the area somewhat, they still had a chance. Perhaps a varmint or hog would come out late to provide the youngster with some excitement.

As the afternoon hours wore on, the youngster became increasingly vocal with the grunt tube. Basically she was playing a symphony with the darn thing. The elder hunter at first tried to get her to use it in a more "normal" manner, but to no avail. After all, it was all for fun, so he just kind of went with it. Still he could still kick himself for not bringing the rattling antlers. That was a mistake he vowed to not make again.

As evening approached, the grunting became increasingly loud, so much so that the elder hunter was beginning to get annoyed with all the noise. "Well we've probably spooked every creature in the county by now" he thought "Might as well let her have fun". And so she did. Grunting almost continuously, even laughing quietly during the brief rests, she was thoroughly enjoying the moment.

And that's when it happened.

That's when – although they were deer hunting – the least expected thing happened.

"Dad, I see a deer". The words shot through our hunter's brain that like a blast of #8 pellets from a 20 gauge. He could feel his stomach knotting up. "What" he thought to himself as he furiously scanned the network of trails and openings in front of them.

Then he saw the slightest flicker in the brush way to his left. The buck hadn't come out where he was expected (they almost never do as any experienced deer hunter will tell you). In fact he had come in RIGHT on top of them. He couldn't have been more than five yards from their stand. "Damn" thought the hunter. All hunters prefer close shots but this was too close. Then he saw the antlers. This was a mature 10 point buck.

All our hunter could do at this point was reach around and take the safety off according to the plan. "Shoot that deer" he whispered. But of course the buck detected the movement – how could he not.

Now it would make for a fabulous ending if I could say that the young hunter got her first deer that day and a nice 10 pointer at that. But like I stated in the first chapter, these stories are based on fact. And the fact is this: that was one heck of a tough shot despite being only a few yards away. The angle was tough, the weapon was wrong (a scoped rifle for a point blank shot), the time window could have been measured in nanoseconds, the shooter inexperienced, and the buck was moving.

The elder hunter knew as soon as the shot went off that it was late and that the deer was unharmed. As the buck bolted, he did get a real good last look at it from the shoulders forward. It was a memory that he would haunt him forever. They would later, of course, perform a thorough search. That was another lesson from this hunt for the young hunter. But as the experienced hunter already knew, there would be no sign of a hit.

There was one last opportunity to teach. As the hunters searched for sign, they were able to make out from the tracks how the deer came in and how it left. The buck had come in cautiously in a manner that allowed it to figure out what was making all that racket while maintaining the best advantage of wind and cover. It was an important lesson and one the young hunter eagerly soaked in.

Then the second guessing began. "Could we have done anything different?" he wondered. Perhaps he should have had his rifle ready to shoot also. Perhaps they should have set up in a different place. But after reviewing everything in his mind he decided that he wouldn't have done anything different. They did get a shot at a good deer. Things just didn't click this time. And that is perhaps the most important hunting lesson of this story.

There would be other deer on other trips. But on this one, although the deer got away, the hunters both got a memory that would last a lifetime.

Chapter 9 - Forgotten in Time

For most of us that live in modern America circa 2000, living means living in cities or the suburbs that ring these cities. Life assumes a hectic, numbingly constant pace. This Wednesday would be no different. No different at all in this Sunbelt mega polis that had sprouted suddenly - overnight really - from a once sleepy mission outpost.

The freeways were already jammed hopelessly with traffic, as the business of city life whirled around as always does each weekday - a frantic chasing after the wind which produces a constant low humming background sound that is so constant that it ceases to be noticed. It becomes, well, normal. In fact it DEMANDS to be normal, leaving no room for any other reality.

The day began like most days for someone who was at one time a Legend. Few knew, or had heard, or if they had heard really cared that he was indeed a Legend. He had done many things in many Interesting Places that most people could not imagine, or if they could imagine them didn't care. They were part of a different reality, and such things that make one a legend didn't interest them anymore.

On this particular morning with its seemingly normal routines, there stirred within the Legend an uneasy feeling. The daily routines were comforting and conveyed a sense of security. However, this morning, they failed to do their job. The unease that the Legend felt grew. Today was not going to be not a carbon copy day in the great blanket of modern existence. Today would be different.

It was partly the weather. The day had started out cool and misty. But on top of that, there was a feel to it - a feel that has no description, one that comes with no warning. The more that the Legend thought about it; the more he became convinced that he should go hunting. After all, the weather was right, and the time of year was right. He calculated that he could drive out to that very special piece of west Texas, hunt the evening, and stay at camp that night.

And so the Legend hurriedly threw his gear in the truck and took off. The drive would be about four hours which would put him there at mid-afternoon. "Perfect" he thought. He had developed a plan to hunt Area No. 3. It was a plan that required an afternoon hunt with nobody else on the place. This would be the opportunity to try out his idea.

One drawback to his plan was that he would be alone on this trip. The others were too busy with the daily grind of life to take off in the middle of the week unplanned. And even for West Texas, the weather could be nasty this time of year. So as he headed west out along I-10, the weather began to turn. It wasn't a blizzard or a legendary nor' easterner like one finds in other parts of the country. No, instead it was a gradual but perceptible change. As the legend drove along those lonely empty highway miles, the clouds hung lower with a drizzly fog filling the air.

Slowly he wound through the empty land of West Texas and through the small towns that dot that highway: Kerrville (well it was once a small town but no more), Junction, Sonora, Ozona. While a different man might have reconsidered a lonely hunt in a far off place in worsening weather, the Legend did not. Instead, he couldn't help but notice that whatever seemed so damn important to be done in the city had faded into the misty winter sky behind him. Instead he became more and more focused on the hunt that lay ahead.

That is always the point, is it not? To loose oneself in a different time, a different world. That was the great irony of America in those days. The most trivial and fleeting things demanded the most time, the most energy, and the most of a person's life - even his soul while the really important things were hidden. Indeed, they had to be sought out in forgotten corners of life. That is why that Rough Piece of West Texas was an Interesting Place. It wasn't pompous and loud. It was quiet, so very quiet, and overlooked. And it was in such a place, like all Interesting Places, that a man could return to somewhere he had lost. He could feel his pulse quicken with the anticipation of the unknown while at the same time, he could feel his mind calming to the task at hand. In all Interesting Places, the hunter can sense a great re-gearing of their soul from one reality to another. That is indeed the point.

Finally, the long miles on that empty interstate came to an end. The Legend left the pavement, and with it most of what little remained of the city, at a non-descript exit. The road suddenly became dirt or on that day mud. Always, there is a strange and unexpected feeling that overcomes the hunter at that moment. It is a feeling that has no adjective which adequately describes it. The feeling must be experienced.

On one hand the anticipation reaches a crescendo. However, there is a pang of doubt even regret. The pull of modernity is strong. The hunter knows that there will not be comfortable beds in climate controlled buildings for awhile. The coming script will be set by nature and its ways, not by the hubris of humans. That pull causes one to have a moment of doubt about the whole affair. That pull is the siren call to turn back, to choose the common path where deep purpose is supplanted by the artificial excitement of activity.

Such was the case for the Legend for while the fog had lifted, the rain still drizzled, the plan was untested, and he was still alone. However, he quickly brushed such thoughts aside. Again he went over his plan "Yes, yes, it is a good plan, one that I should try and now is the perfect time to try it" he thought to himself. The siren call of modern life had been fully rejected. The hunter's soul had been re-geared. What lay ahead was not known or controlled by human factors. What was known was that the Legend would be hunting yet again shortly.

The plan had been worked out over the course of several long stand hunts on Pasture No. 6. The Legend had only hunted on this property for a short time and he and the other hunters were still a bit perplexed by its nature. One the one hand Pasture No. 6 dripped with possibilities. The place screamed at an experienced hunter such as the Legend "Big Buck Country." However on the other hand it couldn't be hunted in the typical fashion by hunting over a feeder. The hunters had had some success previously especially in Areas No. 2 and No. 4.

However, Area No. 3 presented a unique set of problems, and these hunters hadn't quite cracked open its secrets. It was one of those places which every deer hunting lease seems to have - a place that has a lot of deer activity but is hard or next to impossible to hunt. In order to get into the area the hunter would have to trample through half the lease on foot. And once there, the wind, swirling off the irregular cut ridges, always seemed wrong. The unpredictable wind patterns along with the lack of road access had discouraged hunters from investing too much in the way of towers or other permanent structures.

For one known as a Legend this simply would not do. He had become a legend by deed. From bull elk in the Rockies to mountain sheep in impossibly steep terrain to pronghorn taken on wide open grasslands, he had built his reputation by hard work and determination. He was by no means a wealthy man. Instead he had accomplished these great feats on a decent but modest income all the while also dealing with the demands of job and family.

It wasn't just the number and size of the trophies that he had taken which made his reputation; it also was the manner of the take. On many occasions he was the one who did the ground work in locating a property and arranging a hunt. His trophies were the result of planning and scouting as well as skill and luck. And that is what made them special and made him a legend.

For this particular hunt, the legend had worked out a plan. He wouldn't hunt Area No. 3 by going directly there. Instead he would go to Area No. 2 and hike up the ridges to the east and north. Then he would work his way along the ridges, using them to maintain a low profile, until he was even with the Area No. 3 and then hike down the ridge west towards the flat area where Area No. 3 lay. The wind came out of the north that day, so by doing this he figured he would mess up the least amount of area. There he would find a perch along one of the bluffs and set up for a shot overlooking the flat area.

While this style of hunting would become a common method in the years that followed, he anticipated several potential problems with his plan. The first was that it would be one heck of a hike, way out of the way and over very steep and unstable terrain. Secondly, he would have to go right through Area No. 2. Therefore it was a plan that wouldn't work very well if other hunters were on the property. A final problem concerned safety. The ridges and bluffs were covered in fractured shale which was slippery and unstable even in dry conditions. It would be quite imprudent and probably counterproductive to attempt that hike before sunrise. A morning hunt was out of the question. An afternoon hunt was the only possibility. That would give a hunter plenty of time to hike in safely and allow time for things to settle before the evening hunt.

Another drawback was that the plan called for a longish shot. By setting up on a bluff on the ridges, the hunter would have a 300 to 400 yard shot down to the flats. However, the Legend was not a legend for nothing. That kind of shot he had made before and was confident he could do it again. A final drawback to the plan was leaving the area at dusk. The hunter couldn't safely go back the way he came. He would have to hike straight down the bluff to Area No. 3 and pick up the trail that leads back to Area No. 2. That would mean that it was probably not only an afternoon hunt, but a single afternoon hunt on a given trip.

The Legend pulled into the southern gate being extremely careful not to make any noise. Since it was the middle of the week, no trace of hunting activity could be detected anywhere around - neither on that property nor any of the surrounding properties. The mid-afternoon weather was misty cool with darkish grey low hanging clouds. The entire scene evoked a sense of gloom. It was then that the Legend felt deep in his bones just how alone he was. It would be his show today regardless what happened. He decided to go straight away to the pasture bypassing the camp. The heavy clouds meant that shooting light would end early today, so there wasno sense in wasting precious daylight driving to camp first.

Quickly he pulled his truck off behind some brush soon after entering the gate. Quietly, oh so quietly, he prepared his gear. The care and deliberate slowness of his preparations was due to the dead quiet of the afternoon. The slightest unnatural noise would shout through the draws and bluffs for a great distance. He wouldn't be taking much. A hunt like this calls for little more than a gun, a shooting stick, some binocs, and a light backpack with just enough supplies to last a couple of hours. This is how the Legend liked to hunt - not a lot of equipment which tended to just get in the way.

His last act of preparation was to check his trusty 25-06 and after making sure that the chamber was clear, slinging it over his shoulder. With that, he began the hike. He soon realized that it was going to be tougher than he thought. Since the entire property sloped from east to west, he would be going uphill all the way even from the gate to Area No. 2, and that was before he began his ascent up the steep ridges. However, he had time, and so he continued.

Many a deer hunt is spoiled at this point. A clumsy entrance to the targeted area has ruined many a hunter's chance. Pasture No. 6 presented special problems here. The entire place is covered with loose rocks and broken shale slats. It requires extreme care to walk through the area without sounding like a malfunctioning ice maker. With the canyons and bluffs snaking through the land, the sound generated by an errant step can echo for hundreds of yards.

Finally, the Legend reached the Area No. 2. From there he took a brief rest before tackling the steep ascent from the bottom of the draw to the top of the ridge - a climb of several hundred feet. The top of the main ridge consisted mainly of a flat bluff with little vegetation and easy walking. He could drop further to the west, and make good time all the while not to disturb the area along the ridge face with its thick vegetation and numerous draws, canyons and other potential hiding places.

Soon enough, he was even with Area No. 3. From there he carefully worked his way straight toward the ridge's edge using the available brush to hide his silhouette. By this time, the afternoon was wearing on, and he knew by experience that he needed to get set up soon in order to allow sufficient "silent" time before the evening came.

At this point, the Legend had to improvise. He had a general idea of where he wanted to set up. He wanted to drop down just below the rimrock that circled the top of the ridge like a multi-layered band. There he would find a place that provided for a good set up with a commanding view of the flat area below while at the same time using the natural vegetation as cover.

However once he reached the ridge edge, he had a problem. The rimrock formed a shear straight edge drop off for most of its length. Therefore getting down form the top to a perch where he could hunt presented a problem. By design he started his hike early enough in the afternoon in order to allow sufficient time for such contingencies and now he would need some of that time. Without panicking or trying to force the issue he searched for a way down and soon found one.

Carefully he slid down the narrow trail to a spot at the base of the rim rock. There he found the perfect place to setup. Protected from the wind with the rim rock at his back he could use the available vegetation as cover while at the same time have a commanding view of the flat area below. From there he could glass a good portion of the lease, and with his long range shooting skills honed from years in the high country, he had a number of trails within range.

Immediately he loved the spot, and settled in for the long wait. There is something incredibly peaceful about being up on the side of a hill looking out over a wilderness. The sense of being absolutely alone sends a strange chill down to the deepest part of a person's soul. Especially in this instance, the Legend felt that feeling strongly. Here he was by himself. There was no one else on Pasture No. 6 that day nor was there anyone on the surrounding pastures. From where he sat he could have been the only person in the world. Even the roads sat in stillness with no sounds of activity for hours.

Although he had hunted on many adventures over many places, each hunt stands apart. He didn't have to prove anything any more. He was already acknowledged by his peers as a legend, although in the world from whence he came they knew nothing about this and cared even less. But now here he sat once more. Nature did not care of his past accomplishments for it knows nothing of them. It merely sets the stage and prepares the drama. The outcome is always unknown. That is what Interesting Places are – the stage. The participants, including the hunter with all his knowledge, must adjust to the conditions which are presented as the drama unfolds. Hubris has no place here and will be ruthlessly exposed for what it truly is, that is untruth.

Despite all his care and skill to this point, all the Legend could do now is to wait and disappear into the nondescript mesquite background. In that state, the hunter becomes part of the Place. His humanness dissolves away and is absorbed by the land. His mind transforms to a primitive state that is part calm relaxation and part vicious concentration. Here the hunter becomes aware of every little movement no matter how small. Gone is the incessant din of noise in the modern world to be replaced with a smothering quiet. In this state, an Interesting Place can come alive and lightening can strike.

As the afternoon wore on, the Legend slowly lost time of the hour. The clouds which had spit precipitation all day hung lower and darker as the sun advanced. Imperceptibly the wind began to swirl a little faster and the daylight faded into a dingy grey mist. The Legend had seen this phenomenon happen before: the sky and the ground merging into a dull sameness as if the life force of the world was slowly being turned off.

Some might think such a thing as eerie and in some ways it is. It is as if the hunter must be completely consumed into the stage before he can fully become the actor. He must loose his individuality in order to discover who he truly is and where it counts, in his deepest soul.

At the moment where the Legend had finally lost his sense of self, his eyes reflexively shifted to the right. There in the misty grey failing light of late afternoon appeared a huge buck down on the flat far from the ridge. He was barely in range. He had appeared out of the monotonous tangle of worthless thickets like a ghost. It almost seemed that he wasn't actually real, but perhaps a dream.

The silent and sudden appearance at first startled the Legend. Regardless of how many deer he had seen, and there had been many, the vision of a buck always fascinated him. It is as if a person is mesmerized and frozen into inaction by the apparition.

The Legend's experience kicked in at that point. He forced his arms to move the rifle into position. He forced his eyes to look through the scope, but the deer had vanished. Perhaps it had been a ghost after all, or maybe his mind was playing tricks on him. Then it appeared again, this time 20 yards further to the left. How did it get there without being seen? The ability of a deer to disappear in even the slightest cover always intrigued the hunter.

But he couldn't focus on that now. The buck had moved to the edge of gun range, and the Legend needed to act fast before he ran out of light and range. For a moment the large buck stood there. He was mature, heavy in the shoulders. Now the Legend's experience came into play one more time. He quickly calculated the distance in his head and set the rifle solid on the shooting stick he used as a rest. Without warning the silent stillness shattered into pieces as the gun fired. The large buck slumped forward and disappeared in the brush one last time.

Almost immediately after the sound of the shot died away, the gentle rhythms of the scene returned as if nothing happened. The shot was a moment in time, almost out of place in the larger scale of things. The Legend waited to make sure. Eventually he crawled down the ridge face and began to cross the flat area to the spot. He was in no hurry as he picked his way through the sticker brush trying to avoid cutting his aged skin.

He came directly upon the buck as it lay on the shale strewn ground. He was a large one, a real trophy for a low fence lease. His antlers, heavy with mass, could only have been wielded by a large bodied mature deer such as this one. The deer's neck bulged with power. His heft and muscularity impressed even an experienced hunter such as the Legend.

Sizing up the situation, the hunter quickly realized he couldn't move this beast by himself. He fell back on his elk hunting experience and quartered the animal on the spot. Even then, transported the buck out proved to be a challenge. The Legend got the parts to a trail that maybe at one time had been a road, but was barely discernable as such now. Once loaded he headed to camp where he planned to spend the night.

Upon arriving at the campsite, he felt an overwhelming sense of loneliness. Here he was, in deer camp in the middle of the season and he had a huge mature buck in the truck. The problem was that he was absolutely alone. Not only was his camper deserted, but the house used by the hunters on the other pastures howled with silence. Nobody with which to celebrate or to tell stories existed. He might as well have been the last surviving person on earth. For a while he sat and tried to shake off the feeling of isolation. The modern world had faded away but the hunting world was silent also. He had lived up to his status as Legend, but what did it matter without anyone to share the moment.

The Legend sat in the dark hunched over a cold fire pit, staring into the night, forgotten in time.

The modern world with its frantic thrashing about does not care anymore for the wisdom which comes from a life well lived. It no longer values the knowledge and experience of age. Rather it concerns itself only with the present and youth. Only that which is deemed necessary to increase wealth in the immediate moment is valued. What use is there of a Legend when the modern world provides all the needed security of daily physical existence? What need is there of his wisdom built up over countless hours of experience when everything can be had at the touch of a computer?

What does society loose when its elders are no longer valued as a reservoir of life lived? One could argue that the modern ways are better. They produce more stuff, but at what cost? The constant leveling process which the modern world unleashes has no concern or need for Legends or Interesting Places, so they are forgotten and ignored. Of course the modern world and its ways are just as much an experiment on the great stage of existence as any creature or way of life. The verdict on it is still out and unknown. That is a great irony. Our attempts to push back the realities of our physical state cannot be completed. For even that attempt is subject to the same eternal judgment as any other. We may temporarily ignore our nature, but we cannot escape our nature and the physical world in which we exist.

And the Legend continued to sit in the dark hunched over a lifeless fire pit, staring into the night, forgotten in time.

Eventually he decided that he couldn't stay. There was no point in it. He hadn't bothered to unload his deer yet. So he put his still packed duffle bag back into the truck, and slowly drove away with the headlights of his truck illuminating the terrain like a spaceship on an alien world. Within minutes the highway suddenly loomed up in front. It appeared as a shock to someone who had been recently so absorbed by the deathly stillness of a forgotten world. The cars and big rigs roared up and down the roadway in a headlong race against reality. The constant whirring impressed the Legend as a great chasing after the wind. It all seemed so important and yet so futile.

Soon his vehicle joined the great race too, blending into the mix seamlessly. Nobody around him had any awareness of the Legend and what he had done that day. Completely sealed in anonymity each raced ahead into the blackness of the night.

Part 3

Other Interesting Places

Chapter 10 - Turkey Surprise

One of the truly Interesting Places was a lease near Brownwood Texas. It was unusual in the sense that it was not originally much of a property at all. Rather it was an amalgamation of odd scrapes of leftover edge land from adjoining properties. Therefore it was not a typical nice, neat block of land; instead, it was a collection of various geometric odds and ends stuck together. As a result, it ran in a jagged, uneven manner in a large L shape which gave the property a lot of nooks and crannies to set up and hunt.

For a hunting property it was fantastic as long as one was not too concerned with large scoring buck deer. The rancher was an old timer who hadn't fallen prey to the temptation of a big money game ranch. The place was a ranch first with hunting being just an odd source of a little extra income. In that way, the Brownwood lease was one of the last of its kind. And this, naturally, made it a very Interesting Place.

The deer were not managed but they were numerous. The cost was very reasonable even by the standards of that day. There was plenty of game and the lease included all seasons – including quail, ducks (yes they could be hunted on a small pond at the extreme northern most end of the L), deer, and of course turkey.

In fact it was a better turkey lease than anything else. The land undulated through various wooded draws broken by open cultivated fields. There were numerous places in the wooded bottoms for good turkey roosts, and there were numerous quiet, hidden places to set up to hunt them.

So each year the spring turkey season was anticipated as much if not more than the fall deer gun season. Not only was there normally a good deal of hunting action, but turkey hunting is in many ways a pleasant experience. The weather in springtime is generally mild. The pressure to remain scent free was much less. And it was a nice break to be able to hunt in the spring being able to get away and scratch that hunting itch at a different time of the year.

So in this particular year, the hunters gathered at camp the day before the spring turkey season opened with customary enthusiasm. It was great to see old friends, reminisce about the fall season, talk football, talk family, and generally blow off some steam with the guys.

And besides, there was darn good turkey hunting on this lease. What the place lacked in big deer, it made up for in good turkey hunting - at least most years. So the hunter's happily reunited in this Interesting Place, but what they didn't know is that one of them would have a very interesting experience which would make for a very interesting story.

As he normally did every year, the rancher stopped by camp to chat with the hunters the night before the season opened. He enjoyed this. For the rancher, the hunting was an important source of income, but he didn't rely on it heavily. Therefore, he had as much more casual relationship with his hunters than some of the big money operations which were just beginning to come into vogue about that time. The hunters also enjoyed this friendly relationship. For them it was part of a great experience to greet the rancher, invite him for a drink or two, and discuss his thoughts on the upcoming season.

However, this year the rancher, being an honest man, didn't have such good news. "There ain't no turkeys on this lease. Haven't seen one in months, haven't seen as much as a track or a feather since fall" he reported. "In fact there ain't any turkeys anywhere up here on any of the other leases. There're all down along the bayou. If you want I can line you up with a day hunt deal or two down there. You'll probably at least get a chance at one. I don't know why they're all down on the bayou. You know they are strange birds. Most of the time they are up here, but not this year."

That news certainly discouraged the hunters, and they discussed the rancher's offer of a day lease down on the bayou. However, they decided that, well, they were already at their lease and already several stiff bourbons into settling into camp, and well, they'd just take their chances on a lease they already knew. Besides, wasn't one of the most important purposes of a hunt to get away and enjoy themselves? If they spilt up and hunted on different day leases, they would miss out on one of the most important aspects of the entire exercise.

Now don't go and get the wrong idea. These were not "party hardy" hunters who used hunting as an excuse to get away from the wife and kids and who spent an entire hunting trip either drunk, or sleeping off a drunk. Not that I would criticize that or that I would be above that. After all, the great thing about hunting is that there is no "wrong" approach (as long as it's legal). If the "party hardy" types want to hunt that way and enjoy it, more power to them. I wish them well. A least they won't have to waste a lot of time cleaning their guns when they get home, and they'll leave all the big deer for someone else. No, the hunters in this story were serious hunters who each and everyone had paid his dues in the field and had the trophies or at least the stories to back that up.

However, with a discouraging report from the rancher and the decision to stay and hunt their lease, the hunters loosened up a bit – well maybe more than a little bit. The pressures of work, of family, of worry about the future had weighed on them all when they arrived. And now the idea of just enjoying each other's company around a campfire and killing some Wild Turkeys seemed like a good idea, a really good idea. So they did – very late into the night.

One thing about turkey hunting is that like most hunting, one should, if one is serious, get up very early in the morning and get out to the stand before daylight breaks and the birds come off the roost. And so the next morning, the alarm clock went off VERY early, PAINFULLY early. With that the hunters rolled over and went back to sleep – except for one.

Slowly and painfully, this solitary hunter struggled to get up and get ready. His head pounded. He wasn't even sure if he was fully sober yet. Of course the temptation to slide back into his bed occurred to him several times. However, somehow he willed his rebeling body to get ready. After all he had a place to hunt, he had taken vacation to hunt, and he had traveled a good ways to hunt, so he was going to go hunting.

He hadn't even really thought about where he was going to hunt that morning, but it didn't take much consideration since he had the whole lease to choose. He had a favorite turkey ground stand that was located along one of the wooded bottoms on the east border of the lease. It was a well camouflaged area with a good view of a natural turkey ridge.

One important aspect of this story is that turkeys like to walk ridges. They can see danger from below (and boy do they see well as any turkey hunter can tell you), and if they sense danger they can fly down off the ridge without expending a lot of energy – they being big birds and all. Also, important for this particular story is that this ridge was not on the lease but on an adjoining property. Any turkey seen on the ridge had to be lured down by calling onto our hunter's side of the fence.

And so our lone hunter set out in the early morning dark, stumbling along and finding the ground stand. He placed a turkey hen decoy (which would become another important part of this story) the appropriate distance away from the stand, crawled behind the camo netting and leaned up against the big oak tree forming the back of the blind.

It was at that precise moment, he noticed several things: one it was dark, two he felt awful from the previous night, and three he felt like an idiot. This was the moment that every hunter has felt and thought to himself "What the heck am I doing out here"? This feeling was particularly intense this time as the chances of getting any turkey action seemed remote by the rancher's account. Perhaps this hunter should have stayed in bed that morning, oh well.

Our intrepid turkey hunter didn't have to feel like an idiot for too long. For soon after first light, he heard a gobble. Now this did get his attention. At least it took his mind off of his hangover. But being experienced at this turkey hunting thing he didn't get too alarmed. After all it was opening morning of the Texas spring turkey season. There was another property right across the fence line. Chances were good it was just another lonely hunter hoping against hope of calling in a turkey.

So after waiting a little while, our hunter used his turkey call to gobble back. To his surprise, his call was immediately and fairly aggressively answered back with another gobble. This definitely got his attention, but he still tempered his excitement.

So he called again. And again his gobble was answered, and there was no doubt that responding gobble was much closer and if it was a call it sure was a darn realistic call. But before our hunter could think about the implications of what this might mean, he saw a sight so shocking that he wasn't sure if it was real or not.

There on the ridge on the adjoining property strutted a turkey silhouetted in the early morning light. If our hunter had seen a giraffe he couldn't have been more stunned. His hangover was a thing of the past for he had switched into full hunting mode. The outside world and its problems blocked out completely from his consciousness. The hunter's entire focus, his entire soul was on that one turkey. So now on hunting auto pilot, he gave the turkey the lonely hen call.

With that, the turkey froze and snapped his head in the direction of our hunter. Briefly both parties stared, locked in total concentration – one on finding a mate, the other on the hunt. For that moment the hunter lost himself in a forgotten era. Total fixation on one pure point of existence to the exclusion of all else, even the hunter's own existence, this is the unexplainable attraction of the hunt. This primal call cannot be explained, only experienced. This drama can only occur in the hidden, special places overlooked by the never ending rush of our modern time. And here in this Interesting Place in this moment in time, the hunter and the hunted will play out a script that hasn't been written but holds life and death in the balance.

With another soft, oh so soft hen call, the turkey couldn't stand it any longer. The sight of the hen decoy and the wooing of the call's sweetness was all this young gobbler needed. Off the ridge this guy went with his wings fully outstretched (and a turkey is an impressively large animal in flight). The turkey was headed directly, I mean directly, at our hunter. He thought the turkey was going to land in the tree he was leaning against.

Now you might think that things were going just swimmingly for our hunter at this moment and generally you'd be right. However, there was a problem. Our hunter hadn't anticipated that the turkey would come in so fast. Normally it takes work to lure a gobbler into a hen call. Often they "hang up" just out of sight and expect for the hen to make the final approach to them. Our hunter had been through many such scenarios; sometimes he got a shot at such a gobbler, sometimes he didn't. However in this case the gobbler came in so fast, that our hunter was in no position to shoot – his shotgun lying across his lap as the gobbler flopped down just feet from the decoy.

The entire sequence had played itself out in a few small minutes. That can, and often, does happen in hunting. Usually when least expected, the hunter is thrown from thinking about the futility of such a hobby into the very depths of high drama where the next few decisions in the next few moments determines success or failure, determines whether the hunter can add to his legend or add just another sad "almost" story to the evening dinner.

And our hunter was now thrown into the depths of such a moment and events were being dictated by the turkey who was totally absorbed on his own life and death quest. For as soon as the turkey had flopped down in front of the hunter, the turkey began to court the hen decoy. Apparently the turkey hadn't seen another turkey for a while either and didn't bother to examine the decoy too closely before deciding on a course of action. Therefore not wanting to waste too much time on introductions, our turkey began promptly to strut around the hen decoy.

Our hunter could only sit there frozen in motionless astonishment. For as any turkey hunter can tell you, turkeys may not be too bright, but they can pick up the slightest movement and be gone in a flash.

However, in this case our hunter was going to have to do something soon if he wanted this bird. For this young gobbler had just decided that courting time was over, no need for any more romance, let's get on with business. He quickly switched from strutting to positioning himself behind the decoy in preparation for the final act. With this development, our hunter knew time was up. Although turkeys may have the reputation of being rather dense, even a young, dumb gobbler such as this would, in short order, realize something was terrible wrong-like as soon as he tried to mount that plastic decoy.

So, not having much time to consider his options, our hunter made a quick decision and took a chance. He knew it was impossible to get his gun up without spooking the bird at this point. Therefore his only chance was to quickly snap the gun up to a predetermined point and fire. He knew the turkey was likely to do one of two things once spooked: he would scamper away on the ground, or explode straight up into the air.

Now someone that is only familiar with turkeys that come from Butterball might not think much of such a large bird's flying ability. But any turkey hunter will tell you that the wild version of the species can fly quite well, and they often will explode straight up with surprising speed when spooked.

With that knowledge, our hunter swung his trusty 12 gauge shotgun with one fluid motion directly above the bird's head and fired. This was a calculated gamble based on years of not only turkey hunting but also shotgun shooting skills honed with the wildest quail in North America. The turkey and the shot intersected perfectly leaving the bird stone cold dead on the ground. And with that the hunter's morning turkey was concluded successfully. For the bird, well, there would be no amore that morning.

All hunts for larger game that end successful end suddenly. For once the shot is made, well that's it. Although the hunter can then switch off the hunting mode and go back to everyday mode, often this a bit clumsy and there hangs in the air an awkwardness - sort of like a melody cut off in mid-stream.

This hunt was no exception. After all, the hunt had just started only minutes before. Our hunter had just barely forgotten his hangover and locked into the hunt, and now it was over? Some how, it didn't seem quite right.

After retrieving his prize, our hunter didn't exactly know how to proceed next. Surely his comrades were still snoozing away, blissfully unaware of the drama that had unfolded, so heading back to camp so soon was out of question.

He lingered at the blind a little longer to enjoy the rest of the early morning. This is one of the truly enjoyable aspects of hunting: to allow the world to slowly come around on its own pace, to notice the little details as a new day awakens. After the brief flurry of activity had died down, nature began to return to its softer pace. He noticed the songbirds beginning their activity. Male cardinals had already begun to bark at each other, jealously guarding their territories by swooping at any intrusion. The intense struggle between life and death continued in these and other smaller creatures he observed. How strange it was to be human and be able to observe this, especially after so recently being apart of it? A doe with her fawns casually fed near the hunter. "Why is it so easy to see deer during turkey season? Where do they all go during deer season?" the hunter thought to himself.

After a while, the hunter left his stand. He knew he not only had his bird but a great story to tell his friends and often the story is the most important thing to bring back. When he got back to camp, the other hunters were still sound asleep – as expected. When they heard the story and saw the bird, they could hardly believe it. Most felt a little silly and embarrassed, after all why hadn't they been out that morning? For the rest of the weekend the others hunted hard, but not a bird was to be seen or heard, not a track spotted, not so much as a feather was found on the lease. The old rancher had been right after all. There were no birds on the lease that season. Well he was almost right, there was one.

Chapter 11 - Old Eleven Point

One of the rules about Interesting Places is that it isn't necessary for a place to be grandiose, spectacular in size, or exotic in local to be an Interesting Place. Many places that do fit that description are indeed Interesting Places, but it is not a prerequisite. What is important is that the place be capable of producing those special moments in time that shape the lives who cross the path of that place. Sometimes money helps in this regard, sometimes it does not, and sometimes as in the case presented here about the Busby lease, it is completely irrelevant.

You needn't go looking on a map for a place called the Busby lease. It was nothing but a small, tiny by Texas standards, jewel of a place located just on the then outskirts of the ever expanding suburbs. At only 60 acres more or less, it barely would qualify as a place at all, let alone an Interesting Place, but it was in all the important ways that make a place an Interesting Place.

The Busby lease was a roughly square shaped piece of property with stands located at the corners. Each stand was easily accessible from a gravel road. What made the property special is that the bulk of the center part was dominated by an unexpectedly steep canyon with impregnable brush guarding the walls. Essentially, the entire lease was a single massive draw of the wildest nature wrapped tightly by walls on almost all sides.

This made for the most unusual contrast. On one hand, the thin rim that surrounded the canyon was a highly domesticated piece of land located just off the blacktop. However, it transitioned quickly to a forgotten world of untamed mystery. The sudden, steep boundary between these worlds drew a sharp line rarely found presented in such an extreme manner. A variety of game in surprising numbers including hogs, turkeys, and of course deer used these canyons not only as a residence but as a travel corridor. Despite the smallness of the property, several hunters could hunt at the same time. The stands were arranged so that each was looking down the slope to the drop off of the canyon. This kept each stand out of line of fire of the others.

For the three hunters on the lease, it represented the best of both worlds in a rare opportunity that seldom is seen. Not only was it easily accessible from the civilization thus avoiding the hassles of camping, it provided excellent opportunities at game. Although the deer were on the small side (typical for a hill country free range location), the chance at a turkey or hog made up for that. If one was not too overly concerned about antler size, then it would definitely qualify as a great hunting lease.

However, to reach the status of Interesting Place, a property needs something more. It must have an element of that mystery and magic that is rarely found. Many a good lease where a hunter takes a designated stand and hunts a feeder (as is common practice in Texas), simply do not qualify as Interesting Places.

In fact this method of hunting which has dominated many places in recent years is, in fact, the very antithesis of what makes an Interesting Place. Why this method has won out in the market place of hunting is easy enough to understand. As hunting became more popular, ranchers looked at it more as an income source. The easiest way to maximize this income stream was to pack as many hunters as possible into a given property. Of course any property only has so much carrying capacity and only so many good natural areas to hunt. The way to get around this was to create artificial "good" spots with the feeders.

That allowed more income from more hunters but presented another problem. Nobody is going to want to spend money to hunt if they are not going to see any deer of worth. Therefore, the answer to that was to turn the entire operation into a managed herd approach. In that manner, the rancher could assure a certain opportunity for a big deer that would be commiserate with the price. This inevitably led to breeding for bigger deer, which led to the high fence phenomena.

Thus what began as a pastime and an extra for the rancher morphed into a business scarcely recognizable to deer hunters of earlier eras. The focus on antler size alone had replaced the hunting experience as the chief determiner of success. This trade off fit in nicely with the bubble years as the baby boomer generation reached middle age.

They could plunk down a wad of money, and with minimal expenditure of effort and time, have a chance at a "trophy" in the sense of antler size.

Of course, what originally a trophy buck represented was the skill of the hunter. He was the one who expended the greatest effort in knowing the deer's habits. He was the one willing to go deeper in the brush, stay longer, and suffer more disappoints. The reward for his skill, denial, and perseverance was sometimes a trophy buck deer. The antlers embodied the traits of the hunter more than the hunted.

In the modern era, that has changed. Now the antlers embody not skill but breeding; the cost is in terms of cash not effort. All of these factors worked with each other in a feed back loop to create a style of hunting that no longer favored Interesting Places.

However, even in this environment, Interesting Places can be found. Often forgotten places of modest extent, they are shunned or even ridiculed by those who measure success purely in inches of antler. But in these overlooked realms can be found jewels for the hunter persistent in finding the unique hunting experience.

The Busby lease was such a place. Although it had the typical stand with a feeder setup, its smallness along the small number of hunters made it amenable to other manners of hunting.

However, what truly elevated the Busby lease into the ranks of Interesting Places was the presence of that one special deer. This is the one deer that is seen, but for some reason cannot be managed to be taken. These deer become legends themselves, often defining a season or a lease, and with that they receive the highest honor possible – they are given names. At the Busby lease, such a deer existed. This deer was Old Eleven Point.

Old Eleven Point was a decent enough deer by most standards. As the name implied, he had eleven points in a well proportioned rack; however, what made the deer unique was his location. Old Eleven Point existed on this small spit of land with the suburbs encroaching form every direction. By the standards of a low fence, wild chase property on the edge of the hill country, he outshone his contemporaries by a wide margin. In this setting, he could be considered a giant (Of course on any managed, high fence property, he would hardly rate a second look).

Also he had achieved a level of maturity rarely seen in deer in such settings. In fact he had been known for several years; however, he was elusive and had always managed to elude the hunters on this lease and surrounding properties.

Perhaps he had a safe haven in the deepest part of the steep canyon on the lease. Perhaps he had a safe haven on a nearby property that wasn't hunted. Perhaps he had all that and more. The one thing that all three hunters knew is that Old Eleven Point was not a deer that would just saunter into a feeder when the dinner bell went off. No deer that ever reached that maturity in such circumstances could behave so foolishly.

In fact, Old Eleven Point gained the reputation of legend by his habit of popping up from the canyon rim at odd times of the day and in odd places. Obviously he was quite wise to the game that the hunters were attempting to play. Each time he would disappear into the thick brush of the steep canyon sides before a hunter had the opportunity to reposition himself for a shot. Each time the legend of Old Eleven Point grew even more.

During the course of that fateful year on the Busby lease, our three hunters enjoyed great success. Once, the one who was known as Legend, had killed a nice mature six point buck. The taking of such a fine animal was not common for these low fence environs. This elicited much excitement from the rancher who could not stop taking pictures of the kill with the hunter so as to be able to have bragging rights with the other landowners in the area at the local coffee shop. This kill only confirmed to the rancher the status of the Legend from the stories he had heard. Other kills were made: deer, hog, and turkey. All in all it would be considered a banner year by all.

However, Old Eleven Point beckoned the hunters ever more. Once, at the height of the rut in midday, the rancher spotted this ghost of a deer at the edge of the canyon at the far end of the lease. Hurriedly, the rancher raced to one of the hunter's stand and informed him. The hunter then made a careful stalk on foot, but to no avail. Old Eleven Point had given them the slip once again, his legendary status enhanced in proportion to the hunter's frustration.

That was about the last sighting of the deer. Soon the season wore down to its end with the hunter's generally satisfied with the results. Two of the hunters did decide to make one more last season hunt. It would be on Christmas Eve. One of the hunters needed to leave that day to return to his family for Christmas. However, they had time for a quick morning, so they decided to give it one last shot before calling it a season.

The next morning the hunters both awoke early as usual only to find the weather outside to the most disagreeable type possible – fog, thick heavy fog. No other weather condition can shut down a hunt faster than fog. Why hunt if you can't see anything? Hunters can withstand cold, snow, rain, and heat. However, fog is the worst.

The hunter that planned on leaving that day woke first and, upon seeing the conditions, had already decided to pack it in. He was leisurely enjoying a morning cup of coffee when the second hunter came in, dressed to hunt, and raring to go. "Why aren't you dressed, we need to leave." asked the second hunter. "What, in this soup. You can't see anything" was the reply. "Well you ain't gonna kill nothing sitting in the kitchen" retorted the second hunter. With that, the first hunter was shamed into going. You know the old saw "Ain't gonna kill nothing if you aren't out hunting". "Well why not" thought the first hunter.

Quickly the hunters assembled their gear and within a short drive were at the Busby lease. The second hunter had already decided that he would hunt the first stand closest to the gate. It was a short walk from the gravel lease road with the stand being in sight of the road. Therefore, it is normally about as easy a stand to find in the morning dark as one could ask – a straight 50 yard hike. So the second hunter, without giving it much thought, got out of the truck after it stopped to let him off.

As soon as the truck sped off with the first hunter driving did the second driver suddenly realize that he couldn't see a blasted thing. The dark was like the dark in cave tours when they turn off the lights. One literally couldn't see one's hand six inches from the face – that was how thick the fog had become.

Normally there was little need for a flashlight on the Busby lease, but the second hunter carried one just the same. Quickly he fumbled through his backpack in the dark and located the flashlight. Only after turning it on did he realize the full extent of his predicament. The light from the flashlight merely reflected in the fog giving the hunter maybe one foot of visibility amid a blinding glare.

The second hunter then slowly made his way straight ahead, after all the stand couldn't be very far away. However, after what seemed like an hour, our hunter found himself on some smooth rocks sloping down. He had missed the stand and walked all the way to the canyon drop off! There the condensation dripped from the brush like rain. "How can I possibly be get lost trying to find a stand 50 yards form the road?" thought the hunter. With that he started to turn and slipped on the wet smooth stones. Down he went smack on his hip.

It was a hard fall. Instinctively the hunter had done everything to protect his rifle, but he couldn't be sure of its condition. Everything seemed to conspire against him that morning. First the fog, getting lost 50 yards from the road, now this! At that point the temptation arose once again to pack it in, after all who would fault him?

But as he nursed his sore hip, his hunting experience kicked in. He knew that the best thing he could do at that moment was to stay right there until it was light enough to see where he was and where he needed to go. If he tried to stumble around in the murk, he would only mess up the area more - so he stood there waiting for first light. The wait took what seemed forever. After all, the fog only made the night last even longer than normal.

Finally with enough light to see, our hunter could tell that he was way off to the left of the stand having overshot it considerably. He still couldn't see the stand – the visibility was at best only 5 yards or so – but at least he could start to make his way slowly towards the stand.

The one good thing about the thick fog was that it provided cover for his movements. Finally at long last he found the stand when it he came right upon it. Quickly he got in and set up. He checked his rifle and the scope seemed okay. However, he could not see but 10 yards out the blind. As the sun broke the horizon, the fog thickened even more. For all his trouble he knew that it would be all for not.

Soon, he noticed the presence of deer milling about. This was a good sign! Somehow he managed to slip in without completely messing up the area. The deer (certainly does and fawns) normally came out for their morning rituals so this was not unusual. He couldn't make out what kind of deer they were as they only appeared as fuzzy dark shapes in the fog.

Then he noticed that one such shape in the back that hadn't been there before. It was certainly larger than the rest. Our hunter became suddenly interested "Could that be a good buck" he thought.

However, the fog frustrated his attempts at identification. Eventually as the morning wore on, the fog began to break slightly. Our hunter could now make out individual deer in the area close to him briefly in the fleeting openings. However, he still couldn't make out the dark form hanging in the back near the drop off.

Then the fog in that area lifted oh so briefly. Our hunter got a glimpse. His heart dropped, it was definitely a shooter buck much bigger than any he had seen that year. The fog rapidly rolled back in seemingly thicker than ever before the hunter could get a real good look at the rack. In fact all the deer disappeared into the fog once again becoming only dark shadows in the gloomy murk.

Our hunter decided that he would shoot that deer if he got a chance. The question was would he get that chance? Our hunter surmised that the buck was following one of the does – that is why he was hanging back at the canyon's edge. Although the rut was officially over, often there is a second rut late in the season where does that hadn't been bred during the rut come into heat again. This second rut is a great time to trophy buck hunt for several reasons: hunting pressure is lighter, deer are less pressured, and fewer does mean more competition for the bucks. There was no guarantee that the fog would ever lift. Also there was no guarantee that the buck would hang around much longer. The morning was getting long and time was running out.

The fog seemed to grow even thicker! Our hunter could no longer see the dark shape that he believed was the buck. Then it happened. The fog lifted for the entire area in front of our hunter. He could see all the deer in the area clearly. The buck was at the edge of the drop off just about to go back down. The buck was poised broadside. His rifle was poised and ready. He had been waiting for just such a stroke of luck.

The first hunter had long settled into his stand on the other side of the canyon after dropping the second hunter off. His stand was positioned higher on the rim than the second hunter's location. The fog there was thick as well. In fact he couldn't and hadn't seen anything. He had already decided that this hunt was over when he looked over in the direction of the second hunter.

He then saw a strange sight. In the fog a brief streak of light, like someone had stuck a large lighter, shot across the fog. "What the..?" he thought. A loud boom quickly followed the streak, and he knew that the other hunter had fired a shot. At what he had no idea, a hog perhaps?

At the firing of his gun, the second hunter saw the buck start to fall. However, the fog rolled in again before he could see it down – that is how brief a window of opportunity it was. The second hunter had no choice but to wait. It was at that moment that he realized that if the buck ran off, he was going to have a heck of a time locating it in that fog. The next 30 minutes dragged by slowly.

Finally the hunter got out of his stand and moved directly towards the buck's last sighting - the fog still too thick to see more than a few yards. Then he spotted the buck on the ground. Belly towards him, it was definitely a nice one. Then he looked at the rack: one, two, three,....eleven! He had gotten Old Eleven Point – on the last morning of the season in heavy fog. Our hunter could scarcely believe his good fortune, and to think, he almost didn't go hunting that morning. To think, he almost gave up after he couldn't find the stand and fell on his hip. To think, the fog only lifted for the briefest moment for a shot. So many things had to go right, and so many right things our hunter had to do.

Old Eleven Point defined the lease and made it a very Interesting Place indeed. Often a special deer will do that to even the most humble of properties. Such a legendary creature creates the mystery that any Interesting Place needs – a mystery that can define a moment in time.

Chapter 12 - High Country Elk

For most of the stories told herein, the hunter has developed a special relationship with a place over a period of time. Many times a place doesn't start off being an Interesting Place at first. Rather the hunter must first learn about the hidden secrets which often do not reveal themselves easily or announce their existence with pompous fanfare. That is what makes them so unique and different from the modern world where image – loudly blared to all – demands to be noticed. In fact isn't that the whole point of image?

However in this account, the hunter only spent one day in this particular place. But boy, what a day! For what transpired there pushed this hunter to the very limits of his physical and mental limits. Little did he know when the day began the great adventure he would experience in one the world's truly spectacular settings. It turned out to be the perfect combination of the place, the time, and the hunter. Each element combined to produce the most memorial hunt in this person's career. This was the hunt that solidified for all time the Legend's status among his peers.

In fact, in his later years, it was this one hunt more than any other that he loved to tell to anyone who would listen – more than the all the white tails he shot from the swamps of Louisiana to the western plains of Oklahoma, more than all the upland game he shot as a youth in Kansas, more than all the waterfowl he shot as a young adult, more than all the big muleys he killed from New Mexico to Montana, more than the big horn sheep on a limited draw, and more than any other mountain elk hunt. This was the story which defined him as a Legend. Here it is reproduced with as much accuracy as possible for all posterity.

The Hunter

At the time of this hunt, our hunter had already secured a rather impressive resume which would be the envy of any ordinary outdoorsman. In his youth he had the good fortunate to live in a place, eastern Kansas, at a time when it ranked unrivaled as a quail hunting paradise. There he honed not only shooting skills and hunting prowess, but he also developed a fiery passion within which caused him to stand apart from his contemporaries. Many of his peers could match him in knowledge of the game and shooting, but none could come close to matching this hunter when it came to drive and determination once out in the field.

This was the thing set him apart and which would carry him to success throughout his lifetime. His compatriots often spoke in hushed, reverent tones about his incredible drive once the hunt began. No one, and I mean no one, could out hike or out hunt him. Even as age inexorably took hold, men half his years struggled to match his endurance. During breaks in the hunt, they could often be seen shaking their heads, trying to catch their breath while saying "that is one tough old bird!" as he waited impatiently for them to catch up. This passion is the one element which he brought to the drama that day which made all the difference.

Hunting being hunting, he didn't score on every outing. But if anyone shot anything more times than not it would be him. On so many trips he bagged the most quail or shot the only deer and when that wasn't the case, it was news. Of course luck always plays a part in a pursuit like hunting, but often luck is made and it is made from doing a lot of the little things right.

Once, many years later on after this hunt and in a completely different place deep in American Midwest, he was pulled unexpectedly one day into what the locals called a "turkey shoot" contest. This was a contest with which our hunter was heretofore completely unfamiliar. For those of you that don't know what a turkey shoot is (and I suspect that is the majority), it has absolutely nothing to do with shooting turkeys. Instead it is a competition held often in the fall during Oktoberfest festivals in small Midwest towns usually accompanied by lots of eating and beer drinking. The object is to take a shotgun and shoot a paper target at some distance away, say 20 or 30 yards. Each contestant gets one shot and whoever puts the most pellets in a shape on the paper wins.

Obviously a lot of luck plays into the outcome and everyone tends to have a great time. It is one of those quaint traditions which at one time was common in the American heartland but which with time has tended to fade away. Why the name you ask? Well the winner of each round gets a turkey or a ham or some other kind of prize so that is why these contests are called "turkey shoots".

At one of these festivals a local thrust a shotgun into the hand of our hunter and proclaimed "Sir, we've heard a lot of stories about what a great hunter and all from your son. Would you like to give it a try?" Well obviously he couldn't say no, but at the same time he suddenly felt a bit of pressure. After all he would have to live up to his reputation in a contest which he previously had never heard of and in which luck played a major part and with a borrowed gun at that.

Gamely he took his place at the line and examined the situation and the shotgun he was holding. Slowly he took his stance and at the sound of the judge's command he fired along with the other contestants. The contestants chatted and drank beer as the judge examined each target, and our hunter was declared the winner on his first turkey shoot!

The locals, now duly impressed, began to pepper our hunter with questions which he fielded as diplomatically as possible. After all was it only luck? Or perhaps in all those thousands of shots on the range and in the field and in all those different hunting conditions, did our hunter do some little thing right that gave him a slight edge. Luck is made after all.

In his youth he learned hunting small game, and as he entered adulthood, the urge to hunt larger game naturally took hold. In those days, deer hunting wasn't quite like it is today. Due to the intense agricultural activity, many areas which today are known for their huge white tails were back then almost devoid of deer. Nevertheless he began to pursue them with the same intensity which he learned from hunting small game.

He hand carved the stock of his rifle. He did this not just for economic reasons – although at the time that was a consideration – he did it so that his rifle had the very best fit possible to his body. Now most people wouldn't bother with such details, but the wisdom of this extra attention proved many times to be invaluable. Our hunter with his hand carved stock become a legendary shot, killing many deer one the run with off hand shots at impressive distances. This is an example of our hunter's passion and his attention to the smallest details which at the critical moment can make all the difference.

The Time

As a man lives his life, changes can occur at an imperceptible rate to the individual. Yet when one stands back and observes the changes on an accumulated basis, the difference can be startling. One could be in the mist of a great historical sea change and hardly be conscious of it. This is the problem of the daily existence of our lives. We become caught up in the moment to moment necessities and miss the bigger picture.

America has changed since this hunt took place all those many years ago in some ways for the better but mostly not. At that time, she still stood out from the world in many areas in commerce and industry. But more importantly she stood apart in what really counted and that was liberty and opportunity. Liberty means something much more than just words on a document. True freedom means that one can live life without concern of being monitored. A person could travel, work, partake in activities and be completely anonymous. That has been the biggest change. Whether the watchers are helpful or malevolent is not the point. Freedom means being left alone. It means that associations are voluntary. Why is liberty important here? It is because wild chase hunting represents a vision of freedom which few are fortunate enough to experience.

Freedom is also important because when America was free it was prosperous to the point where a man of humble background could succeed to the point of hunting elk in the Rocky Mountains. This unique combination of opportunity and prosperity made for a special golden age where a few souls could test their skill and determination in the most demanding settings.

The Place

When one says the words Colorado Rocky Mountains, one pictures a spectacular mountain range with tall ragged peaks reaching up past the timber line with the top capped by snow and the lower section blanketed with forests of alpine evergreens and aspens. Perhaps in the foreground of this image is an idyllic lake with water such a deep shade of blue that it hypnotizes the mind. In the summer, the mind's eye can see beautiful wild flowers such as Indian Paintbrushes with their vibrant reds dotting the landscape along with a variety of yellow flowers scattered about mixed with delicate Columbines that shower shades of gentle blues. During the winter, the lake is frozen over, and the flowers are replaced with a blanket of pure white snow which caps every tree branch creating a winter wonderland scene that appears to be special made for a movie.

That mental image of the Rockies correctly describes the location of this hunt. It took place not in the eastern plains or the rough wilderness of the western mesas of the state. Rather it occurred right in the heart of some of the highest peaks in North America, the Sawatch mountain range. There may be mountains in the world more youthfully rugged, or more extensive in area, or taller. But one would be hard pressed to find an area that combined these elements together to produce one of the grandest expanses of high mountain wilderness found anywhere. Here in the heart of the Colorado Rockies lies the setting of the most memorable day of this hunter's lifetime.

The Hunt

How did our hunter arrive at this place at this time? Well in those days, the oil industry didn't have the "dirty" label so many associate with it today. A man of modest means could and in this case did work his way through college and obtain an engineering degree without having to go into debt. Then he could, and in this case did, find a job right out of school which paid well enough to support, without a second income, a solid middle class family. Finally, opportunities existed for those willing to work hard to advance and that advancement meant an improvement in economic wellbeing.

And in addition to the normal opportunities, one of the very special features of those somewhat more laid back days consisted of vendor perks - including trips. And these perks weren't only for the top brass; they existed in good numbers for workers on down the line.

That is how our hunter ended up here at that moment. In his dealings as a mid-level manager, he made a number of contacts and those contacts led to more contacts and pretty soon he found himself invited to go on a trip at a private ranch in a valley among these spectacular mountains.

The ranch consisted of a number of individual cabins and a large restaurant / dance hall. An oil field supply company had acquired the land with the idea of building a resort and running that resort as a for-profit venture. However, due to the remoteness and the lack of civilization in the area, that idea never really caught on. It was an example of a company with excess money which expanded into a business in which it had no business. Soon after a few years of trying to run the resort as an independent venture, the place became more and more a nice little place to entertain their customers.

In addition to the cabins and the restaurant, the resort sat on a wide lush mountain valley. And through that valley ran a good size mountain stream which ended at a decently large mountain lake. Trout fishing was the main attraction and the main reason this company took their customers to this place (at least fishing was the excuse, there might have been a bit of partying in the lodge also but we will never know for sure). And that is why our hunter found himself there in the late autumn of that year. Of course, the vendor had made mention of the possibility of hunting should the opportunity arise. So our hunter, always mindful of a possibility made sure to pack his trusty 30-06 with the hand carved stock.

Sometime early in the second evening, after all the guests had eaten in the restaurant and were relaxing with a few drinks, the manager of the resort came in to announce that he had spotted a large number of elk up in a high basin on the mountain range south of the resort. In the back of the restaurant / dance hall existed a telescope which the manager used to glass the surrounding slopes. It was with this device that he spotted the elk. Naturally this created quite a stir among the guests, and none more so than our hunter. They spent the rest of the evening light taking turns observing the elk and discussing at great length how to go about hunting them which they all agreed they should do the next morning.

This is where things began to get a little testy. The manager decided that he would take those with rifles and licenses up to the top of the basin where the elk had been seen in a jeep and from there they would hunt. Our hunter, however, thought that tactic would only bust them up and they would never see anything. He preferred to work up from the bottom on foot and use the timber to mask the approach. The problem was that the manager wanted to keep everyone together – understandably so – and didn't want hunters, who probably weren't in the best of shape, hiking up a rugged 14,000 foot peak through the timber. As the sun sat over the mountain range, the discussion carried back and for in a good natured way as the drinks and stories flowed.

The only female present was the head cook who had developed a rather rough exterior to deal with all the rowdy oil field types who frequented the club – or perhaps she was just born that way. In either case, it became obvious to our hunter that she had heard all this grandiose talk about elk hunting before and that she was less than convinced of their chances. It even occurred to our hunter after listening to her talk that perhaps this elk hunt was a regular feature and that it provided a good excuse to take the guests on a jeep ride to break up the fishing. She even coyly seemed to taunt them "You know that if anyone shoots an elk and doesn't bring me the liver to cook, he can never set foot in my restaurant again. I don't to hear about any of you boys leaving a perfectly good liver up there on the mountain for the coyotes to eat." Our hunter detected a grin as she said this as if it was all part of the show and preplanned. Still it kicked off another round of drinks and hooraying for all the guests.

Early the next morning our hunter woke early raring to go. However the other hunters were less inclined to miss any sleep. After all this was supposed to be a fun trip and this elk hunt thing was really more of a diversion to pass the day – a chance to take a jeep ride up above the timberline. Finally about mid-morning after a hearty breakfast, the guests who would be hunting loaded up in two jeeps and began the journey. And what a torturous journey it became! The jeep trail quickly turned into little more than a rut which seemed at time to go straight up the side of the mountain at impossibly steep angles.

About half way up, our hunter somehow convinced the driver to let him out there. He re-assured him that he was perfectly fit and capable of hunting in this environment and that he could easily hike back down the mountain after the hunt finished. The driver hesitated but finally figured "What the heck. The hunt will be over by noon and he'll probably be right here when we drive back down." He couldn't have been more wrong! In hindsight it was an incredibly foolhardy move. In today's litigious climate, a proprietor would never do such a thing. But in those days, people still had more of a hardy, self reliant nature and assumed that other people could take care of their selves if they insisted. It was a different time then.

Freed from the confines of the jeep, our hunter set forth to hike to a spot at the base of the large basin where the elk had been seen previously. Walking in a path directly away from the trail to the west, he soon found himself at the base of an aspen thicket and there he decided to take a stand. In that time of the year, the aspens had already dropped their leaves. So instead of being the brilliant torches of fall colors seen in postcards, they more resembled ghostly sticks of bare white branches. In fact the entire scene presented a sullen appearance with the bare tree branches and the blanket of snow on the ground. A far cry from the typical imagery of the Rocky Mountains, it held a somber mood which enveloped our hunter with a strange mixture of loneliness and comfort.

However, this is why he chose this spot. It provided cover, and he could see through the branches up the slope. As soon as he set up, he immediately knew he made the right move. For all the while he waited, he could hear the whirring sound of the jeeps as they made their way up the mountain. If he could hear the jeeps, the elk surly could also!

There is something to be said for taking risks, for going against the group, and trusting your fate to your own abilities. It is always tempting to go with the flow and not rock the boat, even if you know better. It is difficult to actually do the right thing when everyone else is going the other way. But in this case, not only did our hunter have the correct strategy; he used the others as unwitting accomplices to improve his chance. While he stood as a blocker at the base of a natural funnel, the jeeps acted as drivers to push the elk out.

Soon elk appeared everywhere from above his location and they were streaming down in large numbers. They had moved down from the basin on top and were looking back towards that direction. Now our hunter's heart began racing in earnest. But the problem was the elk appeared everywhere at once. He only held an over the counter bull tag, but there was no size restriction in those days. Still he temporarily became disoriented at the sudden appearance of all these elk.

Forcing his mind to focus and concentrate at the task at hand, he quickly began to scan the elk for bulls. As the elk moved down he knew the bulls would be hanging back towards the last. He spotted one small group of three or four bulls. Just as he was about to raise his rifle in preparation to shoot, his eye suddenly caught sight of a huge, herd bull elk standing between several of the aspens trailing behind the others. Without hesitating he swung his rifle in position and with one fluid motion fired as soon as the butt of the gun hit his shoulder. So perfect did the rifle fit his body that the entire sequence took only a fraction of a second and presented no need or adjustment after he shouldered the gun. It was as if the hunter merely had to look at the target and the shot would be on.

The big bull turned nonchalantly as if he was completely unfazed and trotted off. Our hunter, momentarily confused by the big animal's reaction, knew he had a solid hit and decided to wait. He then hiked around to the right in order to try and pick up the trail. There he spotted the bull again along with several of the other bulls who were hanging in the same area. Our hunter once again swung his rifle up to his shoulder and fired off hand at the bull which was in a straight on orientation to the shot. Once again, the bullet found its mark with a solid hit. This time the bull did react by throwing its head up and down violently like a bucking horse. And this time, instead of a nonchalant reaction, the bull along with his escorts took off up the slope. Now the stalk was on.

Fortunately for our hunter, thick snow blanketed the ground which made for easy tracking – the blood trail being obvious in the fresh snowfall. Unfortunately for our hunter, thick snow blanketed the ground which made hiking up the steep high mountain even more labor intensive and slow. Slogging along the trail, the aspens turned to evergreens as he climbed ever higher. Once he almost walked up on the elk, but he heard them crashing away through the forest. Not wanting to push them more he found a place to rest and then waited. Hopefully the big bull would lie down and expire.

After waiting several hours, he eased up the trail which by now was at the edge of the timberline. From there he could look up and see the summit of the mountain which formed a sheer rim which wrapped around the upper part of the basin. There he saw something that made his heart sank. He could clearly see a blood trail glowing with crimson harshness in the snow running along the base of this rim. It headed across to the west and over a swag in the rim and there disappeared from view. With the afternoon wearing on, our hunter had to make a decision: should he continue to follow the elk or pull back for the day. He knew that the trail led to another smaller basin above the timberline. The lesson here is that he had studied the topographical maps the night before and had some knowledge of the area. If the elk continued across that next basin, they would be on the other side of the mountain and in a completely different drainage. The time to act was at hand.

Instead of continuing along their trail, our hunter decided to buttonhook around them. He dropped back down to just inside the timberline and proceeded towards the western side of the first basin. The going got rough, very rough indeed. He had to cross an ice covered gulch at one point. From there he crested the rim which although was not as steep there as in other places still presented a challenge. Once into the next basin he worked up to the area where he hoped the elk had holed up. As he approached the timberline from below, he caught sight of the elk in a small swag in the basin. The smaller bulls had formed a tight circle around the big bull, but our hunter could clearly see him. The big bull was swaying back and forth like a drunk – his giant antlers rising and falling. The elks' hooves had left deep bright red impressions in the bloodied snow. At any moment it seemed the bull could drop to the ground and the hunt would be over. However he still stood there! The smaller bulls were looking back down their trial waiting for our hunter to appear once more.

Knowing that this was his best chance to end the hunt before the elk crossed over the ridge, our hunter eased up to the right of the elk in the timber. This put a small ridge between him and the elk. Now the snow, which had caused him to labor so mightily before, acted as a muffler as he ever so carefully eased up the ridge. As he crested the ridge, the elk still stood looking back down the trail. He had done it! He had successfully button hooked around these elk at high altitude using stalking skill combined with physical endurance. Once more he gently eased his rifle up for an off hand shot. With his heart now racing he patiently waited for a shot between the smaller elk. Finally after what seemed hours, a gap appeared between two of the smaller elk right on the big bull's shoulder. Without hesitating the hunter's gun fired for one final time.

Mercifully the big bull flattened where he stood. The smaller elk now thoroughly befuddled wandered around aimlessly for a few moments. They still had no idea where our hunter stood or from what direction the shot had been fired. Finally one turned and bolted right underneath where our hunter stood. The other also decided to book out and followed in hasty fashion.

Our hunter approached the big bull in what felt like a surreal scene. The chase had lasted all afternoon and now with a single shot it had ended. There was, of course, no way could he have retrieved the animal that day, so he dressed out the animal as best he could to leave it for morning. However, as he did this, he remembered one important thing – the admonishment of the camp cook to bring back the liver. Now an elk's liver is no small matter; it weighed several pounds. But into his backpack it went.

Now began the long hike back to the jeep trail where he assumed, wrongly as it turned out, that his buddies would be waiting for him as previously planned. The only problem was that rendezvous was scheduled for the morning and the hour now approached early evening. Those guys had long since returned to camp and to the comfort of food and beverage.

At first he felt a little miffed by this fact; however it presented no real problem for he could simply hike straight down the slope to camp. After what he had been though, that hike was certainly no big deal. As he strode down with the blood soaked backpack weighed down by the elk's liver, he had time to reflect on the day. He had pushed his body and hunting skills to their limits in one of the greatest cathedrals of hunting adventure and he had succeeded. It is moments like this why people give up the comfort of more civilized pursuits. This drama is why he had crossed over from respectable professional to a sort of primitive mountain man. This first elk would be a moment which would define his hunting career and with it, his entire life in a way like few other things could.

With the first shadows of darkness enveloped the landscape, the warm comfort of the lodge glowed in the evening cold as he descended. Still he was in the wild and strange things happen and those things are often good things when one is prepared. You see just as he approached the nose of a small downward sloping ridge a large mule deer buck jumped up in front of him. Without hesitating, he swung his trusty 30-06 with the hand carved stalk into action and the buck tumbled down in the snow. Now he had another problem! Night was now falling hard and he had another animal up on the mountain. Without wasting time he gutted the deer, and once more he remembered the cook's forceful instructions about the liver. So, once again, into the backpack went yet another liver.

By this time the backpack was so heavy and blood soaked that balancing it became a struggle, but he didn't have far to go by now. Very soon, he hit the bottom of the mountain and turned towards the lodge. He could hear the laughter as he approached when he heard someone say "I wonder where John is. Is he still up on the mountain?" Another chimed in "Ahh, he's okay I heard him shooting all afternoon" Then just as he approached the door the cook added "Well I don't want to hear no sad stories about not getting no elk and no liver!"

Our hunter used that moment to burst through the front door like a wild man crashing a fancy ball. The bitter cold wind blew a small wisp of snow across his feet as he stood in the entranceway eying the scene. Everyone stopped and stared in amazement as he pulled off his backpack, opened it up and with a loud pronouncement declared "Well here's your elk liver" and with a loud thump he slapped it on the table next to him. "And here's your deer liver" he added as he threw it down next.

The other hunters let loose with delirious celebration and congratulations to our hunter. However, before any one noticed, the cook snatched away both livers to the kitchen like prized trophies. Next day's evening meal would be the tastiest liver and onions our hunter ever ate.

Chapter 13 – Stories from Squirrel Camp

Squirrel hunting holds a special place in the hearts of American hunters in a way that no other game animal does. While experienced hunters may tell tall tales about monster elk, giant muleys, and that special white tail that got away, they all can recall a time from their youth where they first learned to hunt on small game such as squirrels. And those memories, in moments of quieter reflection, always bring a sense of warm glowing joy that comes from the innocence of youth. How many hunters have for their first special hunting memories of that first squirrel or rabbit or other small game quarry? When they reflect back to those youthful times of exuberance they can remember the total excitement and sheer joy that came from those hunts. Maybe, in ways small and large, these men spend the rest of their lives trying to re-capture that that unique feeling they experienced as youth.

And in a very special way, perhaps America herself tries to re-capture the youthful innocence that those days in the woods represented. For in those days, adults didn't fear a group of young men with guns slung over their shoulders marching towards the local woods. Instead, they would smile a little and know that those boys were off to explore this vast world in a way that would shape their character and help them grow into well adjusted men.

The lure of the unknown adventures which await the brave never really leaves some men. They still, even as adults, long to return to these Interesting Places to hunt the quarry of their youth, to try and reclaim the felling and the special sensations they back then. And they attempt to do this in squirrel camp. In a melancholy reflection, squirrel hunting evokes innocence, a freedom, and an individualist attitude which is uniquely American and preciously rare. Can we really forgive these men – or ourselves – for wishing to return to that era that we may not see again in our lifetimes?

Squirrels on a Plane

Long before America was terrorized from the air and expressed that
fear through movies like "Snakes on a Plane" (sort of like the
Japanese used the Godzilla movies as cinematic metaphor for the
horrors they experienced in the war), air travel in America was a
decidedly less pressured mode of travel. In fact, the basis of this
story – Squirrels on a Plane - which produced a humorous encounter
between some ornery hunters and a flight crew would probably land
the same group in jail and on the no-fly list.

The story began when a group of well-seasoned hunters and good
friends got an invite to travel to a squirrel camp in northern
Louisiana, which had the woods for some of the best squirrel hunting
anywhere in North America. So naturally, boys being boys, they
couldn't pass on an opportunity to relive a part of their youth and
have a good time doing it. To this end, they all flew to this
destination. Now air travel in those days wasn't anything like it is
today. Unbelievably by today's standards, these hunters boarded the
domestic airline with their firearms in tow (although unloaded).
While this elicited some annoyed looks from some of the less
outdoors oriented passengers, it was perfectly common. Could you
imagine such a thing today?

Once at camp, they did what men (or men wishing to be boys) do.
They drank. They swapped stories. They commiserated over the
difficulties of middle age life: the kids in high school, college costs,
the demands of their careers, difficulties at home. All these things
they discussed and as they discussed them and drank, they somehow,
in some small way returned to that age of innocence when they
grabbed a single shot 20 gauge and headed out the door to the local
woods. This was the last bastion of unbridled manhood.

Don't get the wrong idea. These were not mean or bad men. Quite
the opposite, they represented the salt of the earth. These men
played by the rules and worked hard to carve out a little piece of the
American dream so that they could pass it on to their children. But
they needed, from time to time, to blow off a little steam, and
squirrel camp was just the place to accomplish that.

During the next few days they did manage to work in a little hunting. These woods held prime squirrel habitat, and it wasn't long before each hunter began to stack an impressive tally of the little fury animals. Each hunter's success spurred on the others. After all, each hunter did have a little pride, and nobody wanted to left out of the fun once the shooting action got hot and heavy.

Now normally one wouldn't think of squirrels as trophy animals by any means. These hunters had all killed large game animals such as deer and elk, so they really weren't prepared to handle the situation that came up. See, in addition to the normal grey and fox squirrels, one hunter happened to bag a rather unusual black squirrel. These aren't necessarily rare, but they are a little unique. And so it came to pass that during the course of that evening's dinner, this hunter deemed that his black squirrel worthy enough to be mounted for display in his office.

This presented a bit of a problem for the squirrel camp for they really didn't have the facilities to handle such a request. So after some discussion the hunters decided that about the only way to preserve the critter in the warm climate would be set it in the freezer. And so it sat until the end of the trip.

But that presented another problem. Remember that they flew on a commercial flight. Now they had to somehow transport this frozen trophy back home and get it to a taxidermist before it thawed. About the only choice the hunter had at this point was to simply take the specimen onboard with him. If you thought it was unbelievable that some grown men could board a flight with shotguns slung over their shoulders, it was even more unbelievable that one could board a plane with a frozen squirrel.

The hunter did think of placing it in a plastic Tupperware container; however, truth be told, that was more out of concern for preserving his prize than out of concern for what his fellow travelers would think at such a sight. And unbelievably enough the hunters boarded the plane – guns, Tupperware container and all – without a hitch.

Another difference in air travel back in those days concerned the attitude of the flight crew and their relationship with the passengers. They didn't view the passengers as a collection of potential security threats. Rather the attitude was much more relaxed and congenial. It wasn't uncommon for the flight crew to actually flirt a bit – especially on longer flights which were not full (which actually was most flights back then). I know this might be viewed as political incorrect these days, but stewardesses viewed a big part of their job as making the flight as enjoyable as possible and if that meant a little innocent attention then that certainly wasn't frowned upon.

Naturally one of the stewardesses had her attention drawn to the strange sight of this hunter with a Tupperware container on his lap. This provided an opportunity for a little good natured conversation. "What's in there?' she naively began. "Oh, I've got a pet squirrel in here" was the reply. The flight attendant assumed that he was just ribbing her so she played along.

After serving the drinks and snacks, she stopped by again "You don't really have a squirrel in there, do you?" The hunter simply couldn't resist "Yes ma'am I do. I'd let you see him, but I'm afraid he'll get out." He opened the lid just a little and shut it back real fast "Oh, I'm afraid that he'll get out."

The stewardess at this point just knew that he was kidding but she continued to play it up. "Why don't you let me see him? I'm sure it is really cute!" The hunter peaked real quick under the lid "Oh, he's just raring to get out. I can't risk it." And so it went through most of the flight. However, in between these exchanges, our hunter had managed to reach into the container and position the still quite frozen animal in a pose such that it looked like he was standing on all fours.

Finally she couldn't stand it any more. "I don't believe that you have a squirrel in there." she proclaimed. With that the hunter knew that he had played this game long enough. "Well, let me see if he's calmed down." After checking the container again he told her "I'll be. I think he's settled down. I tell you what. I think I can open the lid enough for you to see him, but I'll have to close it back real fast." The attendant thought she was being played but decided to go along with it. By this time, she really was curious about what the container held.

With great deliberation and fanfare the hunter slowly cracked the lid. "Okay, here he is." With that he popped the lid completely off. Probably the last thing the stewardess expected to see was an actual squirrel (albeit dead, but she didn't know that at the time). Predictably she let out a shriek – the kind that only a woman who is truly frightened can produce. She ran up and down the aisle muttering "Close the lid! Don't let him out!" By now the commotion attracted the other members of the flight crew, and after a rather tense moment of discussion about the actual state of the squirrel with the hunter, they calmed down and everyone returned to normal.

The hunter, far from being arrested and removed from the flight, achieved a bit of notoriety for the whole incident. Of course the results would be far different today if someone pulled the same stunt on a plane, but that was a different age.

Great White Hunter

Not every ordinary deer hunter gets the opportunity to hunt with a true hunting legend – a man who earned the reputation of as a Great White Hunter. By that I mean he legitimately had the credentials of a big game hunter in the African Safari sense. He, being a man of great wealth (obviously), had taken the time to go on several extended safaris in Africa, and he did this in an era largely before the various local governments became corrupted with their various socialist-type dictators. In other words, he hunted the Africa of legend, he hunted the Africa of wild game in vast wilderness, he hunted the Africa of Chapwick.

Safaris in that era were grand adventures of the most lavish type which were affordable to only the very wealthy. And this Great White Hunter had the opportunity during his prime to hunt those places, and he had made the most of it.

So it sent something of a shiver of nervous excitement though the a group of squirrel hunters when word came that this Great White Hunter would be joining them on a trip to a squirrel camp located in East Texas. Several members of the invited group had heard second hand stories of his extensive collection of trophies, and needless to say, the tales sounded of his collection sounded like something out of a novel.

A question one may be asking at this point is: this is a story about squirrel hunting, perhaps the humblest of the quarry not about Africa hunting. Why would a Great White Hunter who had taken everything from Springbok to Lions bother with the furry things? Well that is a little hard to say except that, well, hunting is hunting. And if the opportunity arises, a dedicated hunter jumps at the chance to hunt again. Each hunt and each place is unique and special, and one never knows what will happen for nothing is scripted and the future remains unknown. And just maybe, despite the wild adventures hunting overseas, a man in his later years yearns to return to his roots, to capture that special feeling he had on his first hunt in the woods.

Now when you picture the image of a Great White Hunter, what comes to mind? Of course it is some larger than life character with the khaki outfit (perfectly pressed) and the all important safari hat. He would have an impressive build and a commanding – but perhaps genteel – voice. If you had that mental image of the Great White Hunter in this story then, well, you could not have been more wrong. He was everything opposite of the typical image of a hunter of grand African safari adventures.

So it was a great shock to the other hunters when this legend arrived at camp. With glasses as thick as coke bottle bottoms, he stood a head shorter than the others. His thin frame sported ordinary and quite modest hunting attire. Although very polite, he was not talkative at all and when he spoke, it had none of commanding qualities one would assume of a person of such accomplishments. In fact overall he seemed to be a little out of sorts and rather harried from the trip. After a quick dinner and some brief conversation, his main focus seemed to be on getting to bed early.

Could this be the Great White Hunter that they had heard so much about wondered the other hunters? When he did speak, he appeared to be very knowledgeable about Africa and his hunts there. And he obviously knew his stuff. But this was not a man given to bombast. In fact whenever the others pressed him for stories, he looked uncomfortable – almost as if he didn't want to stand out much from the rest. Perhaps that is the mark of a great hunter and a gentleman – knowing when not to boast. However, it puzzled the other hunters at the time and only added to the mystery of this little man they would be hunting with in the morning.

And morning came early enough. At the dinner table, the hunters scooped up scrambled eggs, bacon, grits, and plenty of other grub for the long day ahead. Thoughts and conversation turned to the almost ideal squirrel territory they were going to hunt. Extensive woods which ran along numerous creeks and swamp like pools of water provided an environment not much removed from pre-settlement days. In places there existed even a few stands of old growth trees which, if you have never seen them, are a sight to behold. Giants whose canopies completely block out the light, they have trunks so massive that a grown man cannot reach around and touch his fingers. This was truly an Interesting Place and full of unknowns and potential adventure.

All of these hunters felt very privileged to be here at this place at this time. Each was a guest and was invited for this hunt by the landowner. Naturally there were connections involved such as work, relatives, etc., but each hunter knew how lucky they were to be here. That added to the excitement that morning as they wolfed down breakfast and tried to outdo each other with stories of hunts long past - all that is except for the Great White Hunter. That morning he kind of apologized for his early night claiming he felt a bit out of sorts, blaming it on advancing age and a hectic schedule. He relayed some tales of Africa when pressed by the others, but on the whole remaining fairly quiet.

Despite the long night's sleep, he still appeared to be somewhat disorganized and fumbled about with his gear and personal effects getting ready. The other hunters couldn't help but notice the contrast between what they expected and what they saw before them.

The Great White Hunter joined in one of the trucks heading out into the woods. Soon after leaving camp, the hunters found themselves in the midst of another world. Giant old growth trees turned the early morning into pitch black darkness. The bogs and swamps added to the eeriness of the place. No wonder early pioneers considered the woods to be full of evil and danger.

At the appointed spot, the truck stopped and the hunters dismounted. Each eagerly gathered up his gear and firearm and soon they began to move off in different directions through the woods - all that is except for the Great White Hunter. Appearing to be all thumbs, he had a heck of a time getting unstrung. The heavy mist of the deep woods played havoc with his thick glasses and caused them to continuously fog over. Not wanting to hold up the others he implored them to carry on without him "Don't worry about me. I'll just stay around here until the sun gets up a little and I can see. I'll be okay." Now the other hunters didn't want to leave him alone. Not only did he not live up to their preconceived ideas about a big time African hunter, they weren't sure that he should even be in the woods at all! Eventually however, his assurances that he would be okay convinced them to take off and get the hunt started.

Reluctantly the others began their hunt. Each headed off in a different direction with the agreement that they would meet back at lunch. The place did not disappoint in the fast paced squirrel hunting action provided. Soon after daylight the trees seemed to explode with squirrel activity from every part. Everywhere the hunters could hear the little buggers and occasionally get sight of one as it darted through the branches at high altitude.

Although squirrels filled the woods, getting a clean shot at one is another matter altogether. They often appeared to have a sixth sense on where to go – flitting out of sight just as a hunter got ready to shoot. Of course this is all part of hunting and that is why is it called hunting and not just killing. Eventually, with perseverance and skill each of the hunters that struck out into the woods had a heavy backpack full of squirrel meat. And at the agreed to time, they headed back to the rendezvous point of the truck.

When each hunter approached, he was a little surprised to find the Great White Hunter sitting on a stool not far from the vehicle. Obviously he had not ventured out very far that morning. Now the others didn't know exactly how to handle the situation. Here was the Great White Hunter who had been all over the world and he had hardly moved from the same spot all morning! Their feelings towards him changed from one of awe to one of almost pity. How could they even discus the morning's hunt without implicitly insulting the man? They didn't want to wound his pride. What to do now?

They found the Great White Hunter in a much cheerier mood upon arrival. "How'd you fellas do?" he eagerly asked. Each described in detail the long hikes, the quick chances, missed opportunities, and bagged squirrels. "I ended up with six." stated one. Another hunter chimed in "well I managed to get seven." To which the Great White Hunter replied "wonderful, wonderful, simply wonderful."

Now came the clumsy moment. The hunters were obliged to ask him about his morning, to not do so would be an insult. But they didn't want to force the old man to have to explain how he hadn't really moved much from sight of the truck. Hesitatingly one asked "Well, umm, sir, how'd you do." "Oh I managed to bag fifteen." came the nonchalant reply.

Stunned silence and dropped jaws betrayed the complete and utter shock that the other hunters felt at that moment. "Well, if you don't mind, sir. How exactly did you manage to do that?" one asked in a stammered voice.

"Oh, well, you know at first I couldn't see and all due to my glasses. So I decided to let you boys go on out. After about thirty minutes the woods started to settle down from all the racket. I decided to just sit here awhile and take a moment to get my bearings. After the sun got up some, I finally could see, and I noticed a stand of red oaks about fifty yards off down in that draw. I heard squirrels cutting on those acorns so I moved over there, took a stand, and waited. Pretty soon I could see several squirrels moving around. I waited until I could get a good shot at least two before shooting. After I felled those, I waited until the squirrels came back, which took only a few minutes because those squirrels just couldn't resist those acorns. I repeated the process until I had my limit, and then I went and gathered them all up. For the last hour or so I've been waiting by the truck for you boys."

It was the most the Great White Hunter said all weekend, and it spoke volumes. The others had completely underestimated his hunting skills, despite his resume, due to appearance. Now they understood that they had had the privilege of hunting with a truly remarkable hunter who really knew his stuff. Each knew they had learned a lesson, but it was a lesson learned with a chuckle and a memory they would each treasure always.

Part 4

Cascade Canyon

Chapter 14 - Cascade Canyon

Of all the very Interesting Places we experienced over the years, none could quite compare to one place: Cascade Canyon. I know that from the title of this book you may think that Rough Piece of West Texas would hold the highest honor. Well the truth is that all Interesting Places, if they are truly interesting, cannot compare to each other. Each is unique in its own right, because that is what makes each truly interesting. Each brings out a special feeling in those fortunate enough to hunt them, because each sets the stage for more than just hunting. Each sets the stage for magic. And in that magic, moments would be hung like jewels in the memories of those that lived them – moments in time that defined those that dared to test themselves.

No place tested those that hunted there more than Cascade Canyon. For here, on those rugged, sage brush swept mesas and mountains of northwest Colorado, was the ultimate hunting dream. It was a dream that became achievable to even those of middle class means during one golden era in history. It was a dream to those ready to risk disappointment for a chance at hunting glory, to those who would leave the comforts of the world (at least for a while) for a chance at memories that would define a life.

For close to 35 years, this Interesting Place saw a number of hunters plumb its mysteries. All left very different men than when they came. Over the years, while some passed on leaving only their stories behind, others joined hoping to add their stories to the lore. For in many ways Cascade Canyon defined what an Interesting Place should be – except everything was magnified due to its placement in the Rockies.

The Beginning

Like the paradox of all Interesting Places in that brief golden era, the very modern world that inexorably levels everything into a numbing sameness, provided the means to discover this Interesting Place before it passed. One of the founding hunters, the one who would become Legend, put together the first trip in 1974. This came about as apart of an oil field lease deal back during the first oil crisis. The mesas in this area held within them oil shale which was being eyed as a replacement to America's ever increasing demand for imported oil from rather non-friendly countries.

Of course, to the younger readers, the Arab oil embargo probably reeks of ancient history. However, what is important is the odd juxtaposition of the demands of the modern world in discovering this very Interesting Place. For our founding hunter, it was an opportunity to acquire rights to hunt big game in Colorado. This was truly remarkable, because he had grown up in poorer means during the Great Depression and had only achieved middle class status only through perseverance, skill, and the GI bill.

Of course, the danger was that the oil shale would be developed. This would mean basically tearing down the entire mountain to extract its riches. There was even a pilot plant tested on one of the main ridges in the area. The tailings from even that modest experiment flowed down the bluff face like an ugly scar to the canyon bottom.

Fortunately, the economics of the oil shale operation just weren't there. By that I mean fortunately for our hunters. They were left with a hunting lease in one of the most magnificent settings imaginable while the oil companies had largely abandoned (for now) the property to the ranchers and hunters.

<u>Camp</u>

Far from the popular images of luxuriant camping provided by an outfitter for high paying clients that one may have seen depicted in print and on screen, the camping at Cascade Canyon was of the most meager sort but still quite adequate. Everything, and I mean everything, was provided by the hunters themselves. This was at once both a blessing and a curse.

The curse part was easy enough to see. After all, considerable effort had to be expended in order to provide for a mountain camp in the late fall Colorado season. The climate during this time of year varied from tee-shirt weather to near artic conditions. Also it was a good 30 miles over rough, four wheel drive (real four wheel drive, not TV four wheel drive) conditions over mountain trails to the nearest blacktop. Therefore, every contingency had to be taken into account: propane, food, water, tents, tools, tire chains, rope, gasoline, diesel, utensils, emergency kits, camping furniture, stoves, heaters, etc. In addition, there were other essentials, such as whiskey, which could not be done without. Camping could, and sometimes did, become a major limiter on the hunting that could be accomplished – all the more its charm. Often it was joked that the hunt would end when, either, the propane, the gas, or the whiskey would run out first. There is a reason why hunters with money gladly pay for the niceties of a provided camp, and this camp in this very interesting place demonstrated all too well these reasons.

However, there were definite benefits of doing your own camp. First and foremost was the experience, which was a major reason these hunters chose to hunt here. Many memories were made just in the planning phase alone. Hunters would call each other throughout the year in order to check up on progress for the upcoming trip. In that way, and others, the trip to hunt Cascade Canyon defined the entire year for those lucky hunters (much to the consternation of wives and bosses).

In addition, the hunters acquired a deep appreciation of the adventure undertaken. And let's face it; they also obtained a certain status that comes from the bragging rights of rugged manhood from their more domesticated colleagues back at the office. There was a deep satisfaction that comes from the knowledge of doing something yourself, and doing it well. For these hunters, the camping was an indispensable element in the quest of a wild chase hunt in the back country of the Rocky Mountains.

Each hunter had a responsibility to provide for his part of the camp. One duo (the hunters would normally work in pairs both in planning and in hunting) provided the tents; another duo had responsibility for the kitchen and food for breakfast and lunch. Finally, someone would always be assigned the very most important responsibility of procuring the camp whiskey (of course individuals would have their private stashes also). Costs would be split, of course, but they were definitely on the modest side.

This system had been started in an earlier time, before the era of high priced guided hunts became accessible to a larger portion of the hunting population. So although these hunters, being successful in their trades during their careers, could have opted out for a more genteel style of guided hunts, they choose instead to perfect their chosen manner. When they hunted, everything that was going to happen depended on their actions and theirs alone. This included the tiniest details of the camp, to the locating of game, to planning the stalks and making the shots, to the handling of the meat in the field, transportation, and of course fun. By doing it this way, it could and did create a certain number of problems, but by overcoming these difficulties and succeeding in spite of them, our hunters created a bond between them that few people ever experience.

Food

For example, over the years, the hunters developed what they considered the most optimum manner to handle the food situation. Lunches were basically sandwiches, fruit, and chips. The sandwich material was provided, but each party was responsible for their own. The hunters generally made their lunches before heading out in the morning; after all, no telling if they would be back at camp before dark.

Dinners were handled in a unique way. Each hunter provided one precooked meal sufficient enough for the whole camp. With five to six hunters, this generally would cover dinners for the week. There was never a "camp cook", since everyone was there to hunt, so the hunters had learned better than to try and do any fancy cooking after a tough all day hunt for muleys and elk. With this system, they could plop a meal into a cooking pot to heat, have a few drinks, tell a few stories, warm up by the sheepherder's stove, and generally try to recover from the day's rigors.

The dinners often became a point of pride for the hunters as they (or more accurately their wives) tried to create the best delicacy that could be put in zip-lock bags and frozen for later re-thawing. Lavish praise would be heaped on the hunter who pulled off the feat with much thanks to the misses. The drawback to this approach was that some years it sure did seem like there were a lot of chilies and stews.

Breakfasts were another matter altogether. There isn't a lot to say about them. Like I mentioned before, they were there to hunt, not to camp. And seeing that everyone was always anxious to get to where they were going early in the morning, breakfast consisted of cereal – cold or hot. The biggest problem here was to keep the milk from freezing overnight. Normally, some would be placed in a cooler each night – not to keep cool, but to keep from freezing.

The one exception to this rather utilitarian morning menu came late in the week. If the hunting had been good (as it often was), one or more of the hunters would have "tagged out" by this juncture. Therefore they would have the honor of frying up several pounds of bacon along several dozen eggs in the remaining bacon grease as a treat. No matter how many eggs had been purchased, it never seemed enough.

That went for all the food. By hunting hard in the thin mountain air, these hunters found out a truism lost to modern man: if you are going full out every day, the last thing you need to worry about is your diet making you fat. Basically the real "caveman" diet is everything you can get your hands on – if you are really living as a hunter / gather.

Camping Equipment

As for the rest of the camp, there were two somewhat spacious wall tents. One was the cooking tent with a sheepherders stove converted to burn propane (a homemade innovation not available in stores and not advisable to duplicate), a three burner hot plate stove (also somewhat modified for the service), a foldout table with chairs for sitting and eating, and even storage containers that could be stacked along one wall of the tent as cupboards.

Normally the cooking tent was the general gathering place early in the morning and late in the evening with the corner where the sheepherders stove was located being the most prized location due to its warmth. The other tent served as the sleeping tent. Over the years, the hunters had evolved their sleeping equipment to ever better standards. Most preferred spacious sleeping bags designed to handle the cold temperatures. Originally the prime choice for sleeping bags was goose down. However, synthetics were later developed that were just as good, easier to maintain, less costly, and easier on the geese. This allowed for more spacious sleeping bags that over the course of a week of steady use were certainly appreciated.

Another item that became popular over the years was cots. These definitely made for a better nights sleep than the always uneven ground. In addition, they created a storage space underneath for personnel gear – which made for tidier quarters for all. The main drawback to cots is that one lost the insulating effect of the ground. However, that problem could be managed with air mattresses and good sleeping bags. So over the years, the equipment got better and more high tech. In many ways that made the hunt more enjoyable, in other ways it made it more domesticated. However, no matter how good the equipment, that first night back in town in a hotel room, with a restaurant, with heat, with a bed, is a luxuriant experience that those hunters will not soon forget.

An example of the spirit of that age involved how much of the gear was made by the hunters. Instead of just flashing a credit card and buying on credit, these men didn't have any qualms about making their own if necessary. One example of that was the cook trailer.

This trailer was designed by the hunter that organized the first trip to Cascade Canyon, the one that would be Legend. Not content with just any old rental unit, he designed this trailer specifically for hunting camps in the mountains. On a sturdy steel frame, a wooden box sat. Nothing special about that except that the box was divided with shelves which formed compartments for storing the cook tent gear. These compartments were removable and then could be stacked to form a pantry in the cook tent. This system allowed the hunters to keep the cooking utensils and food items sorted (more or less) instead of having them dumped into a disorganized mess. The cook trailer also held the water jugs, the propane bottles, tables, chairs, propane oven, propane stove, a fold out kitchen table complete with a sink, and all the assorted odds and ends a mountain camp might need. The design of this trailer allowed for a specific location for each of these items. In this way the available space was efficiently utilized.

On each trip over the many years, this trailer proved its worth. However as the years wore on, so did it. Despite many attempts to repair it, the wood finally became too soft and spongy. The little camp trailer had to be retired.

The First Camp

As fate would have it, the first trip to Cascade Canyon back in the seventies turned out to be one of the most difficult. Our hunters had never been there before, so that year, and for a number of years, they were instructed to meet the rancher at his ranch house, located just off the highway first. He then led them up the perilous mountain trail to their destination.

The problem with that first year was that it had snowed a great deal, and it was bitter cold. In addition, the rancher wasn't at the house when they arrived. This led to a significant delay. Eventually the rancher showed up and led them up the mountain.

The road now frozen solid was at least drivable; however, for these hunters the trip seemed to take hours. Finally they turned off down another dirt trail as the evening gloom beginning to settle around them. "You'll camp here" barked the rancher. "I need to go break some ice on the tank for the cattle. I'll be back later" he added. With that the rancher sped off and disappeared in the light snowfall.

Now our hunters really wondered what they had gotten themselves into. The romance of hunting mule deer high in the Rocky Mountain wildness faded away with realization of the task ahead. They needed to clear the campsite of snow, set the tents, and most importantly get the propane heater going. On top of all this they had to accomplish these tasks in the bitter cold of fading daylight.

It was as if the mountain was testing them. "Do you really want this?" it seemed to whisper to them "Do you really want to be here instead of a warm hotel bed in town?" This is where these men made that transition from the comforts of the modern world to a different reality – a reality that that although repressed is still present in men's soul. It is a reality that the modern world frantically seeks to level into numbing conformity and security. It is here at this moment that the hunter must face his fears and press forward. Successfully navigating this transition is a major reason why Interesting Places are still sought out. And Cascade Canyon was a very Interesting Place.

Now was not the time to let these doubts settle too long in the mind. Each member of the party set about a separate task. Each had his doubts about the outcome, but as they progressed, each seemed to draw strength from the others. Collectively they pressed forward. Here also is where their preparation and planning helped. The little cook trailer proved invaluable that year keeping everything dry and organized.

The men caught a huge break earlier in the trip when one man spied an old wheat scoop on the drive in. Sensing that they shouldn't leave that tool – despite its advanced age – on the side of the road, they stopped to throw it in the truck. Now that scoop proved invaluable. With it they could more quickly clear the snow from the site. Was that discarded scoop just a quirky happenstance, or did that mountain, although providing a difficult test, somehow make sure the test was fair by providing that one odd item? We will never know.

With the snow cleared, the tents sprung up quickly. Although these men were from the city, the circumstances seemed to bring forth skills and expertise they didn't know they possessed. And once the tents were raised, the hunters' mood brightened considerably. Soon they had a propane stove and heater running. Now dark, they had a pot of stew warming, and with drinks in hand, they could celebrate their accomplishment.

Imagine that rancher's surprise at seeing the camp at his return! Here were a bunch of flatlanders who had not only set up camp in deep snow and bitter cold, but they were comfortably enjoying themselves! The hunter's gladly offered him a whiskey and a bowl of stew when he stuck his head in the flap of the cook tent. Graciously he declined the offer. After all he had to drive back down the mountain to his home. However he added "Well I guess you guys won't freeze" as he left.

They had done it. They had met their first big challenge and passed. They had made the transition. If the mountain could have, it would have smiled. Tomorrow they would begin the first of many hunting adventures at this Interesting Place. Tomorrow they would no longer be business men, oil men, salesmen, they would be hunters.

And what became of that old wheat scoop? As a gift they presented it to the rancher at the end of the trip. He graciously accepted and added to his tools he kept at a small camp house he used up on the mesa. To this day it remains there as far as we know. This began the tradition of presenting the rancher with a gift on each trip. Over the years these gifts became more elaborate and expensive, but none could ever quite compare to that old wheat scoop.

Hunting Gear

Each hunter, naturally, was responsible for his own guns, ammo, binoculars, etc. In the early years, the first hunters were somewhat novices to the style of wide open, long range hunting required in the Rockies. After all they had grown up on farms and small towns of Kansas and Oklahoma. They were accustomed to a style of hunting that involved quick shots at close range with, let's be kind, not the most expensive of weapons. The skills they possessed had been honed during lightning fast covey rises of quail and deer hunting that involved kicking up a deer while hiking and getting a fleeting shot as it bounded away.

However, they had one among them, Wayne, during that first hunt. He was their expert in this new style of mountain hunting. So they learned from him. And in this learning there exists a great lesson: one should never let one's pride get in the way. Also one should never allow his ways to ossify. There is always something to learn, and the truly great hunters never forget these lessons.

The hunters picked up on the requirements of this mountain hunting quickly. They all became experts in long range shooting and its ways. The rifles they used had to be modified or "accurized" as they called it. This involved floating the barrel, reseating the action in epoxy for a better fit, and most importantly, hand loading their ammunition to fine tune the accuracy. They did all of these things themselves. The process, they refined and improved over the many years. From one expert, Wayne, they produced many experts in the craft – experts who would be legends and who would write their own chapters of memories in those mountain hunts.

The rifles themselves were, of course, a constant source of pride. They became each hunter's best companion in the field. Originally, when Cascade Canyon was only a deer area, the preferred rifles were the 25-06, the 280, and similar calibers. As elk hunting became more prevalent, our hunters tended towards larger calibers such as the 300 H&H, the 7mm magnum, even the 338 magnum. Whichever caliber the hunter chose, each rifle was carefully "accurized" (usually by Wayne), tuned with hand loads, and thoroughly tested at the range in the off season.

Old Reliable

For some hunters, they became so attached to their weapons that they named them. One in particular became a legend – Old Reliable. Old reliable was a pre-1964 Winchester Model 70 in a 300 H&H magnum caliber. Now I understand that this model name probably doesn't mean much to most people. Let's just say that it is a prized and rare piece among gun enthusiasts. A perfect mountain rifle, in the hands of a skilled shooter could create magic.

Ed was acknowledged by all as an expert in the shooting arts. He studied under Wayne and learned his ways. When age finally prevented Wayne from making the demanding trips, Ed unofficially took over as the expert in all things concerning rifles. Of course a person of such exalted status couldn't have just an ordinary rifle, and Ed, being an equipment guru, couldn't have just an ordinary anything. This meant he needed to procure a special rifle, and so he did.
Proud was he when he displayed that rifle the first year. It was a beauty, not in the traditional sense. The wood stock was original and showed the natural scars and wounds of a true hunting weapon. The bluing, although good, didn't have the bright sheen like a new rifle out of the box. It looked old. It looked classic. It looked special.

And it was special. Ed used that rifle on many hunts, but the gun won its title on its first elk. That year, again, the weather turned cold with snow. Ed spotted a nice bull elk from Long's Point road in the area of Conn's Creek. Remote even by mountain standards, the only way to hunt that bull was to hike, and that cold the hike proved difficult.

Still Ed moved into position. Carefully he made the final stalk paying careful attention to the wind and to his line of sight. Once he came around a small ridge he spotted the bull again. He had succeeded in the stalk. Now in the failing light of late afternoon, in the snow and cold, and with a shot in the range of 500 yards, his new rifle would be put to the test.

Carefully he took aim, but big bulls don't get big by hanging around anywhere for long. The elk moved off to the south. Ed decided to follow. Now daylight would be his enemy as much as the elements. Another stalk ensued. Again he spotted the bull. This time he squeezed off a shot which found its mark.

The big bull staggered at the hit. Ed could hear the sound of the bullet slapping the giant's side. Staggering at the force of the hit, the big bull stumbled into the brush and out of sight. Working with another hunter, they trailed the elk along a trail. Ed decided to split off and try and head off the bull. With his partner pushing the animal towards him, it came into view. Barely able to stand it wobbled back and forth. Ed was faced with another long shot.

Swiftly he set up for the shot as cold rain pelted his clothing. Already exhausted from the difficult effort, he had to put that out of his mind and focus on the task at hand. With sunset just around the corner, he needed to finish off the beast or risk loosing him. Drawing a bead on the elk's shoulder, all his experience and skill was pushed to its limit. Calmly his mind became totally fixed on the sight picture in his scope. Windage and distance already factored in he pulled the trigger. After what seemed to be minutes, he heard the slapping sound of the bullet striking the animal exactly where he aimed. This time the animal fell and didn't get up. Old Reliable had performed remarkably well. However, the gun is only an instrument. Its accuracy was no accident. Hours of fine tuning the proper loads and practice at the range had transformed it from an ordinary rifle into a legend. That is what made that rifle remarkable.

As evening fell, he and another hunter quickly dressed the animal. They would have to wait until morning to retrieve the trophy. The hike back to Long's Point road and the warmth of the truck was even more arduous. Ed's clothing now soaked with the perspiration of the effort provided minimal protection from the increasing cold. The cold rain turned to freezing rain as if to only add to his misery.

Still the new rifle had proven itself. Ed's reputation as a shooting legend now enhanced, he christened this weapon as Old Reliable. Of course, some may question if the name referred to the gun or perhaps more to Ed. We will never know.

As the years passed, Ed found it fit to pass on Old Reliable to a younger hunter. That is a mark of a true hunting legend and a gentleman, to leave a legacy. The rifle found a new life and continued to perform up to its name. Old Reliable took more game including elk and a trophy mule deer. It is a story that has not finished.

Optics and Other Gear

In addition to the rifles, our hunters quickly came to appreciate the need for quality optics in these rarified heights. The optics that worked for college football games and hunting out of a stand would not pass muster at all in these challenging conditions. Slowly, each hunter bowed to the need for high end optics. These quickly became a point of pride and debate among them. Numerous discussions of a lively nature would often ensure during the evening drinks about the advantages of Swarovski versus Zeiss versus Leica.

Soon one of the hunters reigned supreme as the undisputed expert of all hunting things optical. Ed became a legend for that reason and others. He was the go to source of information the other hunters trusted.

Of course, a hunter can get a little too carried away with all of his gear, and Ed was no exception. Once while hunting along a particular location called 4 Hole along Long's Point, a giant muley buck jumped out in front of Ed and his partner at point blank range. The other hunter wondered why Ed wasn't shooting when he realized Ed was fumbling around with his brand new Zeiss binoculars in order to get a better look at the deer. After all, what's the point of having an expensive new toy if you're not going to use it on your deer! Fortunately, that particular deer was in a forgivingly sort of mood and so it was dispatched from the gene pool in short order.

Originally the only optics our hunters utilized were binoculars and rifle scopes. The rifle scopes served not only the obvious purpose to magnify the target for the shot, but they also served as range estimators. To this end, the type of scope preferred tended to be a 6x or 8x scope whose reticle contained a thin section. By placing a target in the thin section, a hunter could estimate the distance by how much of that section was filled up. It may sound crude, but it was surprisingly effective with practice. It was always important to practice this skill at the range during pre-season and to be able to perform the necessary calculations quickly based on the scope's magnification. In the field, the hunters would be constantly "shoot" distances using aspens in case something would pop out unexpectedly.

Someone not familiar with this style of hunting may ask "why not just use as high a magnification as possible for the scopes?" Well there are several reasons. The first is that a 6x or 8x scope fit the range of shots typically encountered, which could range from point blank out to 500 yards with a 300 yard shot being typical. A higher magnification is not advantageous for close shots and only creates more wobble for the longer shots. In addition, the ranging method described just seems to fit with the 6x or 8x scopes for the typical sized animal hunted.

Although all became skilled with using the scopes as range estimators, it was only a matter of time before laser rangefinders made their way into the hunter's list of must have equipment. At first there was some resistance to using them. However, it was inevitable that they became ubiquitous as the scopes themselves. However, like any technology, these toys had their drawbacks: the glass could get dirty; the batteries could run out, the light conditions may be such that they don't work, and most importantly, they are another piece of gear to carry.

This raises an interesting question. At what point does the equipment interfere with the hunt? For our hunters, there was a sense of regret of going to the higher tech rangefinders. But what about the scopes themselves? Are they not also a high tech intrusion into the hunting experience? This is not an easy issue to resolve. After all, mankind has been using better technology to hunt from the beginning, so one could ask in the extreme if there is anything that could be considered a true "fair chase" method. Even those that shun certain technologies in favor of a more primitive experience utilize all available technological means at their disposal to make their primitive weapons as good as possible. The best answer to this question is best left to each hunter to decide, for it is the individual who must experience the hunt.

Another piece of gear which gained favor over the years was the shooting stick. Originally, the hunters used whatever happened to be available at the moment for a rest (which is definitely needed for the longer shots). However, often the only thing available in that sage brush country was a handful of branches – not very good. So over time, shooting sticks were introduced. Originally they could be quite primitive: homemade crossed sticks that doubled as a walking support. Eventually, the style that won out in the unforgiving demands of the mountain was the collapsible bipod. This could be folded up and put in a backpack during hiking and quickly set up for a shot. By setting up on a slope the hunter could be firmly seated on the ground with the rifle well supported by the adjustable shooting stick. Many a legendary long range shots were accomplished this way.

At this point, you may ask how on earth a hunter could move at all let alone function with all that equipment. Well that was a dilemma. There always seemed to be a tension from covering every possible contingency to being bogged down with too much stuff. It was a tension played out on every trip, and it was a tension that was never truly resolved.

No discussion about personal gear would be complete without mention of the clothing required for these heights. Our hunters also learned that the Rockies were very unforgiving when it came to clothing just as it was for everything else. Anything that fell short of the required quality would be quickly and brutally exposed by the high mountain elements much to the discomfort of the hunter. The weather could vary a lot during a trip and every contingency had to be planned.

Soon the hunters settled on a system of multiple weights of long underwear to meet the variable challenges. In addition, aside from the obvious need for warm clothes, it became apparent that foul weather water proof gear that covered the hunter head to toe was absolutely essential. There was no reason to go to all that trouble of getting up the mountain, if one was going to be stopped by a little precipitation.

Vital in this regard was the footwear. Ordinary boots simply were out of their element up there. The best system our hunters found was waterproof boots insulated for cold weather with removable liners. After a hard day of hiking, the inside of the boots would be sweaty no matter how cold it was. The removable liners were important because each day the sweat soaked liner could be removed and dried by the sheepherders stove. There is nothing better than a dry pair of boots when one first gets out of the sleeping bag on a sub-10 degree morning and nothing worse than having to put one's feet into boots frozen solid with the previous day's sweat.

Getting to Camp and Setting Up

Other than that the camp was very much organized on utilitarian grounds. All would participate (at least nominally) in setting the thing up. Each year the hunters coming from several states would converge at Grand Junction at a hotel that probably wouldn't make the Chamber of Commerce's list of top attractions (two stars at best) on the Thursday before opening morning. There, the hunters reunited with glee. Whiskey flowed, and stories told to the merriment of all. At this point, hunters would produce their newest prizes of equipment: a new rifle, a new pair of binocs, and in later years, new range finders. There were always admonitions to not tell the misses – best that they not know the costs. The distaff side of the equation could never appreciate the importance of such toys.

Then on Friday, the hunters would solemnly awaken early, inspect their gear one last time and have the perfunctory breakfast at Denny's. This would be their last touch of civilization before ascending the mountain. Many years, the morning discussion revolved around the upcoming weather predictions. The "mountain" at times loomed up as an awe inspiring monument of nature. "We are going up on that!?!?" was often the thought of those involved although never openly expressed.

So up to the mountain, the hunters would go. As they turned off the last blacktop, they encountered the gate. Here they would gather for the last time before the ascent. The mountain before them always looked larger than life. Here there would be a hesitation. Here they made that transition from the world and its ways to the other realm. From now on they would be wild. They would be hunters.

The gate also represented a barrier in a more direct material way. The road, such as it was, beyond the gate provided the only drivable means to access a huge acreage of prime Colorado real estate. The land was a mix of private and BLM land. The BLM land located out on Long's Point, of course could be accessed by the public but only with difficulty. The main method of public access was up a foot trail that went up about 2000 feet to the top of the mesa.

Several times our hunters encountered such hardy souls – usually about mid morning of the first day. They would appear up on top ragged and exhausted from the climb. Usually their main hunting accomplishment was to push deer to our hunters. On one such occasion two of our hunters had just finished loading up a couple of nice muley bucks from a spectacular opening morning hunt when up popped two such rugged mountain men. Imagine their disappointment at seeing, after all that physical exertion, their quarry field dressed and loaded up in the back of a pickup truck!

However, most of the hunting territory was privately owned. Originally it belonged to several ranch families who used the grasslands of the mesa tops as pasture. Once the oil shale interest kicked up they signed the land away for a large sum of money and the ranching rights for a number of years. For them it seemed like a good deal.

It also provided our organizing hunter his opportunity. See, since he worked for one of these oil companies, he had access to the contacts. The oil companies actually owned the land outright which was a somewhat unusual arrangement. So once the oil shale boomlet faded away, the land, now privately owned by the companies, was largely left to the hunters and ranchers to enjoy. Our hunters, via their work connections, had an opportunity that most can only dream about. Although the deal struck between the ranchers and the oil companies helped to create this Interesting Place, it also sowed the seeds for its eventual demise. Once again this is the great paradox of Interesting Places in that era.

In some years the ascent, although steep, was uneventful. If the weather was dry, one could make the drive in any vehicle. However, and a big however, in wetter years, the dry dirt trails would turn to the most gawd awful soupy mud imaginable. In several years, it was doubtful that the hunters could make it to their destination at all. This author vividly remembers topping a hill only to see our fellow vehicles below in various states of sliding to and fro down the muddy slope. "We chain up here" was the retort of the driver, who would become Legend.

Some of you may not have had the experience of "chaining up". Well on the down slope of a muddy road, in driving snow and freezing rain it is barely a describable situation. However, one at once knows the necessity of such action, and so however reluctantly, one will crawl underneath a vehicle in the mud to make sure such chains are properly affixed.

Eventually our intrepid crew would make it to their destination. In dry years, the trip from Grand Junction would take several hours. In wetter years, it could take the bulk of daylight. Camp was ALWAYS in the same place. This place had been set by the rancher at the first trip in the first year. Nobody dared to suggest a different location.

The location was in a draw between two east west ridges located at near the very northern most end of the available hunting territory. Upon arriving at the designated campsite, our hunters always experienced a mixture of emotions. One was relief and excitement at returning to an old friend. It was sort of like returning to a house that one had lived in very long ago. The other was trepidation. After all, the site was a grassy flat (more or less) spot at the base of an aspen grove. Normally it was covered in cow paddies – hardly the site of magic.

So after a brief lunch (it was normally lunch time by the time they arrived), our hunters would set about clearing the spot (of aforementioned cow paddies). Normally there ensued a lively discussion about where to set the tents. Arguments would be proffered as to one arrangement over the other. Finally agreement would be reached (I doubt the actual location of the tents varied by so much as five yards during all those years).

So the tents would be thus laid out and set up. Unbelievably to an outsider, the camp would take shape. Each hunter did his part, the roles cementing into form over the years to a near clockwork perfection. However, there were often glitches. Each year it seemed that the hunters had the devil of a time deciding which aluminum tent poles went with which tent. You see, although the tents would appear to be the same, they actually were different by the slightest margin - a difference that could only be discerned AFTER the poles were tried in the tent. So, each year, our hunters, after a dickens of a time sorting out the mess (much like sorting out Christmas lights each year) would solemnly swear to mark said poles so as to solve the confusion. Of course the following year the dialogue went something like "The poles with the electric tape go with the cook tent". "No they don't, they go with the sleep tent" and so forth. So in the never ending human quest to anticipate problems, our hunters just created more confusion.

But in due time, the camp would be completed. All would stand back and proclaim in the most serious tone they could muster that this was the best camp ever. Someone (someone being the Legend) would proclaim it "Elk Camp 19xx (or later 20xx)". And thus the camp was officially and ceremoniously set. Somehow it would always come together and somehow it always looked great, and somehow it was like returning to a home that you never knew you were a part of until you were there.

In some years, setting up the camp was relatively easy due to mild weather. This might seem to an outsider to be a good thing, but leaving boys with their toys with time to kill – well not so much. You see, one MUST sight in their new high tech deer rifle before opening morning. So with all due reference, there exists a certain large, bright, flat rock on the north slope above said camp – approximately 350 yards out – that is scarred with more bullet wounds than a army training site. It has been hit with more hoop and holler and whiskey drinking than a mining camp brothel. But it has served its purpose. It is like that rock was placed there for that purpose, an almost mystical purpose for a special moment in time.

In other years, camp setting up was rough, very rough. For all those that have gone camping with their families in the summer (and I am one), let me say that nothing compares to setting up elk camp in the late, dark afternoon under a steady driving mix of snow and freezing rain. The only good thing is that such conditions eliminate all dawdling. Camp got set up P. D. Q. Also our target rock got a respite on such years.

If time allowed after camp was set, our hunters simply could not resist the temptation to conduct a "scouting" trip the evening before opening. This, of course, can come to no good end. Inevitably, as according to Murphy's Law, massive bull elk and gargantuan muley bucks would be spotted – never to be seen again. However, for one young hunter thrust into this magical place and time, the images of these magnificent creatures would forever sear his memory. It was a like out of a dream from the Serengeti. Never could he image such a place with its sweeping vistas, its end possibilities. It was here he would stake his claim to being a Legend, like the Legend before him. It would be a rocky road fit for other stories.

Battle Mountain

One year after camp had been pitched; our hunters simply couldn't resist taking a scouting trip. Although the evening light was already failing, they headed out. Some took off for the north and to try and peek into the Pocket. Full of nervous energy and eager to feel the rush of adventure after a year, they hurried out before night fell.

Along the Point road, four members of the hunting party stopped at the familiar lookouts to glass and to test their new optics. At a place known as the radio tower (because as the highest point in the area it had hosted a radio facility the remnants of which still remain), they glassed off to the east and west. Here the mountain treated them to an unforgettable moment.

One of the secondary ridges that tied into Long Point takes off to the west just south of the radio tower. This ridge is a bit unusual for the area in that it has little vegetation on top thus forming a smooth flattish spine stretching out west to its end. There a round peak anchored the end – it also unusually devoid of cover. When these hunters glassed towards this peak, the site unfolding before their eyes left them dumbstruck with awe.

For there a gathering of deer of all types were forming – does, bucks, fawns. They appeared to be agitated and restless. Then these hunters discovered the cause of the scene. Two large dominant bucks had squared off. Each sized the other up and it became obvious that these big boys were going to settle matters here and now. The other deer had gathered to watch the show. Also it seemed that other animals, large and small, were gathered and watching from the edges.

With astonishment the hunters fixated on the spectacle when the two bucks went at each other with stunning ferocity. Their antlers crashed into each other. Their necks, already thickened from the coming rut, strained to twist the other into submission. Here on display and in the open was the struggle of life itself being played out. Each giant muley buck focused his entire being on the immediate task driven by an ancient prima urge. Neither would give in as the battle intensified. The other deer appeared to draw energy from the contest as they ran back and forth around the arena. Both bucks, victor and vanquished alike, would be drained after the fight. For each the fight would reduce their chances of surviving the upcoming winter. Yet they fought on.

The hunters could only watch and admire the drama being displayed for them. Nature does not recognize or understand the hunting regulations of the state of Colorado. They are foreign and artificial to it. Yet to the hunters, these regulations must be obeyed. So partly frustrated but fully enthralled they could only remain and observe. Tomorrow they could hunt, but not today. Such is the power of an Interesting Place. Always there are surprises and challenges. Long Point was such an Interesting Place even when the season wasn't on.

It was a sight that the hunters would always remember, and it was a story that would be retold many times in the future. The site from then on became know as "Battle Mountain". That ridge and knob became the scene of many adventures and successes in the future. However, it is forever known for what these hunters had observed that evening.

Opening Morning

The first night in such a storied place is not one for sleep. Lying on the ground, one heard through the earth the bugles of massive bull elk in the distance; one dreamed of the stories of older hunters in his ears. The pressure of such a situation is almost unbearable, but it is welcomed. Now would be his time, now he would write his chapters in the lore. Now was not known but it soon would be revealed.

Opening morning was always one of high anticipation. Long's Point (that most perfect of mule deer hunting locations) beaconed. The hunters hurriedly downed their breakfast – the younger hunters more so (the older hunters maintained more outward calm). All were pregnant with the expectation of the morning hunt. During its height, Long's Point (which was a very Interesting Place within a very Interesting Place) was the ultimate muley experience.

To the casual observer, all of this was perfectly insane. To those who participated; however, it was the pulse of life itself. Several times on opening morning, the combination of altitude, adrenaline, and the pressure of the unknown produced nausea in a young hunter, even after a kill was made.

This was the moment they came for – the experience whose name they could not speak. Hunting for them was more than just about the trophy, it was about the feeling the pulse of life itself. And in no place did that feeling become more real than in this very Interesting Place. Here great shots would be made, great feats be performed. Here they would become part of the history of this Interesting Place and it would become part of them.

Then, as the years wore on, the property changed from strictly a mule deer place to an elk place also. At first, to see an elk was a story worthy of the evening camp tales. Later, bull elk hunting became available. Then in the last years, elk were numerous and hunting them often was the primary focus.

These tales are too numerous to adequately relay. Some are told in depth. Some are told, simply because they must be told. What do they have to do with that Rough Piece of West Texas? Well nothing, but perhaps everything.

<u>First Night</u>

Almost every hunter that has ever taken a gun into the field has at one time or another dreamt of hunting in the Rockies. Something about the thought pulls at a person's soul in a way that few other hunting destinations can (at least those affordable to an average person). So one hunter finally got his chance to hunt along side this group, he could scarcely believe his good fortune.

However, this immediately created a problem or problems for there was so much to do to get ready. Although he had hunted for a variety of game in a number of locales, he knew he needed just about everything for such a trip. It could be a once in a lifetime adventure. One never knows when another opportunity will come along. Everything needed to be reviewed and updated if required: clothes, long johns, gloves, boots, and of course a sleeping bag. Although he had the advantage of the other hunters' experience, that at times almost provided too much information. Still as the date approached, his preparations became more determined, and he became more confident that he was prepared.

The trip proved to be a whirlwind. Everything was new to him. Imagine his reaction upon first arriving at the camp site! Here was the spot where he was going to spend the next week of his life, and it consisted of an uneven clearing at the base of an aspen thicket bordered by a dirt road. The rancher's cows had obviously been here recently and often. Staring at the place in disbelief he could hear a crow caw off in the distance as the cool mountain breeze whisked by stirring up some dust. At that moment any normal person would have thought "Man I'd give a hundred dollars to be back in town." It is at that moment when the hunter has to decide if he really wants to go through with this. It is here that he must push through his doubts and press forward.

With lingering concerns, he quickly pitched in to help set up camp with the others. Soon his initial fears began to fade as the camp took shape. Each year when the cook tent went up, everyone's spirits seemed to brighten. In the good weather, the hunters had camp set up well before dark. Like most years, they couldn't resist at this point to drive out and do a little scouting.

For this new hunter, that trip served to fill him with awe and excitement. Glassing from atop the ridges, they spotted muleys and elk everywhere they looked – at least that that's what the new hunter thought. The extent of the hunting territory stretched out over endless vistas. "Where do you even begin to hunt this place" he asked. Smiling at the question the other hunters responded "Oh, you'll learn. It appeared endless to me on my first trip."

Our new hunter did have one nagging concern. Although he had been strongly advised, he didn't bring a cot. Now he knew why the others had adapted to their use. The ground at camp was very uneven and not really level at all. It was about the flattest, most level spot around, but that wasn't saying much. The cows had trampled large holes making the ground uneven to say the least. Also the entire site sloped towards the road to the north and towards the west down the valley. At this point he didn't have really much choice except to tough it out.

Everyone heartily enjoyed dinner and washed it down with a couple of drinks. Based on the afternoon's scouting trip, every hunter glowed with anticipation at the thought of the morning's hunt. Everything to our novice hunter and camper was new and he eagerly took it all in. All too early, the hour for bed interrupted the festivities. Each wanted to get a good night's sleep for the day ahead. There would be time enough for celebrating later in the week after the tags were filled and the stories told.

Immediately our hunter knew that first night would prove to be a challenge! The combination of the uneven terrain, the constricting nature of the sleeping bag, the cold, and his nerves meant that he would get very little sleep that first night on the mountain. Maybe that's the way it should be. Such an Interesting Place tests the equipment and excites the hunter. If it didn't, well, it wouldn't be so interesting.

Yet all was not lost. Exhaustion took its toll and he eventually nodded off into a fitful sleep. Several times the sound of elk woke him. Being the only one on the ground, he had the advantage of hearing the echo of their bugling as it reverberated through the ground. Their calls shook his body like the base of a boom box on a city street. Was he imaging all this or was it real? They sounded so close how could they not be real? And how can any hunter sleep with that going on?

The next day would be his first hunting in this very Interesting Place. There would be many more. At that moment he felt the excitement of hunting in such a place; but little did he know how this place would change him, for that is what Interesting Places do.

Chapter 15 - Hunting at Cascade Canyon

As much effort as was placed into camping in this Rocky Mountain hunting paradise, the main reason to be there was to hunt muleys and elk. All that preparation, time, and expense created unbelievable memories, but that was just the appetizer. For any hunter, the mention of an opportunity to hunt mule deer and elk in Colorado sends shivers down their spines. It is a reaction that cannot be anticipated or really understood. For in some forgotten corner of every soul, lies a yearning for just such a promise. It is a promise that not only beacons but also terrifies, for in this promise we hope to discover the hidden truth to our very nature.

The Early Years

For the first year, the original hunters, while they hoped for success, they understood that the trip would be primarily a shake out, a test of the place if you will. They were all seasoned hunters and didn't really know at that time that this place, above all the places they had or were going to hunt, would be the place that dominated their careers.

The first year camp had to be set up in a terrible snowstorm. So right from the start, they were tested in a way that they didn't expect. It was actually one of the coldest years of the entire epoch.

If one could look back on that first hunting day at Cascade Canyon, one couldn't help but chuckle a little. The hunters not being familiar at all stayed within sight of camp mostly hunting the ridges to the north and south. In some respects they were taking off the training wheels a little at a time, just enough to get their feet wet (and rather cold from the snow).

They also had to prove themselves to the rancher before he would let them venture out further. This rancher was a throw back to an earlier time when a man's word was as good as any contract. So modest in his approach was he that he didn't even charge for the hunting access! Such a thing is barely comprehensible in the hunting world today which has in many areas been transformed into a big money operation. This man definitely harkened back to a different time where hunting was a privilege that was obtained by asking and by being of good character, not by the size of one's wallet.

So in order to keep in the rancher's good graces, our first hunters started a tradition of giving a gift in lieu of money. These gifts ran the gamut of items that a rancher could need: pistols, spotting scopes, belt buckles, you name it. As the years wore on, it became increasingly difficult to come up with a new gift idea, but somehow the hunters also managed. This tradition was always well received by the rancher and later his son. It strengthened the bond between the rancher and his guests in a way no amount of money ever could. The mutual respect each party had for the other developed into a true friendship. As such our hunters gave the up most care to follow the rancher's requests and respect the property.

On that first hunt, our hunter's were finally given permission to go down Long's Point after the weekend. The hunting season back then ran from Saturday through Wednesday and was strictly a deer only affair. Driving south from that first turnoff down the point opened up new vistas of opportunity that filled the first hunters with awe. Deer were plentiful in those years, and Long's Point was a muley hotspot. Under the guidance of Wayne, all the hunters filled their tags. Each vowed to return now knowing that they had stumbled onto something special.

However, their first year success didn't continue to the second year. That year the hunters saw large numbers of deer – all does with nary a buck to be had. The weather that second year was completely different. Hot and dry had replaced the previous year's snow and frigid temperatures. It was as if they were hunting in a completely different location. That second year would go down on record as the only year that our hunters got completely skunked. Not only did they fail to take a deer, but they didn't take a shot.

At this point, it would have been tempting to stop going to Cascade Canyon. But these hunters, despite their second year disappointment, knew instinctively that they had something special. It is testament to their determination that they stuck with it. As a result of their perseverance, the mountain rewarded them for many years with many great hunts. Interesting Places do that. They test the person and in this case these hunters were the better for that test.

So they came back. That third would prove to be different from the first two. Now with difficult hunting they all took a deer. Now they knew that they would be hunting at this Interesting Place for a long time.

Those early years continued as such. The quest to succeed at the ultimate mountain hunting adventure drove each hunter to perfect his skills, upgrade his equipment, and master the shooting arts of reloading. Quickly, this Interesting Place became the focal point around which their hunting world revolved. Indeed, it quite possibility became the fulcrum around which their yearly schedule revolved.

Last Day Muley

The early years although productive, were not always easy. After all, this is hunting and hunting is never pre-scripted. That element gives the sport much of its allure. The hunter can anticipate the excitement of a successful effort, but it he must be prepared to accept defeat also. There can be no triumph without denial. There can be no legends without failures.

Still it can be a cruel blow to an individual hunter who after all the effort and off season preparation comes up short on the one big hunt of the year. The hunter maybe can accept this outcome in theory, but nevertheless, the bitterness stings hard when actually experienced. It is yet another obstacle for a hunter to overcome, another test.

Failing to get the "big one" is made even harder when you are the only member of the camp with an unfilled tag. Sure, you can be gracious to others' successes and celebrate with them as they tell the tales of their adventures over the evening meal. Still it gnaws on your soul. Somehow it doesn't seem right.

Also you feel the pressure more as the talk turns to leaving. They want you to succeed; however, after their tag is filled, they begin to feel the pressure to return to family and career.

In one of those years, one hunter at Cascade Canyon found himself in this situation. Everyone had filled their tags, except him. To make matters worse, he had his chances. One seemed like a sure thing, but in hunting nothing is a sure thing. He could kick himself. It was an easy shot on a big muley. How could he miss?

Reluctantly everyone agreed that they should break camp the next morning. Nobody wanted this hunter to go home empty, but they couldn't stay any longer. They all agreed that he could hunt that last morning as they started to break camp.

The hunter knew where he would go – Long's Point. That gave him the best chance. So before dawn he took off down the Point road alone. Certainly it felt different. Gone was the opening morning butterflies, instead he felt a different nervousness. It was an uneasy feeling that he was going to have to face disappointment that year.

Another thing that was different that morning is that he had the Point all to himself. He opted to go all the way to the end. Unfortunately, he didn't see any bucks on the way to the end. Now all he could do was to set up on one of the secondary ridges that teed into the main ridge. He chose the second ridge form the Point's end on the east side. Although it didn't look like much, this little draw often produced. Deer liked to come up from the bottom to the mesa top here. They would pop out of nowhere and appear in this basin. At this stage of the hunt, he felt that this was the best play.

As the minutes dragged into hours, he fought the gnawing feeling of disappointment as it crept into his blood. At some point he would have to call it a day and a hunt. He certainly didn't want to do this, it felt like quitting.

Then in the cold crisp morning air, he caught movement in the brush. He had chosen this slope so that the sun would be at his back. Now that strategy appeared to pay off. Quickly he swung his binoculars on the area. His first instinct told him it was a buck, and his instincts proved correct. Not only was it a buck, it was a darn good buck.

Stand hunting in these slopes provided the hunter with the advantage of a stable rest for his shot. With his rear firmly planted on the ground, he could use his knees as rest for his elbows. This hunter had set up to do just this. He had chosen the spot to not only provide for a good view but to utilize the available brush as cover.

As the buck worked along on the opposite slope, he carefully lined up the scope of his rifle. This time there would be no mistake. His mind now completely focused on the task, he became totally absorbed in the moment. With consciously firing, the gun went off. It was a perfect shot. There would be no unfilled buck tag that year.

The hunter still faced a bit of a problem. You see, it turned out to be a really nice buck which is good, except if you have to retrieve it alone. Still it is was a good problem to have. As he drove back toward camp, emotions of relief mixed with pride washed over him. All the internal struggles that had built up over the last few days had been swept away. It had been a good hunt indeed. As he got close to the turnoff to camp, one question came to mind "I wonder if those guys are finished breaking camp? I'm ready to get to town!"

The Middle Years

As time rolled on, the nature of the hunting changed. Unfortunately, the mule deer numbers decreased. Some years it was difficult to even spot a buck, although most years the hunters managed to fill their tags. Instead elk became more and more numerous as the years went.

At first to even see an elk was a big deal worthy of an elaborate story back at camp in the evening. But of course, the idea of hunting them began to take hold as sightings increased. The first elk tags were the over the counter state wide bull tags which were a bit pricey for their day, and always gave our hunters pause, after all they had all come from rather humble origins and such a cost did seem extravagant.

Such a concern dearly cost Dewayne one year. Although he had gained financial success, he still greatly fretted over the costs of just about everything. This was a hangover from his hard scrabble farm upbringing. So to him the idea of paying such an outrageous sum of $125 for a bull elk tag bordered on obscene. Therefore he resisted bitterly on this score. And wouldn't you know it. There he sat, with no elk tag, one evening on Ed's ridge when a shooter bull elk strolled out in front of him within ridiculously easy shooting range.

After that, pretty much everyone would hunt with both deer and elk tag if they could (some years deer tags were hard to draw). Also they began to get cow elk tags through the draw. Thus became the arrangement of hunting muley bucks and cow elk during those years.

The cow tags had the advantage of being a lot easier to fill but still providing for a truly magnificent hunting experience. Also there was the issue of the ranchers in the area when it came to elk. The ranchers didn't mind at all hunters chasing around for the mule deer; they tended to not get excited about such game (perhaps from seeing them all year). However, when it came to elk, well that was another matter. They themselves got the elk bug bad as their numbers increased.

In addition, one rancher took to guiding elk hunts. His available territory included the area of our hunters. So although there was no hard and fast rule about not hunting bulls, our hunters instinctively understood that they had an unbelievably good deal and it was prudent to not push the issue too hard. Every year when asked about what tags they had, they could answer deer and cow elk. The answer always seemed to be well received, although nothing negative about bulls was ever said. Such is an example of the mutual respect each party had for the other.

We Found Some Sign

Although our hunters concentrated primarily on cow elk, during the best years they would occasionally hunt bull elk also. Usually, one hunter would feel the itch to forgo the cow tag and take his chances for a bull.

One such year, Bill Gentry and his partner Sledge set out on just such a quest. Having already filled their muley tags, they focused on the goal of a bull. Sledge was one of the best "Indian Guides" in the group's history. When he set out on a mission to get his partner on an animal, his effort was legendary, sometimes at his partner's expense.

So it came as no surprise that evening when the other hunters had assembled that Sledge and Bill had not returned yet. They had headed off to that great area known to these hunters as Elk World – a huge stretch of territory on the western side of Long's Point and filled with a seemingly endless supply of draws, drop offs, and hidden spits of heavy cover which could and did hide giant muleys and elk.

However, as the dinner passed and the whiskey flowed freely, talk began to focus more on what had happened to them. Ed, who claimed to have seen them in the afternoon near the pipeline right of way to the west of camp, saw Bill shoot at a bull. Although he was a good ways off, he could easily tell that the shot was a miss, thanks to his newest high tech optics. "I know what they're doing." He proclaimed. "They are out looking for that bull. But I know they missed. I saw it". As the minutes rolled by, Ed became more and surer of this occurrence and more and more demonstrative in stating it.

Just about the time that the conversation had turned to concern about these guys still out in the dark, a truck could be heard in the distance and headlights could be seen shining on the outside of the cook tent.

At this stage the drama, for those in camp, when a truck returned form the field was this: would the truck pull into a parking area and stop, or would the truck circle around to the meat pole to position itself to string up that day's kill? The later always creating great excitement in the cook tent.

So as Sledge and Bill's truck pulled up and stopped, it seemed that the only thing that would be strung up was a story about the big one that got away. "See I told you. I saw it all happen" he restated. Now in hindsight there did seem to be an unusual hesitation in Bill and Sledge's entrance to the tent, perhaps they could hear the talk about the missed shot from outside (how could they not at this point). And also in hindsight, their entrance was a bit odd in that Sledge came in all the way while Bill held back with only his head and part of his torso sticking through the tent flaps and visible.

"I saw it. I saw it. I saw Bill shoot at that bull up on the pipeline. No need to look anymore tomorrow, it was a clean miss" insisted Ed upon their entrance. At first Bill and Sledge seemed a little puzzled. "Well, I don't know Edward. I think Bill got off a good shot. He had a good hold and everything" replied Sledge in his thickest Okie drawl. "No, goddamnit, he missed" Ed argued. "Did you see any sign?" someone asked. "Well yeah, we did find a little sign" chimed Bill trying not to grin. "You did!" Ed exclaimed "What, blood, hair?" "Well, yeah, we found some blood and some hair – actually a lot of hair" replied Sledge.

At this stage, all the hunters in the camp were thoroughly perplexed none more so than Ed. "And we found this" stated Bill after a dramatic pause. With that he pulled out from behind the tent flap a large rack of a trophy bull elk that had obviously recently been cut from the body.

With that the camp erupted in madness and congratulations. Drinks were poured for Sledge and Bill, and of course everyone wanted to hear the story, none more so than Ed. It turns out that Ed hadn't seen Bill shoot at a bull. Bill and Sledge were no where near the pipeline and in fact had no idea what Ed was talking about. Bill had shot his bull late in the evening off of one of the many ridges in Elk World, well to the south. Due to the lateness, they had to field dress the animal and lay it out overnight. They could only manage to get the rack out before nightfall, and hence the lateness of the hour when they returned. The only conclusion that anyone could offer is that Ed had seen someone else, perhaps some rancher's relatives or some hunters that had hiked up from below. In any case we will never know.

The Golden Years

For a stretch of about 15 years, hunting at Cascade Canyon entered into a type of golden age. The mule deer returned to the Long's Point in good numbers, and the ever increasing elk herd provided for endless excitement on the north end. Surprisingly the number of hunters in the area dropped off also. Why this happened is not clear, but our hunters had found themselves in one of the very best hunting arrangements imaginable: light hunting pressure, plentiful game, ridiculously low cost, an almost complete absence of oil company activity.

But the most important factor in their success was the hunters themselves. They and they alone, worked to create this opportunity. They showed initiative in putting together the deal in the first place. Then they demonstrated perseverance in sticking with the place through some lean years. Constantly they worked to become better hunters, better shots, and better outdoorsmen. The system they had for camping and hunting had been carefully worked out over the years. Above all, they always were willing to put aside their hubris to learn from one another and help one another.

During these years, the hunters, who almost always hunted in pairs, would split up on opening day to maximize everyone's chances. The main dilemma was a good problem: which tag to try to fill first. On this point, there were two schools of thought. One was to go down the point and fill the buck deer tag first, not being too awfully choosy about trophy size (of course, everyone wanted a nice buck). Then one would go off for elk.

However, if one was inclined for a true trophy muley, the best way was to concentrate on that exclusively. If an elk opportunity presented itself fine, if not, then that was fine also. Often hunters would use one method one year and change the next – depending on their desire for action or their desire for that once in a lifetime buck. This natural variation had the effect of keeping everyone from stepping on each other. It also showed what a truly wonderful hunting paradise it was. After all, the style of hunting employed was completely up to the hunter. He didn't have to follow any prescribed manner set by someone else. It was up to him alone to hunt the way that mattered to him.

During the golden years, each method produced incredible results. Common was the year where every hunter tagged out on deer and sometimes all tagged out on elk as well. Rare was the hunter who left empty handed - that only happened because the hunter was focused exclusively on a high scoring muley buck or bull elk and passed on a number of excellent opportunities. The era was easily marked by pickups full of game as they rolled off the mountain each year. It all seemed so easy, and it all seemed like it would never change.

Wayne's Last Hunt

Wayne was like a father to the hunters at Cascade Canyon. He not only served as the "Indian guide" for those newbies to the mountains, he became their mentor on the art of long range shooting. He introduced them to the idea of taking more than a 100 yard shot, and he taught them how to "accurized" their rifles to the demands of this style of hunting. He was their go to guy on all questions great and small about shooting, rifles, and training.

Whatever Wayne did to earn a paycheck does not matter at this point. For what he is remembered, he is remembered as their mentor in these things. That was his legacy. Once he stepped out of the "real" world with its constant demands and crises that seemed oh so important at that moment, he became legend. In that sliver of reality left behind by the modern world, he came into his own. Here was where he excelled, and here is where he left his mark on these men.

In the early years of Cascade Canyon, he was already along in years. As those years wore on, the cold of the October mornings became bitterer each year. The hikes became more arduous. The preparations for the trip became more demanding. Eventually Wayne had to bow out; leaving future adventures to those he once mentored.

However, after an absence of many years, something stirred within him. Something told him to take one last trip. In was an insane idea really. Advanced in years, he had no business in the harsh mountain environment. The camp, although luxurious by hunting standards, was unforgiving for an eighty-something. Still he felt the need to make this one last trip.

And so that year, our hunters had an extra hunter. They treated him, of course, with the utmost reverence. At times that annoyed him. After all he wished to do his share from setting up camp to handling game. But no matter how much his mind desired this, his body told him to slow down. Best to let the younger blood handle the work. He had done it before; they still saw all of this as a grand adventure.

Fortunately, fate smiled on the hunters that year. Although, a good cold snap hit the camp early, it didn't produce blizzard conditions, and only served to heighten the hunting spirit of the camp. On that first morning the hunters buzzed with the usual excitement as they wolfed down their breakfast. As usual, they barely slept the night before. Boisterous talk filled the cook tent as the hunters planned their days in the field. Some would go north and glass back at the north ridge for elk. Others would take off down Long's Point road with various pairings turning off down different "holes" or draws. In those days Long's Point was a muley hotspot, and the thought of that morning's possibilities filled those hunters with excitement.

Wayne sat at one end of the table in a surprisingly reserved role. Perhaps it was a carryover of his days as mentor – here these youngsters still thrilled by opening morning. Perhaps he was just taking it all in – here was his hunting legacy in full flower. Perhaps he now didn't feel quite at home as if time had passed him by. We will never know.

The hunters allowed Wayne and his partner the honor of leaving camp first for Long's Point, and he didn't disappoint. Almost as if fate smiled on him, they came across a shooter soon after turning onto the Point road. Of course Wayne put it down with a perfect, textbook neck shot. His body may have been aged, but he was still arguably the best shot in camp, perhaps in Colorado that morning.

He had missed out on the elk hunting in his years at Cascade Canyon. The elk came later. Maybe that is why he took this trip. He felt he had missed out on the elk hunting there. We will never know.

With his deer tag filled, the first of the camp, he moved on to filling his cow elk tag. Ed, his partner, took him to Elk World – that vast area to the south of camp where elk often spread out after "slabbing over" from the pipeline.

It was still early in the week when they came upon that lonesome cow. Why was she there? Did fate place her there for that moment? Once again, a perfect shot and Wayne had his elk. Two perfect shots, two tags filled.

Now an elk, even a cow, is quite an animal to handle for a hunter in his prime let alone an eighty-something. No matter, the call went out, and out of the profoundest respect all of the hunters arrived to assist.

That was the end of Wayne's last hunt on Cascade Canyon. It was also his last hunt. Soon after, he suffered a stroke. He never left the hospital. It was an unfitting end to such a Legend of the mountains. Maybe he sensed this would be his last chance. Perhaps the mountains knew it also. That is why that lone cow elk appeared in Elk World in the middle of the day. We will never know in this world. But one thing we do know is that time is not a friend of Interesting Places, nor is it a friend to the men that hunt them – not even to legends.

Hunting Technique

The hunting at Cascade Canyon was about as far removed from the typical whitetail hunt as it could be. The basic technique was to work the ridges either with a vehicle or on foot and stopping every so often to glass – that is to scan the available area with binoculars. Here is where the newbie often realizes the importance of good optics. It took the very best to see game bedded down in the thick cover.

Also, for the beginner, glassing seemed endless and at times futile. However, there is a technique to glassing. The proper technique allowed one to maximize viewing of potential game laden areas with the minimum of effort, and could only be learned with practice.

This became the pattern for most of the day – glass and stalk, glass and stalk. The idea was to give each area adequate viewing while at the same time covering sufficient ground. It is quite different than whitetail hunting where one hunts for a spot and then stays in that spot. At Cascade Canyon, the first rule of elk hunting was that you didn't hunt elk, you located them first.

Once deer or elk were located, the decision had to be made on how to get up on them. This had to be learned through experience. Many stalks were not successful for one reason or another. Light and wind along with possible shooting positions had to be considered in planning a stalk. Normally, the hunters had to drop out of sight of the game to attempt to get on the best side of them. Only at the end of an arduous hike would the hunters know if they had been successful when they popped into viewing range again. If successful, the moment produced adrenaline pulsing excitement from which many memories were made.

Shooting Skills

Central to big game hunting in the mountains were the skills required to make the shot. In every way this was the big league as far as shooting technique went (at least as much as it gets in North America). A novice quickly realizes this basic fact within minutes of his first hunt, and nothing can really prepare one for it.

The advantage may seem to go all to the shooter with his high powered rifle and scope. However, once in the high country, the mountains at once seem to swallow the meager means of man no matter how sophisticated the technology. What is required still is skill.

That skill is honed year round, not just upon arrival on the mesas. As mentioned before, the rifles were "accurized". This not only improved the absolute accuracy of the equipment, but more importantly it married hunter to his most prized hunting tool – the rifle. It was via this process that our hunters in a very real sense never left the mountain during the year, and in a very real sense, their year revolved around the mountain.

Long distance shooting also requires an ability that comes through practice, and concentration. It is in these moments that the hunter meets the ultimate test of his career, and with success in these tests, the stuff of legends is made. Nothing can quite compare to the new hunters first taste of long range shooting success in these ethereal realms.

Total Concentration

There comes a moment for every hunter that has had the pleasure of hunting an Interesting Place where they remember the shot. That is the one shot that hangs in their mind as the most perfect moment where all the practice and effort pays off. That is the one experience of total concentration that sears their being in its most forgotten corner. That is the one bridge that once crossed forever changes the hunter's belief in himself. After that moment, he can tell himself that he is a good shot and believe it.

For one hunter at Cascade Canyon, that moment came in a rather unlikely setting during the golden era of that Interesting Place. As mentioned, the ranchers, who hardly bothered with the muleys, would become obsessed with elk as the number of those magnificent creatures increased in the area. Of course, being ranchers, their basic method of hunting harkened to more of a "round 'em up" mentality. So typically, during the later portion of the hunting week they would inevitably organize a drive with numerous blockers and drivers.

An elk drive, like everything else dealing with elk, was bigger and more involved than other types of game drives. Typically, the area that the ranchers liked to drive ran from a draw east of camp all the way through the ridge and draw north of camp west to the pipeline. Such an expansive stretch of county required a number of hunters for a successful drive, so our hunters usually got tapped to participate. Those that had tagged out could serve as drivers, while those with cow tags could serve as blockers in the numerous gaps in the ridge over which the elk could pour (sometimes this effect by the elk was termed "slab over"). Due to the number of hunters and the distances involved, it could take most of the morning to set up. However, once the elk got running, the action was often wild and unpredictable.

So on this bitterly cold October morning our hunters took up their respective positions for the upcoming drive. Our hunter set up at the base of the south facing side of the north ridge above camp at a location about in the middle of the drive. Other hunters strung out along the south facing slope all the way to the pipeline in the various gaps in order to catch the elk slabbing over.

After our hunter set up, he had to wait. Normally a single pistol shot signaled the drive's beginning. However, the start would be several miles to the east of our hunter, so it was uncertain if he would hear the drive until the elk got to his location. In fact, if the elk didn't cross (or there weren't any elk in the area) he would really have no idea until someone came to pick him up. All he could do was wait.

And freeze. It was a brutally cold morning, and by just sitting there, our hunter got cold despite his winter clothing. In spite of his efforts, he couldn't help to shiver as he waited.

It wasn't clear what tipped him off. Our hunter didn't hear the drive start, nor did he actually hear the elk coming. But suddenly he became aware that something was afoot, and instinctively got ready. The cold was long forgotten, as he switched into automatic.

A large herd of elk had indeed slabbed over and were trying to slip away by going along the south facing slope just under the ridge top. Our hunter tried to pick out a cow, but they were busting hard. Now if you have never seen an elk run, it is scarcely imaginable that such a large animal can run so fast. It as if they are airborne. So try as he might, our hunter couldn't get on a cow despite his desperate efforts.

That is when it happened – the moment of pure and total concentration. That was when he slipped into a sort of trance where his focus was so complete that he was only conscious of the view in his scope. He had awareness of nothing else: not the crosshairs, not the situation, not even of his own existence. And in this loss of awareness he experienced the ultimate realization.

The gun went off as a cow stepped into an opening 250 yards from the hunter. It turned sharply to its right and went over the ridge without any hesitation or outward evidence of a hit (elk often react in this way and our hunter knew that).

Trailing the elk was an easy matter. Once over the ridge one could see large blood splatters on the aspens from the elk tumbling down and crashing into the trees. It was as if someone had a large bucket of red paint and randomly splattered the aspen trunks with a giant paintbrush. Such was the end of that perfect moment in time. That was the moment that our hunter experienced the purest form of consciousness – a mental state so pure and powerful that it is pursued and at the same time feared.

Ranges, Some Very Interesting Places

Most of the Interesting Places discussed within these pages are wild places located in the field. However some very special Interesting Places for all hunters are the shooting ranges where they hone their skills.

Shooting ranges share the primary components of an Interesting Place. They are unique and rare. Often they are located outside the settled area of civilization. As such they are generally looked down upon and frowned upon. After all they are "messy" and not fitting into the sameness of the leveling encroaching around them. They are disordered and somewhat of an embarrassment of a world that would rather forget such things. They exist on the edges, on the fringes of acceptability. For that they are constantly under assault.

Two very special shooting ranges shaped these hunters. One was the Oklahoma City Gun Club. This was more than a place to sight in a rifle. With ranges out to 600 yards, a hunter could simulate the shooting situations found in Cascade Canyon. In this Interesting Place, many of original hunters learned their craft and perfected their technique.

Another was the Corpus Christi Gun Club. Primarily a shotgun club, it also had rifle ranges out to 550 yards. This was an unbelievably wonderful place to practice long range shooting. However, the ever increasing sprawl of suburbia forced the owners to modify the range so that it no longer presents the long range targets up to 500 meters. This is an example of the great incessant leveling process which is constantly on the march.

Like all Interesting Places, time was not on their side. They belonged to a previous way. That way had a different hierarchy of importance of the things in one's life. One that emphasized risk over security and that rewarded denial over indulgence. Was such a world a dream to fade away forever? The world hopes in vain for this. For the world and its ways, despite its seeming invincibility is the true façade.

The old ways may seem defeated but since they contain within them the keys to the human soul, they will ultimately triumph. I believe that the modern world senses this in its unguarded moments and for that it becomes ever louder in its bombast of sound and light.

These hunting ranges existing on the fringes of the modern world represent Interesting Places at their most vulnerable. For that they take the brunt of the modern world's wrath.

The First 500 Yard Shot

This is what it comes down to, the long shot. For one young hunter, the idea of such a feat sounded impossible. Of course so it came to pass that such a shot presented itself early in the first trip of that hunter.

The custom of each hunting pair was to trade shots. That is one hunter in the pair had the right of first refusal. This minimized confusion during a quickly unfolding hunting chance. For our young hunter it was his turn. And early in the hunt, a shot of 500 yards or there about presented itself to a decent, albeit non-trophy mule deer buck. "Do you want to take the shot?" asked the elder hunter. The only thing the young hunter could think was "Are you kidding?" Such a feat seemed to be from the realm of sheer fantasy.

So the young hunter deferred while thinking that the elder hunter was quite mad. Then the elder hunter calmly set up, and taking all due deliberant action (with a 500 yard shot there is no need to rush) fired the shot which promptly dropped the deer stone dead in its tracks. It was the most amazing sight imaginable for the young hunter. Immediately it opened up new vistas of possibilities. For until one sees such a feat accomplished, it is scarcely imaginable. Once seen it becomes a passion that can last a lifetime.

The Final Years

Cascade Canyon changed slowly over the years. The rancher's gift gave way to a significant trespass fee, which while still quite reasonable, was a departure in kind more than degree from the way business had been conducted. The gate which always beaconed as both a destination and a doorway to unknown possibilities transformed into a check station where one had to sign in and out – a sign of how the world had changed becoming ever more security conscious. The uncertain road which traversed the steep canyon walls in a violent switchback became a well maintained, widened thoroughfare which allowed even 18 wheelers access.

Of course, the big change was the level of human activity. Although the oil shale operation never returned as feared, the level of ordinary gas well drilling increased substantially in the area. Long's Point became littered with active rigs which had to be navigated to reach ever smaller tracts still available to hunt safely. In addition, field installations bloomed all over the area which cut off many of the traditional travel routes for the game. In particular, the mule deer numbers decreased significantly.

In those years, hunting success in terms of filling tags was still available. The hunters kept reminding each other that it was still a great setup compared to what else was available. However, something had changed. They no longer had the feeling of adventure which comes from escape. Instead they felt increasingly like guests, almost like intruders. In such circumstances, the uneasy balance between the two sides of the great paradox of hunting had been lost. The world which had given these hunters the means to find and hunt this Interesting Place was now leveling as it inexorably does, destroying that Interesting Place.

Also the hunters changed. Time is not a friend to Interesting Places, and is especially not a friend to old hunters. The style they preferred - doing their own camp, scouting their own game, stalk and spot hunting, processing their kill - particularly did not suit them in their advancing years. Nobody wished to admit it, nor did anyone want to end it. But eventually, the unbelievably, fantastic gift of Cascade Canyon had to end. In fact the hunters never really did end it – such was never openly admitted. After all, "Maybe next year things will be different and we can go" they would wonder. But each knew that would not be the case ever again.

Perhaps that is one last piece that defines a truly Interesting Place – they must end. The ending can be seen as a loss, or it can be seen as part of the tapestry of a life well lived. The paradox of Interesting Places can be understood but not fathomed. For how can one really understand the makeup of one's own soul?

Elk in the Snow

In the final years, activity in the area picked up considerably. Drilling rigs hummed morning and night. Many areas, especially north of camp, had been closed to our hunters. Obviously this affected the hunting. One of the final years of Cascade Canyon illustrates this change.

During the golden years, our hunters took many elk on the ridge north of camp. Now off limits, their best option to hunt these elk involved going down Long Point road to a place where they could glass back to the pipeline right of way. The idea is to see elk "slabbing over" after they came "upstairs", as the ranchers called it, and spread out over the mesa.

That year two hunters did just that. They saw the elk, in full run, cross the pipeline and disappear below the ridge line. At that moment they had to decide where the elk would probably go, and they decided to move back down the Point road towards camp. Once at this spot, they didn't see any elk cross over Long Point road and head east. Here they took an educated gamble. If the elk had come this way, but not crossed the road, they must be in a small draw just below the road on the west side.

The hunters cautiously moved into position. They split up and each moved north towards this little draw. During the night, it snowed, and now the snow blanketed the ground in a powdery white covering about a foot deep. This helped conceal their approach. Still, after they split up they moved independently so their timing was crucial.

Suddenly, without making a sound, the facing slope was covered in elk moving, but not running, up from the bottom. Spread out of the south facing slope, the combination of the morning sun and snow they stood out in an obvious manner. Here they appeared befuddled. Unsure of what to do next, they hesitated.

The hunter closest took advantage. With a good rest, he settled the crosshairs on a mature cow. Years of experience under his belt now would pay off. Patiently he waited for the right shot. Without conscious effort, the rifle fired. He kept the sight picture on the elk through the shot. He heard the whack of the bullet finding its mark. With the white background, he thought he could even see the bullet in flight. A shot that in earlier years would have proved to be a challenge now was executed perfectly by a veteran.

In the sight picture of the scope, he saw the elk flop straight down and tumble to the bottom of the draw. As it fell, the loose powdery snow gave way and formed a mini avalanche beneath the falling animal. Another shot rang out from the other hunter and the elk portion of that hunt was over.

When the hunter hiked up to the downed elk, he at first didn't see it. Then as he followed the trail down the hillside, he spotted it tucked between two large sagebrush plants. There it lay in the snow. The sight is memorable to anyone who has experienced it. The hunt now over, the elk lying in snow, to a hunter this is what hunting in the Rockies is all about.

Yet, this time, the moment was also bittersweet. This scene of the wild Rocky Mountains was being disturbed by the sound of a drilling rig just quarter mile away. This Interesting Place seemed to be melting before their eyes. Each year it was a little smaller. Each year it was a little less interesting. Time was not on its side and the hunters knew this.

Chapter 16 - John's Pocket

Perhaps no place exemplified what an Interesting Place is all about more than John's Pocket. This unique location was actually an Interesting Place within an Interesting Place. Located on the north facing side of the north ridge above camp at Cascade Canyon, this pocket not only was the site of numerous big game hunting adventures over the years, it formed the nucleus of a wider area of superb elk country that stretched for several miles east to west.

The western end of this stretch ended at a drop off from the mesa to the valley below which can only be described as spectacular. The entire draw narrowed towards this drop off becoming a large trail leading to the edge. From there, an unbelievably steep descent wound down the mesa cliff for several thousand feet to the valley below. The property available to our hunters at Cascade Canyon ended just to the north of that ridge with a fence that snaked from the drop off along the bottom of the draw and wound around north of a smaller ridge that jutted out to the east. On top of that smaller ridge sat two gas well sites. Our hunters often used those locations to glass back south to the north ridge above camp.

Elk would use this trail to come up from below to the mesa top. From there they could go in multiple directions which fanned out over the vast countryside. Often they would head north to properties not available to our hunters at Cascade Canyon. Many were the times that our hunters could only watch from one of the well sites as enormous herds of elk streamed up the large slope to the ridge to the north – on another property and untouchable. However frustrating, watching these animals on the move still provided our hunters with many special memories. After all, part of what makes for an Interesting Place is not only the animals you hunt, but the ones that you see.

John's Pocket sat at the epicenter. It acted like the central stage in a huge theater where a variety of hunting dramas could be played out. Elk coming up from the drop off could spread out along that north facing slope which allowed our hunters to be able to glass them from the well sites. Other times the elk coming up from below would, instead of spreading out along the north facing slope, turn south and go up over the ridge around the pipeline right of way. From there they would continue south crossing several other ridges. Many times our hunters sat up on the pipeline and points further south when this happened with great success.

Or, if the elk sneaked up without being seen, they would often settle into John's Pocket. The hunters referred to this unique piece of geology as a pocket for good reason. Although it occupied a surprisingly spacious piece of real estate, it is best described as a pocket due to the steep walls which form a very tight deep canyon. The walls wrap around the pocket in sharp folds that form a protective pocket that is difficult to access. Indeed, if one didn't know it was there, it would be easy to miss. From the well sites to the north, our hunters could see into the pocket a little; however, the walls folded around it so tight that it became impossible to see into the pocket's mysterious depths.

Aspens ran up the center of the pocket from below, stopping about half way up. On the east end, the pocket walls folded so sharply that they almost formed a roof. This area was full of deep thickets of tall brush which provided amazingly good cover. So tall was the brush it formed a canopy over the numerous trails cut by the elk. Often a large herd of elk would hole up in that area and remain completely unseen despite the numerous pairs of binoculars scanning the ridge. The base of the pocket narrowed considerably and flattened out at about the point that the aspens began. As the pocket rose to the top of the ridge, it widened and became much steeper. At the top, the wall became almost vertical.

Although the aspens ended halfway up, the rest of the pocket still contained thick, gnarly cover. The west side of the pocket, although still steep and protective, didn't have the extremely deep folds of the east side. At the top, the pocket formed a saddle between two higher points on the ridge top. These high points seemed to have been set there for the express purpose of marking the location from on high.

When a mere mortal stepped into this mystical realm, it was like stepping through a portal into another world. The light shone in a more diffuse, eerie manner. The air temperature became noticeably different. An almost ghostly clamminess hung in the air. Once a hunter had crossed over to this metaphysical existence, he often felt like a trespasser in a foreign dimension. Experiencing this effect, it is easy to see why the ancients would pronounce such sites as sacred. What was truly disturbing to the moderns that visited John's Pocket is that they, despite their sophisticated knowledge, felt an overwhelming desire to do the same.

Hunting the pocket required specialized knowledge. The first thing special about the Pocket was simply the knowledge of the Pocket's existence. With its deeply undulating sides, it practically didn't exist as part of this world. For that reason, many are the hunters which could be counted that quickly glassed the area and didn't see it as anything worth probing further. Any attempt to move on the pocket from below or from the sides was doomed to failure. The game held all the advantages in these attempts.

Really, the only way to hunt the pocket entailed a coordinated, well timed pincer attack with two hunters. More than two hunters would only mess up the effort. The hunters would first have to endure an arduous hike from the east before beginning the hunt. The only way to get into position was on foot. One hunter would approach from the east side and drop down to the lower portion of the pocket. From there he would have to push forward at just the right speed into the cover. Often, this hunter would never see or even hear anything despite what happened. The second hunter had to come up over the saddle above the pocket. From there he would carefully work down the incredibly steep wall to a spot where he could set up for a shot.

The tricky thing about this move is that the two hunters have to split up well before they each reached the pocket. Therefore each hunter had to pull off his part completely blind to what the other hunter was doing. If their timing was off or if either's approach not precise, then the entire effort would be for naught. However, if they hit their timing correct, the elk would be pushed out of the deep cover on the east side to the pocket bottom or up the slope on the west side. From there, the hunter at the top could take a 200-400 yard shot. If everything went exceptionally well, the first hunter could possibly get a shot if the elk streamed up high over the west end. That shot was considerably longer and more challenging since that hunter must first find a way to see that slope. The pincer move also had to be carefully planned so that each hunter knew where he could and could not shoot. Several times, the game did not cooperate in the manner described and therefore our hunters had to pass on a shot for safety reasons.

Another important factor in a successful pocket hunt included when the hunt would take place. If the hunters attempted the move too soon in the week, nothing would be there, and the area now contaminated would probably not hold any elk before the week's end. Therefore, the hunters had to resist the temptation to hunt the pocket directly too soon. Our hunters had to realize that, although the pocket formed the center of the elk activity along that slope, it itself was fragile and easily messed up. Once messed up, our hunters could only wait to the following year for another attempt.

What really happened in each pocket hunt is that the place changed the hunters. Gone were corporate employees, managers, salesmen, engineers, and bureaucrats. In the pocket, there was no organization to loose oneself. Instead, the modern man receded and a different soul emerged in the same body. This reawakening always startled the hunter. It was as if he had rediscovered a lost friend, a friend whose ways can be quelled but never entirely extinguished. This untamed piece of the human soul startles not only the individual but the entire modern world which relentless seeks to level such untidiness.

Success in John's Pocket depended on a rare balance of caution and aggression. The pocket tested the hunter's patience, shooting skills, physical fitness, and determination. However, nothing could compare to the end of a successful pocket hunt. The feeling of accomplishment overwhelmed a hunter as he stood above his elk lying at the base of the pocket. He had entered another (dare we say sacred) realm and come away profoundly changed, and isn't that the main purpose of a really Interesting Place?

These facts alone would qualify the pocket as an Interesting Place. However, in addition to its location and its special physical features, the stories of the hunters who trod there truly established John's Pocket as an Interesting Place within an Interesting Place.

Giant Muley

Giant muley. Those words strike a shiver down every hunter's spine in a way that no other description of a game animal can match. Elk may be the Imperial Deer and masters of the high Rocky Mountains. White tail deer may epitomize big game hunting in North America. However worthy and awe inspiring these and other big game trophies may be, nothing quite compares to the excitement generated at the thought of a giant mule deer buck in his hidden mountain lair.

They exist almost as regal ghosts in the minds of hunters. They combine the elements of rarity in number, difficulty in reaching, and requiring the best stalking and shooting skills to take, which gives them a unique status among big game animals. They exist in the high mountains like elk, but the monsters of their breed hide out in nearly unreachable solitude like white tails. They do not exist behind high fences nor do they congregate in giant herds in the open. For these reasons, a giant muley trophy is always seen as legitimate in the eyes of hunters for rarely can they be taken in an easy manner.

When hunters were asked in an informal poll "If you only had one last hunt in your life, and had to choose between a once in a lifetime elk, white tail, or mule deer..." Without finishing the question, the hunter so queried almost always answers "muley". A trophy mule deer often defines a big game hunter's career and validates his status as a legend among his peers. And one special giant muley defined not only a legend's career, but defined John's Pocket as a very Interesting Place for all time.

During the fourth year at Cascade Canyon, our hunters definitely began to feel more comfortable with their surroundings. They began to get the camp organized in a more efficient manner, and they were sorting out how to hunt this vast wilderness effectively.

Their early attempts had been successfully but only because of a combination of two things: beginner's luck, and Wayne's experience in the art of long range shooting. Now in their fourth year, gone were the white tail weapons fit for close range shooting. Instead each hunter had upgraded, under the expertise of Wayne, to high barrel velocity, flat shooting, accurized rifles fit for taking a mule deer at long mountain ranges. From their first timid steps out to Long's Point, now they ventured out more freely, increasing the range of their hunting realm.

One hunter that year, the one who would become Legend, was a particularly adventuresome sort. His experience in all types of hunting involved a style that was more "flush 'em out then shoot them like quail" than traditional deer hunting. Never wanting to be still, he preferred to be constantly on the move.

Actually this style of hunting, properly applied, is a very good technique in an environment such as Cascade Canyon. A white tail hunter in more civilized settings must first hunt for a place to hunt and then figure out how to slip into that place and sit tight. Hunting in this high mountain terrain, involves a more aggressive approach. The hunter must cover a lot of ground first to locate the game and then figure out a way to stalk them. Our hunter's style once properly refined was ideal for success on the mesas.

He had always been intrigued by the ridge north of camp. It jutted up about 800 to 1000 feet above the bottom and ran the length of area from the road to the mesa drop off. To our hunter, it just looked like great hunting country. In fact, the first morning of the first year, when our hunters first timidly ventured out in their snow covered paradise (staying within sight of camp) he had jumped a small buck by hiking along the camp side face of the ridge. He had vowed to hunt its length and to see what lay on the north facing slope of this intriguing feature.

A word must be added here about a hunter's fitness, by that I mean physical fitness. In any setting, fitness equals access to more hunting opportunities. The ability to move on foot and cover ground is an advantage whether one is hunting muleys in the Rockies or squirrels in a forest just outside the suburbs. However, to hunt that north ridge, required top level fitness that not all hunters possess. This is one factor about high mountain muleys that is almost true, and that is one reason why a giant muley trophy is so coveted. It can't be faked, or acquired with any lesser means. It must be taken by matching one's abilities and fitness to the world of the muley. This is why a giant muley embodies the very mystery of the Rockies.

The planned hunt that day began several miles to the east. The hunter would then ascend to the ridge top and then carefully work back to the west by ducking just below the ridge line on the south side and crossing over at various points to the north side. All the while, he would be careful to hunt methodically each nook and cranny. Eventually he would end up at the mesa drop off on the west side and then hunt back to camp. Just to walk this route in the thin mountain air while carrying about 70 lbs of gear would be difficult enough. However, he would also need to maintain complete mental sharpness as he carefully worked out every possibility. The circuit would take most of the day, and he planned for that by taking food, water, and everything else needed for an all day ordeal.

After all the other hunters sped off in the predawn dark, our hunter prepared for the effort to come. Sitting alone at camp his mind couldn't help but race with thoughts about what could lay on the other side of the ridge. He quickly tried to excise such flights of imagination in order to maintain his calm.

Once sufficient daylight unfolded, he began his quest. The initial ascent was more difficult than anticipated. This slope's beginnings were gentle with only sagebrush to navigate around. However, once he climbed up about half way, the slope steepened considerably. The brush there turned savage. It quickly thickened into an almost impenetrable tangle of sharp thorny branches that seemed to reach out and grab each piece of clothing with every step. He had to be careful of his gun in this brush. Several times he had to hold it low while he bent down almost to the ground to pass through a particularly bad patch.

With effort, our hunter worked through this obstacle with stealthy effectiveness. Suddenly near the top, the thickets broke open and hiking became easier. He emerged from this tangled mass of brush scratched and bleeding from several wounds. Now his effort would be rewarded. He could now begin to put his plan into action. Now the hunting would begin.

Slowly he worked his way along the ridge top in a stalk and glass fashion. He would stay on the south facing slope in order to maneuver west to the next area he wanted to hunt. Once there he would move over the top of the ridge to the north. From there he would pause to glass the area. Several times he did this. Each area he glassed looked interesting for he was definitely in good hunting country.

He noticed that the north slope had a different feel to it altogether. While the south facing slope was dominated by sagebrush and thick heavy brush, the north slope was more wooded with aspens. Each area he checked out carefully before moving on, but in the early going he had no luck.

As he worked west, he noticed that he was definitely working uphill. The ascent became arduous when he reached a high point in the ridge line. Instinctively, he moved in a cautious manner to check out what was behind this peak. On the other side he noticed that this high point formed one end of a very distinct saddle. Below the saddle, there seemed a good area to hunt. He had arrived at John's Pocket.

As before he dropped down to the south below the ridge line and worked his way to the middle of the pocket. Then he carefully came up over the saddle to view the other side. The view below astounded him. Completely hidden from view until he came right up on it, lay the most magnificent pocket imaginable. Here he lingered, careful to glass every corner.

However, he didn't see anything. Our hunter simply couldn't believe that such a wonderful area could not hold any game. "Did I bust it up?" he thought. Still he waited, and glassed. He couldn't quite bring himself to leave. The area just looked too good.

The minutes rolled by, and still he waited and glassed. Several times he moved slightly from one side of the pocket to another in order to get a better angle on the cover below. And still nothing appeared.

After what seemed like hours, he began to wonder if he should move on. He would make a mental note of the area and come back in the future he thought. Then just as he began to move on, he caught a glimpse of movement at the very bottom of the draw on the east slope.

The old buck which had holed up in that pocket had detected the hunter before he even moved over the ridge. You might think that a deer would bolt at that point, but he didn't become an old, seasoned buck for nothing. In the thick cover of the pocket, the buck had all the advantages. He was well hidden, and had the wind in his favor. Nothing was going to sneak up on him. No, the best course of action was to sit tight and let this unknown danger pass by - as similar dangers probably had many times before.

However, the longer the hunter remained at the top of the ridge, the antsier the buck became. For one thing, this unknown danger should have moved off by now. Maybe the buck wasn't undetected after all. Another thing was the scent. The longer the hunter stayed there, the more his scent wafted into the area.

Finally, the buck couldn't take it any longer. He felt that he had to make a move. Still experience had taught him not to just bust out and make a run for it. No that is a sure sign of youthful inexperience. Instead, the old buck tried to use the cover to his advantage by quietly slipping out the bottom of the pocket unseen.

It could have been a flick of a tail, or perhaps a quick flash of brown in a tiny opening. Whatever it was, our hunter swung his full attention to that area on the west slope of the pocket. Frantically scanning between the thick cover, he finally caught a view of the deer. The hunter's jaw nearly hit the ground. It was a true giant – the kind of muley that normally graces the cover of magazines.

For a minute he had to make sure that it wasn't a bull elk, but there could be no mistake. The neck of the monster grew thick and imposing connecting to a massive chest that looked more like a bull's body than a deer. The hunter quickly got into position for the shot. He quickly put all thoughts about the deer's size out of his mind and focused exclusively on making the shot, for he was no rookie at this game either.

The hunter got a good broadside view as the deer had to cross though a small open area. The cross hairs of the hunter's new accurized, long range rifle settled on the deer's shoulder. All of the off season's work of shooting practice, "accurizing" a new rifle, and trying new loads would now be put to the test. He didn't have time to find a rest for the rifle, so this would be an offhand sot. Then without warning to the hunter, the gun unconsciously fired. With the hit, the giant muley turned 180 degrees and ran straight underneath our hunter. Quickly our hunter reloaded and fired at the deer on the run. The bullet found its target. At the hit, that deer did the most remarkable thing. It flipped end over end and crashed into the brush. End of story.

Well not quite. You see, the first adventure in such an Interesting Place as John's Pocket just couldn't end in such non-dramatic fashion, and it couldn't end without demonstrating at least one more lesson in high mountain hunting. A less experienced hunter, anxious by such a once in a lifetime trophy, may have been tempted to quickly claim his prize. That would have been a big mistake, because although the shot was well placed, the deer was not exactly fully broadside. The bullet hit behind the lead shoulder blade and passed through basically severing the front leg. After it turned and ran it was only on three legs.

The second shot at first appeared to put the animal down for good, but the hunter waited. Soon he noticed movement. Then the buck appeared to stop moving. Our hunter, still cautious, remained at the ridge to make sure his trophy was down for good. And a good thing he waited, for he then spotted the buck, on its belly, crawling through the grass toward the bottom of the pocket. If the deer made it to the aspens, there would be a good chance that the hunter would loose him. Horrified at this development, the hunter fired several more desperate rounds at the unseen target in the grass. Soon the movement stopped. End of story.

Once again, not quite. Incredibly the buck got up one more time. Our hunter could see that the deer was now on two legs – one front leg and the opposite back leg. The second hit, although it caused the deer to spin around, had hit the buck in one of the back legs rendering it useless. Now things were getting really testy. The deer by now had worked his way down almost to the aspens making the shot longer and more difficult. Also, our hunter had to be concerned with his ammunition supply. Carefully the hunter lined up shot with his next to last round of ammo. The deer now barely able to move turned to show a perfect broadside. Calming his nerves, the hunter carefully took and aim and fired. The deer fell straight down again crashing in a thicket of fallen tree branches. End of story.

Well it wasn't quite the end of the story yet. Our hunter, more cautious than ever, waited for hours, or so it seemed. His body was now shaking visibly from the wild swings of emotion from the ordeal. Part of him wanted to rush down, and part of him, still leery of a creature that seemed to be impossible to kill, wanted to wait. At last he regained his composure. There had been no sign of movement from the area where he fired that last shot.

Finally he left his perch to hopefully claim his prize. Slowly he worked down the step rim of the pocket, stopping occasionally to glass the area and make sure that the deer hadn't started to move off again. Soon he worked down to where the aspens began. Then he saw it. It loomed up like a dream "Could I have really done this" he thought to himself. Then looking at the huge wide rack sticking up from the tree branches, he had a terrifying thought "Oh my God, I killed an elk." Quickly he reassured himself that it really was a deer.

It is a peculiar mix of emotions that any hunter feels when he comes up on his kill. The scene is surreal. At once the deer appears to be a normal part of the environs and at the same time, it seems oddly out of place. For it is at that moment that the drama just played out becomes all too real. No longer just a theoretical chess match, the finality of the act infuses that drama with a primal sense of accomplishment that cannot be duplicated anywhere.

The muley buck was a true giant. Not just a good buck or a trophy, this was the very definition of a once in a lifetime trophy. This may sound odd, but that hunter, who would become Legend, never sized the antlers. In some strange way, such an act seemed both unnecessary and somehow unseemly, like desecration. It was unnecessary because one look at that mount brought face altering expressions mixed with silent awe. It was desecration because it seemed belittling for such a magnificent symbol of the wildness of the Rockies. No, the majesty of this regal animal cannot be measured in inches and is best kept unknown – a sign of respect.

The deer's body was enormous. So much so that our hunter then realized that he had no way of effectively recovering it from this remote mountain slope. At that moment, our hunter felt just how alone he really was, and just how magnificently wild and special was that pocket. After he found his deer at the foot of the aspens, our hunter carved his name along with the date and a description of his trophy on the trunk on the biggest aspen. The inscription remained for many years, and it always brought back fond memories to the hunter when he passed by (usually after another successful pocket hunt). However, time would not be a friend to the inscription as it is not to Interesting Places or Legends.

Eventually, he went back to camp to find help. The hunters found a deeply rutted and long abandoned trail that came in from the other side to the base of the draw. That road would be the scene of many successful recovery efforts in the future. By now, late in the day, our hunter with help from two others loaded the deer into the back of a truck. Somehow that act sent a shiver of emotion through the hunter. He had done IT. He had hunted a giant muley in its environment. He had planned the hunt and successfully executed the hunt, a hunt which demanded skill, patience, preparation, conditioning, and luck.

Our hunter had the giant muley mounted which was not common for him. Hunters who have seen many impressive deer mounts are always amazed by this one. Not only large and massive but very symmetrical, many comment that this was the finest mule deer they had ever seen. Today that mount resides at a feed store in a small town. Somehow it never fit in a home. Such a specimen demands to be seen in public as testimony to that day's hunt in the Pocket.

For our hunter, who would be known as Legend, his memories about that hunt in latter years weren't the antler size. Instead he remembered an epic struggle in an untamed wilderness in a very Interesting Place. And he would always remember his name carved on the trunk of that large aspen in the Pocket as a mark of his personal triumph.

That hunt defined John's Pocket for all time as an Interesting Place in an Interesting Place. Many other successful hunts would be had there over the years. However, that one giant muley remained as the symbol of high mountain big game hunting and of John's Pocket.

Race to the Top

Not all pocket hunts utilized the normal tactic with two hunters hiking up to the pocket and performing a two man push and bloc maneuver. One memorable hunt involved quite a different approach that resembled more of an Olympic track event than traditional hunting.

The Pocket formed a central point in a larger area of fantastic elk hunting. Often the ranchers would form a drive late in the season over this area. They would begin far to the east and position blockers at strategic saddles on each side of the valley. Then they would drive down the valley to the west and hopefully push elk out over the top of the ridges to the shooters. John's Pocket sat on the north facing slope of the south ridge of this valley and often the action on these drives revolved around the pocket.

On this hunt, it had been particularly cold and snow covered the ground in patches, becoming deep in the more shaded areas. It was a about mid-morning and two of our hunters were glassing for elk just off Long's Point road, not far from camp. This was a good area to glass because one could look back to the northwest and have a clear view of anything that crossed the pipeline (located along the same ridge as the Pocket but to the west). Suddenly another truck with two other hunters in the party came racing toward them. Barely slowing down they yelled out the window "They're driving the ridge north of camp". As they started off, our two hunters asked "where are you going"? "Pipeline" was the answer as the truck sped off.

How these other two hunters found out about the drive is still a bit of a mystery. Perhaps they had seen the ranchers set up. Perhaps they crossed paths with some of them. No matter, there wasn't any time to waste on figuring such things out. Our hunters needed to act and act fast.

Basically they had two choices. One was to stay about where they were at. They could glass and see anything coming over the ridge and possibly intercept those elk as they crossed Long's Point ridge. The other was to try and get in position along the ridge also. They elected, without much debate, the latter. If they could reach the ridge and get into position, they would increase their odds significantly. If they were late, well, they would have to listen to everyone else's stories that night. The race was on.

Rapidly they piled into the truck and drove to where the road intersected the ridge. Without taking much more than their rifles and backpacks, they sped off up the slope. Normally to hike up this ascent was a grueling enough workout. However, they were not hiking, they were running – well running as well as one can in full gear and heavy mountain boots. Still they only slowed down to crash through the thick brush near the top and to catch a couple of short breaks as they made their way to their final destination – the Pocket.

Once on top of the ridge, the hiking, er, running was easier along the main game trail there. At this stage, their lungs screamed at the lack of oxygen available in the thin air. Still they knew that time was short – all their effort to this point would be wasted if they didn't press on.

Finally they reached the pocket. One hunter dropped down the slope just to the east of the Pocket. This was an area that elk would often double back and "slab over" the ridge. The second hunter continued to the Pocket and got in position just below the ridge in the Pocket's saddle.

Once in position, the first hunter immediately located an aspen that he could use to brace his rifle. As his lungs heaved from the exertion, he quickly checked his shooting lanes through the brush. Straight in front, he had two really good shooting lanes almost to the bottom. He then swung his rifle to his right to check what lanes he had. The picture in his scope made him completely forget his burning lungs.

To his right, about 20 yards away, stood an entire herd of elk that had stopped just below the ridge top (so much for long range shooting expertise). They were all ready to "slab over" but had stopped to look back down to the bottom. If the two hunters had been two minutes late, they would have missed them. Without breaking stride, the hunter picked out a cow and fired. Down went the elk.

With that, the entire mountain side erupted in elk frenzy. The elk had no idea from where the shot came and had no idea where to go. For the next 30 minutes, elk ran back and forth along the ridge in utter confusion. Some went over to the pocket where the second hunter picked one out and dropped it. After that the two hunters filled their cow tags, they could only watch as the elk franticly ran around them. At times they became concerned that they could actually get run over! Once, a nice bull stood in front of one the hunters for several minutes unsure of what to do.

Soon enough, the two hunters heard shots from all directions around them. One in the rancher's party took a bull, maybe the same one our hunters had seen. The two hunters that had gone to the pipeline also got action and filled their cow tags.

All in all, it was an exciting and action filled elk hunt. Far from the typical day in the field where patience is in a virtue and slow, deliberate movements are best, this hunt rewarded determination, fast action, and physical fitness. Of course such an unusual hunt had to occur in an Interesting Place, and no place was more interesting than John's Pocket.

Putting on a Show

Not all hunts followed such a typical script of course. One such hunt happened late in the week in John's Pocket.

Normally late in the week, the hunters had pretty much tagged out and had started to think about returning to town and the warm hotel beds that awaited them there. However, there still existed a cow elk tag to fill, so our hunting pair decided to put on a stalk on John's Pocket the next morning.

After discussing this plan the night before, several of the other hunters who had heard such great tales of the Pocket, wanted to witness the act for themselves. They decided to drive to a gas well location well to the north in order to be able to see back to the pocket to the south. The hunters making the stalk would hike from the base of the ridge to the east and make their way along the top until just before reaching the Pocket before making the final stalk.

On that morning, the hunters set out on their hike while the other hunters, now spectators, drove to the well site. Once at the well site, the spectators glassed back into the pocket in vain for any sign of game. There didn't seem to be any elk anywhere along the length of that slope. Still they waited, knowing that it would take the hunters to make their hike along the ridge top.

When the hunters got close to the Pocket, one dropped down below the ridge to the south, circled around and came over the ridge a shooting location directly above the bottom of the Pocket. He was the blocker. The other shooter dropped down low on the north facing slope below directly to the east of the Pocket and went straight into it. He was the driver.

The spectators could easily see all this take place from their viewing perch. The two hunters had appeared suddenly from the south facing slope; however, the spectators, having not seen anything, didn't expect much of a show.

There was a reason they didn't see anything. The Pocket with its deep and sharply defined sides could blanket even an army of elk out of sight. Elk loved this area as it provided maximum protection, and they often flowed into it during the gun season after being pressured to come up to the mesas from below.

As they split up, the hunter at the top began his trek first. The idea was to coordinate both hunters' movements so that they emerged from the brush at approximately the same time. However, this time the top hunter got to his perch early. There he set up and waited for what seemed to be much too long. Slowly disappointment seeped into his mind. "Well looks like there'll be no show today" he thought to himself. Any moment he expected to see the driver emerge from the impenetrable brush below.

Just then, something caught his attention, a sound perhaps. Quickly he readied his rifle. Soon the Pocket filled with the sound of crashing elk. He couldn't yet see them due to the thick brush, but elk being large animals do not run through the brush silently. Then he began to see animals appearing at the edge of the thick brush. They hesitated before entering the clearing in front. No doubt they did not want to bust out in the opening; however, they felt the pressure from the driver to their rear.

Finally the lead cow leaned forward just enough for the hunter to fix the crosshairs of his gun on its shoulder. With a startling bang, the rifle fired. In the misty, early morning shadows of the Pocket, the hunter could see the flames at the end of his rifle as he concentrated on seeing the bullet all the way to its mark. At the moment of truth, the total focus of these hunters often was so intense that they could see the bullet in flight. It was too dark for that in this case; however, the hunter did hear the bullet strike the elk with a loud and unmistakable WHAP.

The cow crumbled to the ground without taking another step. Elk continued to pour out and stream over the west slope in amazing numbers. However, the hunt was finished. Tag filled, the hunters met at the bottom of the Pocket where the elk lay. There they congratulated each other. It is always an oddly strange feeling at the end of a successful hunt. All the preparation, effort, and anticipation now are over in a single moment. Standing over his trophy, the hunter's mind begins to experience a flood of emotions which can be alarming and overwhelming.

Soon though, this hunter's mind cleared with the thoughts of the task ahead. That is one element of elk hunting. The enormity of dressing and transporting such a beast quickly brings the hunter back down to earth. As the old elk proverb goes "Once the shooting stops, the fun stops and the work begins". And that was true enough in this case. After the celebratory handshakes and pictures, the two hunters quickly set about dressing the animal and quartering it for transport.

The hunters dressed the kill in short order and soon were carrying the various pieces down to trail for transport to the old abandoned jeep trail. It would take the balance of the day, but they had plenty of time. The hunt now over, they could afford to let down their guard and enjoy the spectacular views of a true mountain wilderness as they went about their work.

Each time someone passed through the Pocket, they always stopped at that aspen which had the inscription carved by the hunter of the first Pocket hunt. Each time it brought back memories of previous hunts there. For the one that carved the inscription the memories held even more meaning. That aspen now was much older and the inscription was becoming more difficult to read. Still it was like seeing an old friend.

Once back at camp, the two hunters met up with the other hunters who had been spectators. They were amazed. "How did you know there were elk in there" they asked. "We didn't" was the reply. "Well you guys put on one heck of a show".

The Pocket Experience

That last quote wasn't only true of the hunters in the story; it was true of John's Pocket. Every time hunters stepped into that extra-worldly realm, magic seemed to always happen. The Pocket provided the unique and almost perfect balance between hidden mountain wilderness and accessibility to the modern hunter. It combined the best elements of adrenaline pumping excitement with the uncertain nature of a true wild chase hunting experience. The Pocket always put on one heck of a show. In the purest way, John's Pocket epitomized what an Interesting Place is all about.

Chapter 17 - Lightening is going to Strike

Many times in life, we are faced with turning points. Often times these take the form of a crisis such as a personal tragedy or setback. They may also take the form of something positive like a new child, marriage, or career. It is at these turning points that a person's life is shaped. These moments act like the thin portion of an hourglass which delineates two distinct regions from each other, so that although they are connected, they are separate. Once a person passes through, they are changed. What used to feel so normal and permanent now seems distant, like it was a different person in a different life. And in a very spiritual sense that feeling is true.

In hunting, these moments can often take the form of a loss of confidence. The pressure that a hunter often feels can transform the experience into a type of burden. This sense can be magnified by the setting and by the expectations. Of course a setting like Cascade Canyon can magnify these expectations like no other. That is a strange thing about Interesting Places. To be truly interesting they must test the hunter, but in that test lies the possibility of failure and disappointment. Interesting Places change those who pass through them; however, the outcome is neither scripted nor guaranteed.

One may think that it is quite a leap to compare a crisis of confidence for a hunter to some of the other crises that people face. How can going home empty handed possibly compare to a natural disaster, a layoff, or a loss of a family member? And you would be correct. We all face these turning points whether we want to face them or not. Often we avoid them at all cost, but no matter, they will find is one and all. It is as if these moments are necessary to prepare us for something else beyond this life.

The difference is that hunters will place themselves in these situations voluntarily. They crave the challenge. There is a piece of each man's soul that wishes to be tested. There is a need to for each man to discover who he really is. Hunting fulfills many people with this challenge.

In hunting the future always remains unknown. What lies beyond the next ridge, what waits in the early morning light remains hidden until time unveils it. No matter how much the hunter has prepared for that moment, he does not know how he will react or what the outcome will be.

That is why Interesting Places matter so much. Those places that have not been leveled to the point where everything is safe and predictable hold the key to this experience. That is why these places shape the person and not the other way around. That is why there can be no true hunting experiences without these Interesting Places and why they are so valuable.

Because this need to discover one's true person is so basic, many search for substitutes such as sports, or they launch into their work. Perhaps they seek out this testing in more destructive avenues such as crime or violence, or they shirk from the challenge altogether by "dropping out". In a strange way, nothing civilizes a man quite like hunting, which many consider a needlessly bloody pursuit. Hunting provides that outlet with a true test posed by nature and causes a man to channel his instincts towards positive ends.

In hunting a crises of confidence can start out in many ways. Maybe a blown opportunity or a missed shot starts the process. Or worse, a wounded animal that is lost can shake a hunter and cause doubts to enter his mind. Perhaps he suddenly finds that he has developed "buck fever" – that horrible nervous shaking that can overtake even a seasoned hunter without warning.

However it starts, once the doubts begin, they seem to feed on each other until the hunter finds that he is in a slump. Here is the turning point. Here the hunter must face his fears and conquer this challenge or risk leaving the sport. For one young hunter at Cascade Canyon, a turning point like this appeared suddenly on one trip. For him, this expedition to the mountain would either be a disappointing failure or a personal triumph. This Interesting Place would pose the test; the hunter would have to face it.

In hindsight, one could see that this hunt would be a challenge. Despite a hunter's passion for his craft, the constant drumbeat of everyday life angrily demands all of one's time. This year was a particularly bad one for preparation. For one thing there was a new job in a new city. All the pressures of moving and of adjusting came crashing down on this young hunter just before the trip. He had little time to prepare, and he would pay a price.

Off season preparation does more than just sharpen the physical skills, as important as they are. Target practice does more than just improve shooting skills. It focuses the hunter's concentration. With each shot he replays a scene from the mountain in his mind. The time spent testing new bullet loads does more than just improve accuracy. It creates a bond between hunter and rifle. The effort expended in maintaining his equipment does more than just keep it in order. It forces the hunter to constantly imagine the upcoming challenges on the mesa. These acts prevent the normal rhythms of daily life from breaking that connection to the mountain. That is the true value of preparation.

However, that year he didn't have time to worry about preparation. Besides, he now had several successful hunts under his belt. He had taken white tails in Texas, muleys in Colorado, and of course elk. By any measure he had to be considered an experienced hunter. All in all he was making a serious mistake – complacency.

The mountain will not tolerate that, it will not consider past glories. It does not care about the individual's desires. The hunter cannot reason with the mountain, for it takes no notice of him. The drama that the mountain will provide only lies in the future. Each season, the hunter is tested. Each day of that season, he steps onto the stage – novice and grizzled veteran equally treated. Hubris is a weakness that the mountain will seek out and expose, and that formed the context of this hunter's crisis.

Despite the hurried and last minute preparations, the trip went smoothly enough. It certainly felt good to see the old familiar sights along the way. That is one of the pleasures of a yearly hunting expedition. The familiarity of the travel part of experience brings back past memories. Each stop along the way becomes like seeing an old friend. Even seemingly ordinary places, such as a certain breakfast diner, can mark a stage in the long trip. This almost repetitive ritual while traveling provides an almost necessary balance to the uncertain and unknown adventures that lie ahead up on the mountain. The ritual involved can seem almost necessary to a successful hunt.

This year the traveling went off with the usual ritual. The hunters stopped in the same towns and in the same hotels over their multi-day travels. They ate at the same restaurants. They even stopped at the same gas stations. Once all the hunters rendezvoused in Grande Junction, they would even have their last dinner and breakfast at the same locations. At times one would swear that they ordered the same darn thing each year.

However, once this hunter stepped out of the truck at the campsite, he instinctively knew that something wasn't quite the same. Normally the arrival at the campsite is a cause for a quiet celebration in the mind. Here he had returned once again to this old familiar clearing with the familiar covering of cow paddies. In this moment of arrival, one's senses become alive in a way forgotten since the last trip. The aspens behind camp form an eerily beautiful sight. Their leaves, long dropped, blanket the clearing in a thick mat which creates a sweet aroma full of nature. The hunter can almost taste the mountains in the shockingly fresh air. Yes, there is always something special about being in the mountains. And that special feeling is only amplified by stepping onto the mountain the day before opening morning. The long journey over, the hunter could begin to look towards the week's adventures. "What will we find tomorrow out on the Point? I wonder if there are any elk up in the Pocket?" he would say to himself. Each member of the party felt the same electricity of what lay in the future as they briskly worked at setting up camp.

This time it was different for our hunter. Instead of anticipation, he felt a strange unease. He felt like he had been suddenly uprooted and plopped down in this strange spit of wilderness in a flash. He hadn't crossed that invisible boundary from the present world to his primitive past to face the challenges of the future. Here the sod beneath his boots felt strangely unwelcoming. Instead of feeling reinvigorated by the mountain, he felt as if he were going through the motions as if in a trance. It was in that moment that our hunter sensed his lack of preparedness.

Still he participated in the usual activities of setting up camp and preparing for the next day's adventures. Dinner tasted great as the hunters sat around the cook tent swapping stories of hunts past. They caught up on all the personal news from the year gone by, and generally tried to warm themselves by the sheepherder's stove. Already it was proving to be a colder than normal year. Soon our hunter found himself in the comfort of his sleeping bag dozing off with visions of giant muleys dancing in his head.

Opening morning came with the usual rude awakening to a noisy alarm clock. The first morning always seemed so cold up in the mountains. Maybe it is one more test to see how much the hunter really wants this. Will he leave the warmth of his sleeping bag and face the sub-freezing temperatures, or will he, after making it this far, decide to hang onto that last sliver of civilization? Each morning is a challenge, but the first more so as these flatlanders learn to acclimate once more.

With breakfast progressing, the hunter's excitement only increased. Opening morning normally was a great time to hunt down Long's Point road, and this year our hunter would be one of the first down that special path. The plan seemed straight forward enough: go down to the Point first thing and fill a tag, then spend the rest of the week hunting elk. It was a plan that he had executed several times before with success. Thinking about this reassured him "It'll all work out" he thought.

However, as they drove down the Point road things didn't go according to the plan. That is why they call it hunting after all. One never really knows what will happen.

First he and his partner spotted a really nice muley buck crossing the road. The sun had just begun to peak over the mesa top. Its brilliant hues of oranges and yellows illuminated the deer barely well enough to be spotted. Our hunter quickly got out of the pickup as soon as it came to a stop. With nothing but rifle and shooting stick in hand, he hurriedly began to work through the brush on the west side. Here the mesa drops off steeply close to the road. As he worked through the brush towards the last sighting of the deer, he felt the sting of the cold air on his face. Clumsily he struggled to gain a rhythm on the slope as his boots and heavy clothes slowed him down. Clearly it had been a while since his last such attempt.

Then he caught another glimpse of the buck. It was a really nice one. However, by now, it was located right on the edge of the drop off with its rear facing the hunter. The deer couldn't have been more than 100 yards away at this point. Franticly he tried to get his rifle in position; his fingers seemed to move in slow motion in the cold morning air. But he was too late. Just as he began to swing his scope on the animal, it disappeared into the brush below. "Damn" he thought, but he felt encouraged by the early close call.

Finally, the hunters made their way out to the end of the Point. By now the sun was clearly visible in the eastern sky. At one of their favorite highpoints, they glassed the surrounding area. Then our hunter's partner spotted a fine muley on a secondary slope to the east that teed into the main ridge. It was working along just below the top of that secondary ridge. Our hunter couldn't see it, but off they went. They got into position on the opposite slope. Still our hunter never saw the buck. Frustrated, he glassed the hillside. Finally he spotted the buck as it crossed over the other ridge - another opportunity gone.

The hunters scored later that morning. Our hunter's partner took a decent muley with a perfect long range shot. This certainly warmed the heart of our hunter. They spent the remainder of the morning and part of the afternoon dressing the deer and transporting it back to camp. The day was too far along to go back down the Point road, so they spent the rest of the day hunting the north end for elk.

On the second day, the hunters tried to repeat the same tactic as the first in order to fill that second buck tag. However, the deer were much scarcer. In the late afternoon, they took an evening stand with each hunting a different slope down at the end of the point.

Here is where our hunter's trouble really started. Late in the evening, two muley bucks suddenly appeared working up the opposite slope from our hunter. The shot was lengthy but eminently make able. However, our hunter simply couldn't get on one. Why, this is hard to say. He had never experienced this sensation. The scope refused to settle on the shoulder! Finally as the deer neared the top of the ridge, he let off a wild shot. The deer didn't move. Franticly he fired again, this time they scattered. Both shots were clean misses and he knew it.

The third day almost repeated the second, except this time our hunter missed a relatively straight forward shot at the Point's southernmost edge. At the time, he couldn't understand what went wrong; however, it was a case of inexperience. The angle of the shot was almost straight down. These types of shots need to be treated as shorter than the actual yardage due to the angle. He had shot over the deer.

Now three days in the hunt were passed. Other members of the party had started to pile up the game in camp. Deer filled the meat pole on the east end of camp and even several elk had begun to appear hanging on the big meat pole west of camp. Each evening after dark, the successful hunters pulled their pickups around to these poles as they came into camp. There they, with great fanfare and celebration, tell the tales of their hunt as everyone pitched in to string up the animal.

And now our hunter was really beginning to feel the pressure. Although he genuinely expressed great happiness with the others' successes, he couldn't help but feel that he was being left out. He was now the only one with both tags unfilled, and talk had already begun about what day would be best to break camp.

Then the next day, nature played her card in the continuing frustration. During the night, everyone heard it snow. They awakened to a good foot of snow covering the landscape – and the snow kept falling harder. This would make for a very rough day in the field. Everyone went out that morning, but most soon returned. It was simply not possible to do much good in the every increasing blizzard with visibility dropping by the hour. Our hunter and his partner stayed out the longest. Finally they gave in when they couldn't see more than a few feet in front of their vehicle. It was then mid-afternoon. Another day had passed and still our hunter was skunked.

Now things were getting really serious. The next day would be Wednesday of the week. That morning the hunters awoke to clearer skies but bitter cold temperatures and snow piled thick. However, it would turn out to be a good day overall for the camp. With the game on the move after the storm and the white background highlighting movement, hunting proved excellent. Several hunters filled their remaining tags. Our hunter had a great chance that day. A not-so-big but okay deer wandered out along the top of the ridge line as he worked up a draw on that slope. He used the snow to muffle his setup. Again, a fairly straight forward shot, again a miss. The frustration mounted.

That afternoon, his partner filled his cow elk tag. They spent the balance of the day dealing with that. While they were at camp, our hunter double checked his rifle – Old Reliable. Normally everyone checked their rifles upon arrival at a rock located some 400 yards up the slope north of camp. Old Reliable checked out fine then, but still maybe something had happened. Perhaps the zero had been thrown off in the process of taking the rifle in and out of the truck. Or perhaps it had gotten bumped while the hunter was going through some brush.

There was a problem with re-checking Old Reliable again. With all the plain and fancy missing, our hunter now had to be a little concerned about his ammo count. It was an embarrassing thing to admit, but still he had to consider it. Still he had to check the zero again. One shot at a makeshift target at 100 yards demonstrated that Old Reliable was still reliable. The gun wasn't the problem.

With the elk hung on the pole, our hunter had time for a very quick evening hunt. He decided to go down to the pipeline. That would be close enough to make an evening hunt, and it provided a good chance for either deer or elk.

To stand hunt the pipeline, a hunter normally would go straight west down the same valley that held camp. Just before the drop off, the pipeline right of way crossed the north ridge heading south. Elk moving up from the bottom up to the mesa top often crossed over at this spot before spreading out to the south in "Elk World". The hunter would set up on the opposite slope and wait. The site was ideal for a single hunter to stand hunt; however, the view was restricted. If elk didn't move through there, it would be a long, lonely hunt.

Once set up, our hunter then noticed just how cold it was in the growing shadows of that north facing slope. The loneliness, the cold, and his exhaustion began to take its toll. With the slope in front of him empty, his mind wandered off to the first time he had been here on his first trip to Cascade Canyon. It was another stand hunt with no success. That day, his partner had taken him all the way to the edge. There a tiny creek which ran along the valley bottom ran off the mesa forming a waterfall down to the bottomlands below – a distance of 2000 ft.

Of course, the water didn't make it but a few feet – maybe a hundred – before the liquid vaporized in the dry air. To peer down on this site from above, well it is almost a religious experience. Looking down, one can see the tortuous trail that elk used to go up from below to the mesa top. He still remembered his amazement at the thought of anything being able to traverse such a wild, twisty path. Such a sight brings soul searching awe and will always be remembered until a person's last moment.

That evening was made all the more special by a another critter – a porcupine who simply wouldn't budge from the trail as the hunters hiked back to camp thus forcing them to pass the stubborn rodent by hiking up the slope a ways.

Looking back, that hunt seemed now so carefree. Then our hunter felt little pressure. Everything was a new and a unique experience. The wildness of the mesa seemed to hold limitless opportunities. Here he had seen his first elk, his first mule deer, his first golden eagle fly. Nothing can prepare one for the flood of emotions upon seeing this Interesting Place for the first time. Any animal would have only been a bonus on that trip with no shame in not filling a tag. Whether it was beginner's luck or the kindness of the mountain, this hunter got that bonus with a cow elk – taken, naturally enough, in the Pocket.

As the sun began to set, the cold fell harder. Suddenly it forced our hunter to shiver and come back to this hunt in this place. The clear night ahead would be the coldest of the hunt as the front now passed would give way to clear skies. As they say "Clear as a bell, cold as hell, hardest frost that ever fell".

Without warning, our hunter noticed something different high up on the opposite slope. Then he realized what it was. Several long, camel like necks poked above the brush. They were elk that were crossing over. His plan was working. Quickly he got his rifle ready. Very carefully he took aim and fired – nothing. Again, he steadied the crosshairs on a cow, again nothing. Finally the elk sensed that something was amiss and wandered off.

As any responsible hunter would do, he hiked up to the area and thoroughly checked for any sign of a hit. The hike, although not lengthy, was steep, and the long period of inactivity had stiffened his leg muscles. Laboriously he made it to the area where he last saw the elk. There he found their tracks and could make out their movements. Very carefully he checked every possibility, but he found no sign of a hit. With weary resignation, he gave up the search. Dark was coming fast.

Thus, in the gathering night, he began the long trek back to camp. This time there would be no special moments to remember. The hike back seemed cruel. Completely frustrated, he didn't even want to go to camp. What would he tell them? Never in his life had his confidence been at such a low point.

Nonetheless, he eventually arrived at camp and entered the cook tent. Everyone had already settled into the evening ritual with drinks in hand. This year's hunt had been successful by any account. The meat poles sagged beneath the weight of the hunters' success. Tomorrow the game would be loaded up on trucks for they had decided to break camp. Several of the hunters had to get back to their jobs and everyone felt the tug to return to loved ones. Also, the threat of more hard winter weather made the hunters more than a little anxious about getting off the mountain.

Our hunter accepted this fate as he tried to explain what had happened. Several hunters suggested that he try one more time in the morning. With his confidence shot and his body exhausted from the long hunt, he almost declined. Still he felt that it important to keep trying. "Where will you go tomorrow? One asked. "Well I guess I'll go down the Point one more time" he replied, his voice not sounding at all confident. "Maybe I'll see a deer there".

That was a good plan. Nobody had been down to the Point in several days, so the hunting pressure down there had been reduced. Still our hunter didn't have any confidence that the plan would work. Everything had gone wrong and he felt snake bit. If only he had connected on that very first deer on opening morning he thought. Still it was too late for that. Everything had seemed to conspire: the weather, the game, the timing, and of course his own lack of preparation. And it was that last point that it seemed as if the mountain itself had punished him. He had learned many lessons that he would use in future hunts, but there was one more important lesson to learn on this trip.

"No, goddamn it" bellowed Ed who was already several drinks into celebrating the hunt. "There's no maybe about it. If you go down to the Point tomorrow morning, you will see a deer and you will get it" he added. "Well I certainly hope so" chuckled our hunter his mood humored by Ed's response. "No, no, goddamn it. There's no maybe at all. If you go to the Point tomorrow, you WILL get a deer. Lightening is going to strike"!

With that, our hunter could tell that Ed wasn't kidding. He was dead serious and he was right. Part of what had happened to him on this trip is that his attitude had changed. As more failures occurred he began to half expect more to follow. It had become a negative feedback loop.

Keeping a positive attitude doesn't sound all that important at first in the sport of hunting, but it is vital. If you don't think that something good is about to happen, you get sloppy in the little details. These add up over time until the hunter begins to think the entire endeavor is hopeless.

"You're absolutely right, Ed" our hunter replied "If I go to the Point tomorrow, I WILL get a deer. Lightening is going to strike". He was now fully convinced, and with that he double checked his gear to make sure everything would be ready. That way there would be no wasted time in the morning. He then went to bed to get a good night's sleep. "Tomorrow", he thought "lightening is going to strike".

Our hunter and his partner were the first ones up that morning. They would be the only ones going out to the Point. They went through the normal preparations, but now with renewed energy. Soon enough, they headed down the road. They didn't see any bucks on their way out. A few days ago this development would have disheartened our hunter. Today, he didn't let any doubts enter his mind. He already knew where he would score and that was out on the end of the Point.

With the early morning sun just peeking over the mesa, the hunters split up, each going to opposite sides of the last secondary ridge before the end of the point. Our hunter went to the south facing ridge. It was the same area where he had the shakes early in the hunt. He didn't have the sun in his favor, but they felt it was the more likely of the two slopes to spot a buck. His partner went to the north facing slope. With his deer tag filled, his job was to glass. If he spotted a buck he would go back and get the other hunter.

Each took up a stand and waited. As the first hour passed, our hunter began to feel the doubts creep back in to his mind. He fought those thoughts. He fought the early morning cold. "Lightening is GOING to strike" he thought. Continuously he scanned the opposite slope.

Suddenly his heart dropped. Silhouetted in the morning sun, at the very top of the ridge he spotted two bucks. Neither could be considered a monster by any stretch. Still he made up his mind to hunt them.

He faced a problem. They were working to the west and the end of that secondary ridge. If he couldn't quickly get into range he wouldn't get a shot. It was now or never. Deftly he worked down the slope to his left. He had to wait until neither buck was looking in his direction and quickly move between clumps of sagebrush. It was an agonizing process. The sun was definitely working against him now. Its brilliance filled the southern sky to the point that the deer were difficult to see.

The last gap he needed to cover was one of the biggest. As soon as both deer looked away, he darted towards a large clump of brush. There he paused. Not sure if he had busted the deer with that last move. If he hadn't, he figured he had about a 350 to 400 yard shot. Definitely within range, but he had missed easier shots than that this week. However, he had to take a shot now. There was no more brush between him and the bottom of the draw, and both bucks were nearly at the end of the ridge.

He slowly turned around and laced his gun in position. The deer were still there; however, something must have alerted them because they both had fixed their gaze in the hunter's direction. Maybe they saw a flicker of the gun or a movement of the brush. The hunter would have to take a shot now. This was it – the last chance of the last day of the trip.

At that moment he felt a calm overtake him. By completing a successful stalk, he had regained a part of his lost confidence. It had taken all week but finally he had melded into this world and its rhythms. He had, at last, crossed that boundary, which exists mostly in the mind, between the modern world and the mountain.

Just as he was about to fire, he backed off. One more time he calmed his nerves and made a slight adjustment to his aiming point. Now the previous years of practice and experience were coming back to him. Now he was doing the little things right. Once again he settled the rifle on some brush used as a rest. Once again he settled the scope on the larger buck. Then as his mind reached a completely clear state, the rifle fired. The suddenness of its retort startled him. That was the first time all week that he had no conscious sensation of the gun firing.

However, as he regained his composure he saw a deer bolt over the ridge. His heart sank. His limbs went numb. Had he missed yet again? Then he was startled again. The other hunter had walked up behind him and kneeled down and whispered "Nice shot". Immediately the realization of what happened dawned in him. What he had seen was the smaller deer run. Since he only saw one deer run, the other deer must have gone down.

You may think that he would be filled with joy at this point, and he was to a certain extent. However, what he felt bordered more on relief or emotional exhaustion. Slowly he gathered his wits, checked his gear, and began the hike over to the end of the opposite ridge.

As he approached the bottom of the draw, the slope became noticeably flatter with only short sagebrush. Then as he ascended the other side, the climb became terribly steep. This time, his legs felt light as be maneuvered up the rocky slope. Since he hadn't seen the buck go down, he had to rely on the directions of his partner. The buck had been at the very end of the nose of that ridge when it went down. Now another fear suddenly stormed his mind "What if it tumbled off the edge several thousand feet to the bottom?"

As he reached the same contour as the buck (based on hand signals from his partner), he noticed that the morning sun had begun to melt the ice and snow which had for days gripped Cascade Canyon and been his constant companion in his misadventures. This forced him to step carefully on the steep incline. Eventually as he rounded the corner, he had to actually sit down and scoot around in spots as the snow rapidly melted in the ever increasing sunlight of morning.

Then he spied the deer lying in a game trail. It lay just a few feet from the ledge in the snow. Such a sight always seems to startle a hunter as much as thrill him. The animal seemed at once out of place and at the same fully part of its environment. Maybe it has to do with death in general, or perhaps it is difficult for a man to wrap his mind around what he has accomplished, but the sight of a buck in the snow on top in the Rockies is a sight no person will ever forget. Our hunter allowed himself a small moment for self congratulations, but he had to quickly set about dressing the animal and getting it off that ledge.

Dressing the animal took only a short while. Just before he finished he heard the strangest sound – like a loud crashing. It was then he looked up and saw the most unbelievable sight. The sun had been shining on that west facing slope for several hours now and the temperatures had finally warmed up above freezing. Icicles which had formed over the past week were melting. They had grown to impressive lengths of dozens of feet. As they melted, they broke off from their weight and fell hundreds of feet to the ledges below. There they crashed with such force that the sound echoed off the mesas for miles around.

Phenomenal is the only way to describe the sight. Rapidly the temperatures climbed, as the icicle symphony reached a crescendo. Our hunter paused and sat in the snow to take in the spectacular, orchestral opera that played before him. No amount of money or technology could ever duplicate this show. It was if the mountain was rewarding him for his week long frustrations.

At that moment the thought occurred to him that he was probably the only person that was witnessing this sight. It is at moments like those that a person cannot help but feel the special nature of creation. This sight convinced that man for all time that our being here is no accident. Whenever he began to doubt the reason for existence, he would think back to that sight. That was his trophy from this hunt – a trophy not measured in antler size or bragging rights but one of immeasurable value.

Eventually he drug the deer off the ledge and up through the draw that he had moments before stalked so carefully into range. With the snow now almost completely melted in the warming sun, the ground had turned to slop. By the time he reached a trail capable of supporting a vehicle, he was almost completely covered in mud mixed with blood. In addition, his clothes, selected for the cold morning, were now half off and soaked with perspiration from the effort. Not a pretty site. After loading the buck in the truck, he slumped against it in exhaustion from not only that day but from the ordeal of the entire week.

Before leaving, he looked back to the east one last time as the sun shone brightly in the mid-morning sky. The entire landscape had been altered from the time he first arrived that morning. He thought about the incredible opera that the icicles performed just minutes before. Already it seemed surreal, like a dream. He knew even then what a special moment in time he experienced. It was a turning point in his life. From now on he would always be considered a hunter of the high mountains.

More importantly he now understood his own being better. What had been revealed to him on that ragged ledge cannot be put into words. He had come here to this Interesting Place and it had changed him. This place created by God for a purpose.

And in that one perfect moment where everything, for a brief second seemed so clear the hunter could only think "I guess they're right. It really does rain fire in the sky".

In later years visitors to that hunter's home can admire many of his trophies. Many times they are puzzled by one: a rather non-impressive mule deer antler mount. Our hunter sometimes tries to explain, but often times not. This trophy is THE jewel of the collection. For it is what the trophy represents – the experience and how that experience changed the hunter – that makes it a trophy. And that experience can only happen in Interesting Places that are wild and free and created by God.

Believe always: "Lightening is going to strike".

Part 5

Conclusion

Chapter 18 - Final Thoughts

Where did all the Interesting Places go? That is a question that I ask myself a lot in the quieter moments. At one time it seemed like they along with the flower of youth would never end although I knew in my mind that wasn't true, the heart is not so easily convinced, or perhaps it is more easily deluded by the concerns of the here and now.

In the selective distillery of a person's memory, the special moments of the good hunts remain while the not so special hunts tend to be weeded out. That is our nature. Not all the places we hunted qualified as Interesting Places; in fact a number did not. We had the unique perspective of hunting a variety of different places in a number of different states. This was not by our design; rather it just worked out that way. Some hunters have the financial means to hunt pretty much anywhere anytime. For them they can afford the best accommodations, guides, and exclusive properties. On the other end of the spectrum, there are those that have a good setup and hunt the same place year after year.

We fell somewhat in the middle. Due to our living circumstances, we never connected on a place that was permanent. Also we certainly never had the means to be the Great White Hunter on safari. Neither of these opposing poles are necessarily wrong, it is that we always seemed to bounce around somewhere in the ill-defined middle. We always knew that each place was temporary and wouldn't last as we moved from one deal to another like some sort of hunting version of migrant workers. While this certainly had its disadvantages (foremost among them is that a quite a few of the places we tried turned out to be duds or worse), hunting in this manner gave us a unique perspective. We came to appreciate each Interesting Place, no matter how fleeting, for its own special reasons.

And we became better hunters in the process for we had to constantly adapt to each place we hunted. Sometimes this was easy, and at other times we were forced to put aside some preconceived notions. That was one thing we learned about Interesting Places – you had to adapt to them, they didn't know you or care about your hubris. In that way these Interesting Places not only made us better hunters, they made us better people. Looking back was all that effort and activity worth it?

Like what is written.

> *Yet when I surveyed all that my hands*
> *Had done*
> *And this what I had toiled to achieve,*
> *everything was meaningless, a chasing*
> *after the wind;*
> *nothing was gained under the sun.*

No, I would answer. It was not meaningless. We gained a great deal. Not the trophies or even the entertainment, although they are special. What we gained was how these Interesting Places provided us with authentic experiences and in those experiences we became different people, better people. Our souls were molded in many imperceptibly small ways. No it was not meaningless activity simply to pass the time. It was something much more, and it was something that is permanently etched upon our souls for eternity. Much was gained under the sun and in heaven.

Within all of us there lies this need for authentic experiences. It is programmed into our DNA. Yet at the same time we often shirk from these challenges in fear of what we might really find out about ourselves. That is when we drift aimlessly from activity to activity desperately seeking meaning, trying to justify what we are with what we believe that we should be. Hunting at these Interesting Places has been one of the few truly authentic things that I have done in my life. I cannot imagine the person I would have become if I hadn't hunted. But I know I would be different and incomplete. I am thankful to God and to my family for the opportunity to have hunted these places. Although I would love to do so again, I know how rare truly Interesting Places are. If I never have the opportunity to hunt them again, apart of me would be sad, but another part of me would understand that I have been very specially blessed to have lived part of my life hunting on Interesting Places. I make no apologies at all for having done so or for the great sport of hunting.

And where did the Interesting Places go? That question is still there. Some maybe are still there in some form. The hunters in this story, being creatures of the modern world didn't stay in one place all their lives. As they moved due to careers or family, they left these places behind.

Some of them changed. At times they changed slowly as when the modern world crept upon them in its relentless leveling. Other times they changed suddenly as with a change in ownership. In most cases, the constant economic pressures were at work. This leveling process which is constantly at work may seem to have the upper hand in the long struggle. However, it too is subject to the judgment of nature. There is no guarantee that it will prevail ultimately.

The Brownsville lease long ago ceased to be an Interesting Place when the old rancher passed away. In his place, the new leaser wanted to create more income and run the place more in line with other Texas leases. To that end the price went up, the number of hunters on the same land doubled, and these changes forced one to hunt over a feeder from a box stand – similar to so many other leases these days. Our hunters moved on to search for a better deal, one where they could hunt more in the style they wished.

Old Eleven Point ended up being the very last deer shot on the Busby lease. Our hunters knew their one and only season on that place would be the last season anyone hunted on that small but Interesting Place. Suburban sprawl encroached from all sides. The hunters could actually hear the construction work on new condos and town homes as they hunted late in the year. That Interesting Place lost forever to a housing boom that turned out to be nothing more than an overheated housing bubble that popped several years later. Was the loss of that Interesting Place worth the frenzied chase of short term profits – profits which turned out to be entirely an illusion – a chasing after the wind?

Other Interesting Places, like the Weimar, succumbed to the same temptations of money. In fact one hunter in these stories swears that he saw that very property on a hunting show. In place of the modest middle class hunt club that ran the place all those years ago, the land now caters to higher end cliental complete with professional guides. And what became of that Rough Piece of West Texas? Well it is hard to explain. The neglect that made that overlooked scrap of land so unique didn't last. Ever increasing fees and the desire to add more paid guns eventually forced our hunters off. That is an example of the paradox of Interesting Places. For an all too brief golden age, ordinary people from modest backgrounds had the financial means, the time, the liberty, and the places to do extraordinary things. But as that golden age ended, all of these things for the average person dried up. That is the final act of this great leveling process: more control, less liberty, and fewer opportunities. America was a different place then, perhaps it was an Interesting Place in its own right.

Of course, not only have these places changed, but the hunters have changed also. Despite their best efforts their bodies slowly succumbed to the same entropy which affects all living things and all of existence. For the physical world is the means to the end, not the main thing itself. As such it is temporary and fragile. This is a hard lesson that we would wish to ignore, but we cannot. In a very real way, all of physical existence is one big Interesting Place which is here for a short while to serve a particular purpose. Our goal should be to live our lives as best we can in accordance with the unchanging Natural and Moral laws which our Creator has set forth. Interesting Places are here to help us to learn these eternal truths and prepare us what lies beyond.

Ultimately time is not a friend to Interesting Places, but we are left with those special moments in time which hang in our memory like stars glittering in the night.

Last Toast

In many ways it had been a difficult trip. For years our hunters had traveled out to Colorado to that very Interesting Place called Cascade Canyon. However, as the years wore on, our hunters aged. Each began to have the normal array of problems that plague our species – cancer, joint pain, and the rest. Every year the trip grew a little less fun and a little more arduous.

Also the place was slowly changing. In its prime, this Interesting Place produced like a newly struck gold mine. Every year, the hunters found great success of legendary proportion. But then that began to change. Human activity began to increase. The modest gas field that had long occupied the mountain was becoming crowded with more and more drilling activity. New pipelines stretched out each year along the ridges. New production facilities filled the canyon bottoms which disrupted game flow. Long Point, which had always been such a muley hotspot, was now almost devoid of any deer, doe or buck.

The last ridge before the Point, the one where one hunter had witnessed the icicles melting and falling one morning, now had a new pipeline right of way slapped over it. No longer did the deer cross that ridge, and no longer did anybody bother hunting there.

On the ridge north of camp where one hunter killed an elk on the run during a drive, now sat a well site right in the spot where he fired the shot. It jutted out of the hillside in an artificial manner. Gone were the heavy thickets of brush which proved so difficult when the hunters climbed the ridge there. In their place stood a well maintained road to service the well.

Perhaps saddest of all to our hunters is what happened to John's Pocket. In this Interesting Place within an Interesting Place, a place that seemed to be almost separate from this world when one stepped into it, now sat another well site. The site sat directly over the spot where the elk had once made a virtual city under the massive thickets. Now they came there no more. The hunters did not hunt there anymore either.

Each year there was more activity. Each year there was less area to hunt. And each year security increased. That didn't kick in right after 911, but soon enough the hunters noticed more and more security measures up on the mountain. In place of the gate, which at one time represented the last boundary between the modern world and the potential adventure beyond, now stood a check stand with guards. In addition there was another check stand further down the road. Gone was the neat separation from the world. Now the modern world and its hectic pace flowed seamlessly up the mountain. Each year they felt less like hunters free to pursue their quarry according to their own skill and more like strangers intruding where they weren't really welcomed.

All the hunters knew this as it unfolded, but nobody wanted to bring it up in open conversation. Cascade Canyon was such an Interesting Place that none of them wanted to let it go. This despite the fact they were aging and the place was changing. It is hard to say good bye. Instead as they sat in the cook tent after dinner they hinted around with words like "Well there may be more drilling along the Point road next year" or "I hear the gate fee is going up again". It was an indirect way to get one of the others to make the final call.

Towards the end of that trip one hunter convinced his father, the one who was known as Legend to take a late afternoon drive out to the Point. At first he objected. Hunting down Long Point had been poor all week, why go out now? "Let's take one last trip down the Point. We might see something" the hunter replied. Reluctantly the Legend agreed. Slowly they drove down that road like they had so many times before. They stopped and glassed at the usual spots, but they saw nothing, not so much as a doe. It would have made a wonderful final story, kind of like the last five minutes of a hunting show on television, if a big bruiser muley came out. But this wasn't television. It was a real wild chase hunt. And all they found was the wind.

Once they got out to the drop off overlooking the Point, they stopped one last time to look. Then our hunter produced a bottle of cognac he had carried all this time. The two hunters toasted Long Point. They reminisced about all the great hunts, many of them occurred within sight of where they sat. So many great moments, some told here and many not. Each hunter took turns in recalling many of these hunts.

There was the time that the younger hunter had shot a large mule deer buck, the largest deer he had ever shot, not too far from that spot.

The Legend recalled the many deer he had shot on Long Point as well as the others that he didn't quite get. Now looking over the rugged sage brush terrain, it all seemed like a dream. Could all of that really have happened in a place that now looked so barren and forlorn?

As the sun dipped below the mountain ridge, they made one last toast. It was time to leave.

CPSIA information can be obtained at www.ICGtesting.com
Printed in the USA
BVOW08s1442220713

326624BV00014B/466/P